SOCIAL MEDIA FOR ACADEMICS

SAGE was founded in 1965 by Sara Miller McCune to support the dissemination of usable knowledge by publishing innovative and high-quality research and teaching content. Today, we publish over 900 journals, including those of more than 400 learned societies, more than 800 new books per year, and a growing range of library products including archives, data, case studies, reports, and video. SAGE remains majority-owned by our founder, and after Sara's lifetime will become owned by a charitable trust that secures our continued independence.

Los Angeles | London | New Delhi | Singapore | Washington DC | Melbourne

SOCIAL MEDIA FOR ACADEMICS

MARK CARRIGAN

Los Angeles | London | New Delhi
Singapore | Washington DC | Melbourne

Los Angeles | London | New Delhi
Singapore | Washington DC | Melbourne

SAGE Publications Ltd
1 Oliver's Yard
55 City Road
London EC1Y 1SP

SAGE Publications Inc.
2455 Teller Road
Thousand Oaks, California 91320

SAGE Publications India Pvt Ltd
B 1/I 1 Mohan Cooperative Industrial Area
Mathura Road
New Delhi 110 044

SAGE Publications Asia-Pacific Pte Ltd
3 Church Street
#10-04 Samsung Hub
Singapore 049483

Editor: James Clark
Editorial assistant: Robert Patterson
Production editor: Tom Bedford
Copyeditor: Audrey Scriven
Proofreader: Caroline Stock
Indexer: Anne Solamito
Marketing manager: Catherine Slinn
Cover design: Naomi Robinson
Typeset by: C&M Digitals (P) Ltd, Chennai, India
Printed and bound by Ashford Colour Press Ltd,
Gosport, Hants

Library of Congress Control Number: 2015948980

British Library Cataloguing in Publication data

A catalogue record for this book is available from
the British Library

ISBN 978-1-4462-9868-8
ISBN 978-1-4462-9869-5 (pbk)

Contents

About the author

Mark Carrigan is a digital sociologist and consultant. He's a research fellow at the Centre for Social Ontology at the University of Warwick and digital fellow at *The Sociological Review*. He convenes the Independent Social Research Foundation's Digital Social Science Forum. He edits the *Sociological Imagination*. He's social media associate editor of the *International Journal of Social Research Methodology*, assistant editor of *Big Data & Society* and a founding member of the editorial board of *Discover Society*. His past research interests have included the emergence of asexuality, the ontology of social movements and the sociology of internal conversation. His current project is an inquiry into digital capitalism, exploring how the micro-politics of digital distraction are shaping political and economic life. He is a regular blogger and podcaster.

www.markcarrigan.net

@mark_carrigan

Acknowledgements

I began this project a few months before the end of my PhD thesis. At the time, my level of focus in the face of the most solid deadline I had ever been subject to in my life (i.e. if I didn't submit the document, I'd have wasted six years of my life) made *Social Media for Academics* seem like it would be comparatively easy in comparison. How wrong I was. Therefore thanks are due to James Clark, not only for suggesting this project to me in the first place but also for remaining cheerful and encouraging in the face of my apologies for what became perpetual delays. Thanks also to Rachael Plant who was my editorial point of contact for the first half of the process, as well as Robert Patterson who took over after she left. You were both supportive and encouraging at all stages, and apologies for what I'm sure was my frustrating inability to hand over the manuscript on a chapter-by-chapter basis.

This had been harder to write than I expected. Much harder. Thanks must go to my friends and family who have listened to me complain about this project at many difficult points over the last year and a half, particularly Marta who never fails to be an amazing friend, even when I'm being anything but. Then there's Sam who persuaded me to explore social media professionally in the first place, who I still so frequently miss talking to and suspect always will.

Nothing did more to develop the ideas in this book than the six months I spent at the LSE's Public Policy Group as editor of the *British Politics and Policy Blog*. I'd be lying if I said it was the happiest six months of my life, as I was driven slowly mad by a four-hour daily commute which I had naively assumed would be four hours a day in which I could do my PhD while working full-time, but I learnt so much from this experience and the people I worked with there. Thanks to Pat Lockley who encouraged me to develop some initial ideas with him, the first time I'd ever tried to think systematically about these issues, even after many years of blogging as a hobby. It set into motion a whole new strand of my professional life which has proved enormously rewarding. Thanks to many people who I've had interesting discussions with about these issues over the past few years, as well as those who've helped and encouraged my work on them: Jennifer Jones, Martin Eve, Ernesto Priego, Melonie Fullick, Karen Gregory, Jessie Daniels, Tanya Palmer, Catherine Baker, Emma Head, Les Back, Deborah Lupton, Martin Weller, Dave Beer, Sierra Williams, Chris Gilson, Rob O'Toole, Cheryl Brumley, Milena Kremakova, Steve Fuller, Sadia Habib, Andy Coverdale, Ruth Pearce, Warren Pearce, Simon Bastow, Stuart Brown, Jane Tinkler, Patrick Dunleavy, Mark Knights, Christina Hughes, Sarah Burton, John Holmwood, Salma Patel, Stephen Barnard, Bev Skeggs, Marcus Gilroy-Ware, Imogen Tyler, Rachael Kiddey, Matthew Wargent, Su Corcoran, Esther De Smet, Nadine Muller, Martin Price, Angèle Christin, Mark Murphy, Pat Thomson, Sasha Roseneil, Jon Rainford, Nick Mahoney, Lucy Mayblin, Michael Burawoy, Kandy Woodfield, Monder Ram, Azumah Dennis, John Field, Noortje Marres, Niahm Thornton, Kim Pawlak, Matt Phillpot, Graham Scambler and Lachlan Smith. Apologies to the many others I have undoubtedly forgotten. Petra Boynton, Sarah Lewthwaite and Helena Webb all made extraordinarily useful contributions to the book at later stages, ones which I wasn't able to use as fully as I'd have liked due to my rush to meet the impending deadline. Particular thanks go to Daniel Little, Gurminder Bhambra, Dave O'Brien, MJ Barker, Ele Belfiore, Stuart Elden and Charlotte Mathieson for letting me ask them an endless series of slightly tedious questions about how they used social media.

Social media and digital scholarship

1

Chapter themes

This chapter will:

- Explore what social media are and why they matter
- Discuss the concept of digital scholarship and its implications for higher education
- Explore some significant characteristics of social media
- Introduce the topics covered throughout the rest of this book

Social media are everywhere. At least it can often seem like that. In under a decade, what were once online novelties have become taken-for-granted parts of everyday life for many, something which is reflected in the sheer scale of their use. In 2011, 1.2 billion users worldwide logged into a social media site and the numbers across platforms have continued to rise ever since (van Dijck 2012: loc 123). Here are some facts about the day on which I wrote this paragraph, courtesy of the Internet Live Stats (2015) project:

- Over 3,351,200 blog posts have been published
- Over 696,800,000 tweets have been sent

- Over 7,581,700,000 videos have been viewed on YouTube
- Over 165,378,000 photos have been uploaded to Instagram
- Over 148,408,000 Tumblr posts have been posted
- Over 132,686,000 Skype calls have been made

These numbers increase at such a pace that they're out of date by the time I've finished the list. I'm returning to the live counts at the end of writing this paragraph and they've already increased, in some cases to a degree that can initially seem baffling when you consider the investment of time and energy implied in each single case that registers. But it shouldn't be surprising in a world in which there are 3,147,131,306 internet users, 1,425,892,583 active users of Facebook, 312,852,100 active users of Twitter, 1,184,050,501 active users of Google+ and 75,085,140 active users of Pinterest. Those numbers give us some insight into what the buyers who have purchased 600,855 computers, 4,347,556 smart phones and 816,142 tablets today are likely to do with their new products. The sheer quantity of the data involved in social media can be difficult to grasp. Cory Doctorow, activist and co-editor of Boing Boing, offers a useful comparison:

> A really top-notch cable operator might carry two hundred to five hundred TV channels, each one airing ten to twenty-four hours of programming a day. Assuming your cable operator had two hundred channels, that's a minimum of two thousand hours of video a day. As of March 2014, YouTube was adding that much content *every twenty minutes*. (Doctorow 2014: 73)

Many have argued that we even need a new social science for a world in which Facebook processes 2.5 billion pieces of content, 2.7 billion 'Like' actions and 300 million photo uploads each day (Kitchin 2014). Given how central the imagery of 'the cloud' has become to what we once talked about as 'cyberspace', it's easy to forget how brutishly physical these processes are. Not just in the sense of the physical networks which make up the internet, and the enormous amounts of money and power tied up in their construction and maintenance (Blum 2012, Lewis 2014), but also the environmental impact of all this blogging, tweeting and sharing. At the point of writing, 2,599,804MWh electricity has been used so far on this day alone for the internet and 2,392,471 tons of CO_2 emissions have been generated (Internet Live Stats 2015). Incidentally there are almost a billion websites at the time of writing, leaving me oddly enthused by the knowledge that this arbitrary but nonetheless resonant milestone will have been long passed by the time you read this book.

It's remarkable how rapidly the terminology of social media has entered everyday life. Much as 'googling' has become a verb which ubiquitously characterises the activity of using an online search engine, so too has 'tweeting' come to define micro-blogging with what appears to be becoming a comparable degree of penetration. Operators like '@' (addressing a user) and '#' (indicating a hashtag) increasingly function as a syntax for social media in general (van Dijck 2012: loc 1484), as opposed to being restricted to Twitter as the platform on which they originated. But the related terminology of 'retweets' and 'hashtags' has been appropriated into the common lexicon in ways that would have been difficult to predict in the early days of social media. Despite being immersed in Twitter, I was amazed to learn that the hashtag has been widely taken up by young children as 'a device for adding comment and emphasis in stories', in spite of the fact that many or most of them do not use the service themselves (Brown 2015). Terms which were only recently used by those immersed in internet culture are sufficiently recognised to merit inclusion in the *Oxford English Dictionary*. Words like 'astroturfing' (a fake grassroots political campaign) and 'sock puppet' (a fake social media account) have been recognised in this way and, through doing so, the social possibilities which this new technology affords are becoming more widely understood (Reed 2014). Some phrases with a long history within internet culture change as a result of their recognition. For instance 'troll' was once understood to be a deliberate provocateur, someone who sought to provoke discord and incite reactions in a planned way (Coleman 2014). It is now more commonly used as a generic designation for those who behave in anti-social and offensive ways online (Bartlett 2014). The meaning of existing words change as a result of social media as well. Terms like 'sharing', 'friending' and 'liking' were part of the common vernacular long before Facebook and yet their meanings have begun to shift in ways that are still ongoing. It might seem that the change is subtle but I'm persuaded by van Dijck's (2012: loc 307) argument that what we mean by terms like 'friend' and 'follower' are in the process of what could be a radical change as a result of social media:

In the offline world, people who are "well connected" are commonly understood to be individuals whose connections are gauged by their quality and status rather than their quantity. In the context of social media, the term "friends" and its adjunct verb "friending" have come to designate strong and weak ties, intimate contacts as well as total strangers. Their significance is commonly articulated in one indiscriminate number. The term "followers" has undergone a similar transformation: the word con-notes everything from neutral "groups" to "devotees" and "believers," but in the context of social media it has come to mean the sheer number of people who follow your twit stream.

That social media are exercising such an influence over language shouldn't be a surprise. As we saw earlier, the sheer number of users active on these services and the volume of communication taking place through them mean it would be confusing if they *weren't* leading to changes in language and culture. Nonetheless, there are important social and cultural questions posed by this influence, which we should keep sight of when we think about using social media as academics.

It is easy to become wrapped up in the scale of social media, breathlessly celebrat-ing this explosion of human communication and collaboration. The iconoclastic critic of internet hype, Evgeny Morozov describes this as 'internet-centrism': the idea 'that we are living through unique, revolutionary times, in which the previous truths no longer hold, everything is undergoing profound change, and the need to "fix things" runs as high as ever' (Morozov 2013: 15). To internet-centrists, technology is some-thing outside society leading inexorably to radical change due to the unfolding of its internal logic. On this view, the internet becomes something we cannot resist. Social media will change everything in their wake, as we're all forced to adapt to the radi-cal new world they have created. However, as many critics of technological capitalism have pointed out those most loudly proclaiming the inevitability of 'disruption' are also those with the biggest stake in the game. If radical change is on the horizon, indeed if it's already here, we inevitably need guides to help us 'weather the storm'. As one particularly crass statement of this I encountered recently put it, 'Above all, we hope to prepare you so you can survive and thrive through the coming titanic storm' (Scoble and Israel 2014: loc 223).

The problem is that higher education is not immune from this way of thinking and writing about technology. Far from it. Indeed I've spent the last year and a half concerned that I might slip into this mode when writing the present book. Hopefully I've managed to avoid it but only you can judge whether I've actually succeeded. Internet-centrism is most apparent when it comes to Massively Open Online Courses (MOOCs) and the radical changes to the delivery of higher edu-cation which are assumed to inevitably follow from digital technology (Bady 2013). But some critics have suggested that we can see the same trend with open-access, a potent mix of technological hype and commercial concern, part of a broader climate in which all manner of storms, avalanches and tsunamis of change are on the horizon (Holmwood 2013a, 2013b). The problem is that as

Morozov (2013) observes, these technological solutions to perceived problems have a tendency to change their object in the course of 'fixing it' and their preoccupation with technology works to shut down debate about the acceptability or otherwise of these changes.

So we shouldn't be preoccupied by technology. But given that I'm writing this book about social media in higher education and you're reading it, there's clearly something to be said here that goes beyond the level of hype (Daniels and Feagin 2011). The way I approach this is to look at how new technology *has* changed, and *might* change, how each academic conducts their working lives on an everyday level (Weller 2011). In part this is because I'm a sociologist who studies the internal dialogues of individuals in a social context: how we *become who we are* through the mundane business of everyday life (Archer 2007, Carrigan 2014a). But it's also because social media have become integral to my working life. As I explain further below, research blogging became increasingly central to how I worked over the long course of a part-time PhD, while I also began to immerse myself in Twitter and podcasting. Writing this now, as a post-doctoral researcher, I find it increasingly difficult to imagine how I would work *without* social media. In fact I tried to give up blogging in the final stages of writing this book, wondering if the time commitment involved was making it difficult to retain my focus through the challenging process of concluding a writing project. But I soon realised that without blogging, I found it much more difficult to clarify my thoughts, develop provisional arguments and sustain the research process whilst juggling multiple commitments. Now a cynic might see this as a negative thing (the phrase 'internet addiction' springs to mind) and in a way I wouldn't blame them (boyd 2014: loc 1337–1388). My point is only to make clear where I'm coming from in writing this book.

Social media are central to my working life as a scholar and this is something which I, as well as many others, have found enormously beneficial (Lupton 2014a). This book is an extended attempt to explain how this can be so, by mapping out how social media can be integrated into different facets of scholarly activity in a helpful and productive way. In this sense, it's a practical guidebook to what Weller (2011) and others describe as *digital scholarship*. As he admits, 'scholarship' is a slightly old-fashioned term. It's also one that's difficult to define in a non-tautological way. Scholarship is what scholars do (Weller 2011: loc 105). So digital scholarship refers to the activities undertaken by scholars, experts within a given field, utilising digital media or tools in some way. In defining digital scholarship in this way, Weller intends to recognise that digital scholars will not necessarily have an academic affiliation. My decision to title this book

Social Media for Academics is by no means a rejection of this impulse. But it's a recognition that the *practical* dimension of social media use, which will be the concern of this book, relates to questions which arise for *academics* pursuing *academic careers* within *universities*. This book is about *why* you might use social media tools, as much as *how* to use them. This has the additional benefit of allowing me to sidestep the perennial problem that any book about social media faces: things change at such an immense pace that overly specific steps about how to use particular platforms risk becoming outdated soon after publication, if they're not already so by the time a book has been released. That said, my motivation for this isn't a pragmatic attempt to preserve the shelf life of my book (though it's nice it has that effect). As I explain below, the basic steps involved in using each platform aren't challenging, at least once you've familiarised yourself with them. The challenge comes in knowing how to use them in a way that's helpful and appropriate for *you*. That's what this book is about, though of course I unavoidably get into specifics at points. In the interests of keeping this content up to date, as well as giving me a productive way to procrastinate from my next project, I'll be returning to these themes regularly in the *Social Media for Academics* section of my blog at www.markcarrigan.net. If you have questions, suggestions or disagreements about the book (or anything else really) then you can find me on Twitter @mark_carrigan.

In the rest of this chapter, I lay the groundwork for the book as a whole. The next section is the most traditionally academic part of the book, in which I introduce some useful concepts from the interdisciplinary literature on social media to clarify exactly what it is we mean by this nebulous term. I discuss the current state of play, major trends and some important critiques that have been made about social media and the implications all of this holds for social life. Then I say a little about my own pathway into social media and academia, hopefully in a way that's useful for understanding where I'm coming from, before offering an overview of the book as a whole.

What are social media and why is it so dangerous to try and write a book about them?

At the start of her 2013 book *The Culture of Connectivity*, the media scholar Jose van Dijck bemoans the fact that 'Every time I look at my screen, the world of social networking and online sociality has changed and begs to be reinterpreted' (van Dijck 2012: loc 68). I share her frustration. The risk inherent in writing a book about social media is that the discussion will be out of date by the time the book is read, let alone a year or two later. But as I've already suggested, this particular book is not intended to be an instructional manual for particular services, but rather a guidebook for navigating a rapidly changing landscape. If certain references come to seem passé only a year or two later then I hope you can overlook them because in a way they're incidental. The real concern of this book is how existing scholarly activities (things like *writing*, *publishing*, *networking* and *engaging*) can be enhanced thorough social media and perhaps transformed in the process. The social media scholar danah boyd makes a similar point in her book about the social media practices of contemporary teenagers: 'Even though many of the tools and services that I reference throughout this book are now passé, the core activities I discuss—chatting and socializing, engaging in self-expression, grappling with privacy, and sharing media and information—are here to stay' (boyd 2014: loc 189). In other words: while social media *will* change, the core activities for which academics will use social media will remain the same, even if they might come to look somewhat different as social media become a mainstream part of academic life. This is why I find Weller's (2011) focus on *digital scholarship*, that is to say the things scholars actually do, a useful way of approaching this subject matter. Scholarly practices are being changed through the use scholars make of digital technology (Greenhow and Gleason 2014). As Weller (2011) writes:

> Whenever I ask someone to think of scholarship they usually imagine a lone individual, surrounded by books (preferably dusty ones), frantically scribbling notes in a library. This is somewhat removed from the highly connected scholar, creating multimedia outputs and sharing these with a global network of peers. (Weller 2011: loc 100)

Patrick Dunleavy, chair of the group at the LSE who run a popular family of academic blogs, invokes similar imagery when he bemoans the persistence of 'academic hermits' who refuse to embrace the possibilities for 'shorter, better, faster, free' scholarship (Dunleavy 2014a, 2014b). But I think it's more helpful to see this as a spectrum rather than a binary opposition. At the one extreme there are Dunleavy's 'hermits' and on the other there are Weller's digital scholars. Most fall in between. Nonetheless, it's important not to forget the ways in which most if not all academics are already digital scholars in some sense. The impact of technology upon scholarship isn't something new (Veletsianos and Kimmons 2012). How many people still read paper journals? How many people's first recourse for searching a literature is to physically visit a university library? Could the modern university function without e-mail? How many people *ever* forego digital tools for writing? These aren't trivial changes. As Katherine Hayles observes, 'print-based scholars increasingly compose, edit and disseminate files in digital form without worrying too much about how digital text differs from print, so they tend not to see the ways in which digital text, although superficially similar to print, differs profoundly in its internal structures, as well as in the different functionalities, protocols, and communicative possibilities of networked and programmable machines' (Hayles 2012: 5). In fact Berry (2012: loc 427) has argued that there is an emerging recognition of the 'cultural importance of the digital as the unifying idea of the university'.

Digital technology is already an integral part of scholarship in part because of what Weller (2011: loc 2612) describes as 'network weather', namely 'changes in your environment are occurring because of other people's use of these technologies and the behaviour they facilitate, even if as an individual you are not engaged with them'. Expectations begin to coalesce and pressure is exerted, even if unintentionally, over those who fail to meet them. This can be subtle. Even trivial. But these pressures are nonetheless real and their cumulative effect is to create a drift towards the diffusion of technology, at least past a certain point. Yet once this technology is taken up, it influences the activities which are undertaken using it, often in extremely subtle ways such as those highlighted by Hayles (2012). This explains an emerging sense of pressure surrounding the use of social media, a theme which I return to in the final chapter (Lupton 2014a).

Once we start to think about digital scholarship, it begins to seem as if we are all *already* digital scholars, at least to some degree. Many digital technologies are so taken for granted that they have become all but invisible to us, becoming so tied up in the routines of our working lives that we don't really stop to think about what they are and how we use them (Jones and Hafner 2012). Social media are more unfamiliar. They are a particular subset of these other media, with their own distinctive characteristics. What can make them exciting is the opportunity they offer to reflect on what we're doing and why. Their very novelty invites us to consider how we might use them and why we would do this. As the internet scholar Nancy Baym (2010: loc 148) puts it, 'these moments in which they are new and the norms for their use are in flux offer fresh opportunities to think about our technologies, our connections, and the relationships amongst them'. My approach in this book is to try and explore social media in these terms, considering how they might be used by academics to extend and even change the scholarly practices which they are already engaged in. In this sense I share the conviction of Jones and Hafner (2012: loc 284) that 'the best way to become more competent users of technologies is to become more critical and reflective about how we use them in our everyday lives, the kinds of things that they allow us to do, and the kinds of things they don't allow us to do'. The evidence we have suggests that researchers using social media recognise the distinctive characteristics of these platforms, but there remains a broader lack of clarity about what the value of their use is and whether this outweighs the costs involved (RIN 2011). This is particularly problematic because some of those who might benefit the most from using social media, such as doctoral students, still seem often not to engage despite recognising the potential value in doing so (JISC 2012).

The technical aspects of using social media, in so far as they exist, remain fairly trivial. If you can use a software package like Microsoft Word then you can use any social media platform. The former is one of those everyday technologies with which we are so familiar, that it's easy to forget what a bulky and cumbersome tool it is. Most users barely scratch the surface of the capacities built into the software, at least in everyday use rather than when doing things like preparing book manuscripts, without this posing any sort of problem. If you have a clear idea of what you want to achieve with Word, the fiddly details of precisely how you'll do it largely take care of themselves, at least once you've familiarised yourself with the software. This isn't to say users don't have questions and run into problems. It's just that these are relatively peripheral. Most of the time they simply get on with it without problems. Hopefully this book will help you feel the same way about social media and the technical challenges posed by them. These are trivial. What matters are the more substantive questions, *what* you are doing and *why*, which become clear once you develop a reflective understanding of what social media will allow you to do as an academic, what they won't allow you to do, and what a broader context (within which digital scholarship is becoming the norm) is likely to mean both for your working life and your career.

However this leaves a rather important question unanswered: what *are* social media? The obvious response is to reel off a list along the lines of the one I used less than a couple of pages ago to convey a sense of their scale and speed. What we mean by 'social media' are things like Twitter, Facebook, YouTube, Tumblr and Pinterest. The next step on from listing examples is to categorise these in a way that distinguishes their various features. Jose van Dijck (2012: loc 208) offers a helpful set of categories to make sense of their variety:

Social Network Sites 'primarily promote interpersonal contact, whether between individuals or groups; they forge personal, professional, or geographical connections and encourage weak ties'. Examples include *Facebook, Twitter, LinkedIn, Google+, Foursquare.*

User Generated Content supports 'creativity, foreground cultural activity, and promote the exchange of amateur or professional content'. Examples include *YouTube, Flickr, Myspace, GarageBand, Wikipedia.*

Trading and Marketing Sites 'principally aim at exchanging products or selling them'. Examples include *Amazon, eBay, Groupon, Craigslist.*

Play and Game Sites: host games which are intrinsically social. Examples include *FarmVille, CityVille, The Sims Social, Word Feud, Angry Birds.*

However, as van Dijck admits these categories are far from exhaustive. There's also overlap between them. For instance, as anyone who uses Facebook (SNS) will likely have noticed, it's a platform upon which games like FarmVille and CityVille (PGS) are played. Furthermore, much of the impact of user generated content comes from its capacity to circulate through social media (Jenkins et al. 2013). Taxonomies are useful, particularly with something still so relatively new as social media. But there are nonetheless limits to their usefulness. They can help make sense of a messy picture but these categories can't be seen as set in stone.

Social media are often discussed in terms of *web 2.0* (Beer and Burrows 2007), with social media being internet-based applications which build upon these foundations to offer a 'new online layer through which people organize their lives' (van Dijck 2013: loc 125). But web 2.0 is itself a highly contentious term, functioning as both marketing device and ideological lens through which 'internet-centrism' of the sort critiqued by Morozov (2013) has extended its influence even further, helped along by the cultural lure of the tech scene and its alleged economic promise at a time of endemic crisis for capitalism (Keen 2015, Lanier 2014, Marwick 2014). Plus much of how the phrase *web 2.0* has come to be used is in order to categorise and make sense of social media. Therefore it's not much help to turn to this in order to address the more fundamental question of what social media *are*.

Another way into the question is to consider the phase itself. What are *media*? The concept has a long and complex history, but Jones and Hafner (2012) have a helpfully concise way of conveying its essence: 'A medium is something that stands in between two things or people and facilitates interaction between them' (Jones and Hafner 2014: loc 284). So what makes media *social*? Fuchs (2014) highlights four different dimensions to how the term is used: *information*, *communities*, *communication* and *collaboration*. He suggests that what makes social media *social* is an extremely complex matter, reflecting different under-standings of sociality and how they are used to interpret platforms which are social in different ways and to differing degrees. Those with an interest in social theory will likely find value in his discussion, but for more practical purposes it might be necessary to look elsewhere. Baym (2010) offers a range of concepts which can be used to make sense of the differences between various kinds of media: *interactivity*, *temporal structure*, *social cues*, *storage*, *replicability*, *reach* and *mobility*. A full discussion of what she means by these terms would eat away at a limited word count for this chapter. But it certainly points us towards a more useful place, in which we're not contrasting 'traditional media' with 'social media' as if these are two radically distinct types of things, as much as looking at the precise ways in which types of media differ from each other. Social media are still media. But they're media with very specific and exciting characteristics, ones which the social media scholar dana boyd (2014: loc 237-267) usefully describes as *persistence*, *visibility*, *spreadability* and *searchability*.

Persistence means that content cannot be assumed to be forgotten over time, something which Mayer-Schönberger (2011) observes has been true of most information throughout human history. In a later chapter, I explore the idea that the experience of Twitter is similar to that of being at an academic conference, but a conference in which our conversations linger on indefinitely in the room. Assuming we are not being recorded, surreptitiously or otherwise, face-to-face communication leaves no persistent content other than the memo-ries formed by those who participated in the conversation or overheard it. In contrast, communication on social media leaves content as a persistent residue that cannot be assumed to ever disappear.

Visibility means that this persistent content is widely accessible, not least of all because the social media platforms themselves have been designed to ensure that this is the case. As boyd (2014: loc 249) notes, '[m]any popular systems require users to take active steps to limit the visibility of any particular piece of shared content' in sharp contrast to 'physical spaces, where people must make a concerned effort to make content visible to sizeable audiences'.

Spreadability means that these platforms have been designed to ensure that this content can be easily circulated (Jenkins et al. 2013). Not only will the con-tent persist and be visible, unless deliberate steps have been taken to prevent this, it will be easy and enticing for others to circulate it in a way that might lead far beyond the initial context for which it was intended. Hence the many ethical questions which have been raised about live tweeting at academic conferences, to pick on one of many possible examples (McGeeney 2015).

Searchability means that these past communications, as well as being persistent and visible, can often be easily searched after the fact. So even if the visibility hasn't been intensified by others spreading the content online, it's still possible for someone to deliberately find it at a later date or even stumble across it unintentionally. As boyd notes, '[s]earch engines make it easy to surface esoteric interactions' and they do so in a way which systematically strips these interactions of context (boyd 2012: loc 260).

Between them these characteristics offer many opportunities for academics. They allow us to connect with large and/or engaged audiences without having to negotiate established gatekeepers. They offer new ways of working collaboratively within our fields and beyond them. These opportunities are exciting and this book has been written from a perspective that sees them as intrinsically valuable. But they also represent profound challenges. An environment in which communications are *persistent, visible, spreadable* and *searchable* constitutes a radical shift from one in which many, or even most, publications are locked behind journal paywalls and non-citation of papers is rife (Remler 2014). To go from talking to very few people through closed channels to, at least extremely, talking to 'everyone' risks being potentially anxiety-inducing because of the impossibility of knowing how what you publish will spread, what sort of attention it might receive, and what sort of reactions it could provoke. It might be likely that we'll actually provoke no reaction at all. There's a possible hubris underlying our sense of these risks, assuming that the ideas we communicate are so challenging and radical that all manner of consequences might come to fall on us if we communicate them in public, whereas in reality we might entirely fail to be heard. But the number of cases in which the communications of academics have created very real problems is growing with each passing month (Grollman 2015a). So too are attempts by universities to regulate social media, often in ways that could be argued to be motivated more by protecting their institutional brand than by safeguarding the interests of the academics concerned. We'll be returning to these themes at length in later chapters.

Things are changing fast. They'll have changed even more by the time you read this. Given this, it can help to put this in historical perspective. It wasn't so long ago that the internet was seen as a virtual world, divorced from the mundane reality of embodied life. As the social media researcher Jamie Bartlett puts it, 'Users saw it as "a new kind of place", with its own culture, its own identity, and its own rules', and it was for this reason that '[t]he arrival of millions of "ordinary" people online stimulated fears and hopes about what this new form of communication might do to us' (Bartlett 2014: 7). We'd jack into 'cyberspace' and 'surf the web'. To remind yourself of metaphors that were probably once quite familiar, try typing 'surf the web' into images.google.com – it all seems a bit strange in retrospect doesn't it? In large part this is because the way in which we access the internet has changed so radically (Couldry 2014). Lee Rainie and Barry Wellman describe this as the 'triple revolution': 'the turn to social networks, the personalized internet, and always-available mobile connectivity' (Rainie and Wellman 2012: ix). The internet isn't something we have to sit down at a desktop computer or plug our laptop into a cable to use. We don't have to wait for a modem to dial up before we can get on the 'information superhighway'. The ubiquity of wireless internet in public and private spaces, the dizzyingly fast normalisation of the smartphone and the subsequent expansion of tablet computers, have brought about a condition in which the internet is experienced by many, if not most, as always there. It's important not to forget that those who are not 'many' (or 'most') are substantial in number: the digital social inequalities which find expression in what is usually called 'the digital divide' will become ever more central to concerns about social justice in a society where digital technology is ubiquitous (Lupton 2014b: 123–127). But the numbers for whom the texture of daily life is being changed by Rainie and Wellman's 'triple revolution' are far greater still. With a personalised web, accessible from any device, there is no such thing as 'offline'. When the internet is always with us, as opposed to being something to which we deliberately connect, all manner of new social and technical possibilities are opened up. It is these possibilities which are the subject of this book.

How did I come to write this book and how do I hope it will be read?

I began blogging in 2003 when an undergraduate student. It was initially a result of boredom and curiosity, two things I experienced in great abundance as an undergraduate philosophy student prior to discovering sociology. My initial blog was a home for quotes I liked, political rants, music lyrics and random observations. Some of this seemed remarkably cringeworthy when I went back to the blog last year with the benefit of twelve years of hindsight. But this is an occupational hazard of blogging because, as Rettberg (2014) insightfully observes, the fact that blogs are written in real-time means the narrator does not know what the future holds. We don't know the kind of person we will become, who will one day re-read what we have written (Gilbert 2009). Over a decade later I look back upon those early blog posts with a generalised embarrassment. But that's because I do so from a perspective that has in part been shaped by over a decade of blogging. As I went further into the university system, the content of my blogging became increasingly academic. The quotes I gathered became much more likely to be academic ones, as did the issues I addressed and the manner in which I reflected upon events. While I continued in a philosophy department, there was a sharp distinction between the blogging I did as an activist and the blogging I did as a graduate student. It was when I made my transition into a sociology department that this weird tension in my experience, in which I tried to bridge a gap between activism and theory, began to dissipate in the face of a discipline that in an important way refused this separation. As I began my PhD, my blogging became increasingly academic but in a much less narrow sense than had once been the case. It was also increasingly informed by the ideas that now inspired me. The notion put forward by C Wright Mills (2000) of the sociological imagination, linking 'private troubles' to 'public issues', as well as the public sociology of Michael Burawoy (2005) left me with the conviction that sociology should be engaged *with* and *for* the public(s), even if I wasn't entirely clear about what on earth this meant in practical terms. My fumbling exploration of this issue rapidly led me to see that my longstanding hobby could be profoundly important for my growing academic plans.

This led me to set up *The Sociological Imagination* in 2010, soon joined by my good friend and fellow sociologist Milena Kremakova, which we've kept updated on a daily basis for the last five years (Carrigan and Kremakova 2013). Developing a Twitter presence @soc_imagination eventually led me to register a personal Twitter feed and micro-blogging soon became a key part of my working life, helping me find others with similar interests, share the blog posts I'd written, and offering usually helpful interruptions to the rhythm of my daily working life.

My work with a small funded scholarly communications project at Warwick in the arts faculty introduced me to podcasting, something which soon became a favourite hobby of mine as well as a central part of *The Sociological Imagination*. I was hired to maintain a Twitter feed and blog for my department, as well as taking on a variety of social media responsibilities within my professional association. I maintained a Twitter feed and blog for a research network I ran. I began to use social media in a campaigning capacity and got involved in a number of new projects which all used social media. Towards the end of my PhD, I worked at the LSE's Public Policy Group, the team behind the LSE's popular blogs, where I managed the LSE British Politics and Policy blog. My research blogging became ever more significant to me throughout this time and I ran regular training sessions, with *blogging as a research notebook* being a particular focus. I guest blogged regularly on the LSE blogs, even after I left. In more recent years, I've consulted on social media for various journals and research centres, including implementing a completely new presence for *The Sociological Review* which has radically increased its visibility in a fairly short space of time. What was once a hobby has become utterly central to my working life. But rather pleasingly, it still feels like a hobby.

Inevitably then this book has been suffused with social media from the outset. As the media scholar Jose van Dijck has observed, what was once 'a pretty isolated activity' involving 'hours, days, weeks in virtual isolation in archives and libraries or sitting behind a desk' has become 'an intensely social venture at all stages of the process: researching, archiving, communicating ideas, contacting sources, and, of course, endless chatting over different kinds of online media' (van Dijck 2012: loc 64). All the more so for a book like this, which has been reliant on social media for its construction as well as its topic. I couldn't have written it without the many people who have suggested ideas, offered interesting links, and responded constructively to the many occasions upon which I've played with ideas out loud.

However it would be going against the spirit of *Social Media for Academics* to fail to admit that social media have also been a problem. Those many occasions when I've found myself trawling Twitter in lieu of difficult editing, switching mindlessly between channels as I struggle to retain my focus or writing blog posts that skim the surface of a challenging issue rather than addressing it directly in the text. Much more seriously, many other academics have been subject to harassment and abuse through social media, as well as on many occasions being subject to an institutional backlash within their university (McMillan Cottom 2015). Between the triviality of procrastination and the severity of online harassment, there remains a diffuse sense that engaging in activities like blogging can be damaging to academic careers (Rojas 2015). I engage with these questions substantively in later chapters of the book.

Given all this, if the present text reads as a hymn to the virtues of social media then I have not produced the book I set out to write. Nonetheless, I agree with Deborah Lupton (2013a) when she says that 'Academics are now digitised, whether we like it or not'. This stuff isn't going away. In later chapters I discuss some of the negative things on the horizon, particularly the way in which universities risk stifling the creative possibilities of social media in their concern to manage the risks to corporate identity which they pose (Docherty 2015). The present difficulties and future possibilities are ones that have implications for all academics, not least of all in the sense of the 'networked weather' discussed by Weller (2011): the technological environment is changing and this will have important implications, even for those academics who have no interest in engaging on social media. As I discuss in the final chapter, the possibility that social media might be something people increasingly feel forced to do really worries me, not least of all because it seems obvious to me that no one who does it for this reason will extract any enjoyment from it. Nonetheless, I'm aware that digital scholarship will likely prove to be increasingly influential as a marker of capacity for engagement and impact, something increasingly in demand across higher education systems. As McMillan Cottom (2015) puts it, 'Academic capitalism promotes engaged academics as an empirical measure of a university's reputational currency'. The environment is changing and I hope this book will serve as a useful guide which you can dip in and out of, helping you understand these changes and how to respond to them in ways that you find enjoyable and that help you as an academic.

What are the different ways in which you can read this book?

Inevitably, talking about the practical uses which academics can make of social media encourages a tendency to think in terms of tools. What can I *do* with these things? There's much of this in the book but I've tried to incorporate such discussions into a broader framework: what do *you* want to do with these things, *why* do you want to do it? The risk of tool-talk is that we become preoccupied with what we see as *the* uses of the 'tool' and all the other possibilities are foreclosed because we see entirely through this prism. If you're holding a hammer, everything looks like a nail. But unlike hammers, the social media platforms we discuss in this book have *many* uses, though they're not infinitely plastic.

Instead, I've structured this book around *activities* and *challenges*. The first considers scholarly activities which academics engage in and how social media can be used to carry them out and enhance them. In some cases they might even transform them entirely, though I leave it until the final chapter to explore this possibility in any depth. I spoke at length to a number of scholars whose use of social media I admire about their own practice. I have used their experiences as illustrations wherever possible, hopefully in a way which brings to life the issue under discussion and offers examples which can easily be found online.

These are the activities around which the next four chapters revolve:

- Publicising Your Work
- Building Your Network
- Engaging With Publics
- Managing Information

This list is far from exhaustive. These are the activities for which I will argue social media have the most profound implications. An obvious omission here is teaching. But this is such a huge topic that it requires a book in its own right (for example Poore 2016).

The subsequent three chapters address the *challenges* confronted when using social media as an academic:

- Professional Identity
- Communicating Effectively
- Finding the Time for Social Media

Facets of these issues are discussed in the prior chapters. But in these three, I enter into them in a systematic way, addressing their different dimensions and how these impact differently upon people. The final chapter then discusses the changing landscape of academic social media, addressing the likely outcomes of trends which are still only in their infancy. 'Potential Pitfalls' boxes appear throughout chapters highlighting aspects of using social media that need careful consideration – these should help you avoid some of the common errors and obstacles that can beset both beginning and more experienced users. I also offer suggestions for further reading at the end of each chapter.

Further reading

- *The Digital Scholar: How Technology is Transforming Scholarly Practice* by Martin Weller (2012) offers a fascinating overview of the emergence of digital scholarship.
- *The Culture of Connectivity: A Critical History of Social Media* by Jose Van Dijck (2012) is a sophisticated analysis of social media that places each platform in a much wider context.
- *It's Complicated: The Social Lives of Networked Teens* by danah boyd (2014) is an extremely readable and insightful account of how social media are transforming human connectedness.

2

Using social media to publicise your work

Chapter themes

This chapter will:

- Explore how social media can be used to publicise academic work
- Discuss the opportunities for engagement social media offer above and beyond traditional forms of publishing
- Offer some practical guidance on publicising your work, and on using some popular tools that can support this
- Consider some of the risks inherent in publishing your work online

This chapter discusses how social media can be used to publicise academic work and how, in turn, social media can become part of this work. It was difficult to decide upon the word 'publicise' in framing this chapter. To talk of publicity has negative connotations and if the phrase 'self-publicist' has associations these are rarely positive. It's not unlike 'networking' as a term associated with careerism and instrumentalism. However, in the same way that we might distinguish between 'Networking' and networking, as the difference between an aggressively instrumental activity and simply seeking to cultivate connections with others who share your interests, it's helpful to distinguish between 'Publicising' and publicising. While we might see 'Publicising' as involving aggressive, continual and untargeted announcements of your research and your publications, we can distinguish this from simply seeking to ensure that *those who might be interested know about your work.*

Part of the problem here is that social media are often equated with triviality and narcissism. The prominent British journalist Andrew Marr once opined that 'A lot of bloggers seem to be socially inadequate, pimpled, single, slightly seedy, bald, cauliflower-nosed young men sitting in their mother's basements and ranting' (Plunkett 2010). A strand of common sense which sees social media in such terms, or as providing means for 'people to talk about what they had for breakfast', has been reinforced by a literature of cyber-pessimism of varying degrees of sophistication, accusing social media of bringing about a state of 'digital vertigo', 'the shallows' or 'the big disconnect' to name but three examples (Carr 2011, Keen 2012, Slade 2012). Careers can clearly be made from this: for instance, Andrew Keen developed his arguments into a further, slightly gloomier book, *The Internet is Not the Answer* (Keen 2015), which despite being a bit better was remarkably reliant upon internet sources. As Morozov (2013) and others have pointed out, these cyber-pessimists are the mirror image of cyber-optimists like Clay Shirky (2008, 2011). Both see technology as leading inexorably to certain outcomes. As boyd (2014: loc 310) puts it, 'Utopian and dystopian views assume that technologies possess intrinsic powers that affect *all* people in *all* situations the same way'. We need to avoid this for reasons that are obvious, at least once the assumption is stated explicitly.

Nonetheless, the characteristics of academics and of higher education are going to have a big impact on how academics use social media within higher education. So for the purposes of this book it's useful if we can at least partially step back from our notions about social media in general and consider the particular kinds of uses to which these technologies may be put within the particular surroundings of higher education. These uses might be trivial and narcissistic. But they probably won't be. What's more likely is that they'll build upon existing things that academics do, helping in some ways and hindering in others. They'll suggest new ways of doing these things and change how we see existing ones. They'll also suggest new things we can do, with this novelty entailing all sorts of consequences for long-established professional practices and standards.

In the case of the present chapter, which considers how social media can be used to help publicise our research and publications, we immediately run into the question of what it means for something to be 'public'. Underlying the widespread equation of social media with triviality is the fear that, as the novelist Jonathan Franzen (2007: 50) puts it in a discussion of privacy and cyber-culture, '[r]eticence, meanwhile, has become an obsolete virtue'. So when we see self-promotion as something negative, it perhaps reflects a more pervasive unease with the emphasis placed upon being visible; in our quest to be seen, to be recognised in public, we perhaps leave something important behind. On this view, publicity is seen as something suspect and questionable, to be contrasted with an intrinsic worth that doesn't require visibility to legitimate it. But then the 'ivory tower' has always had a complex relationship to privacy. After all, as the sociologist Les Back suggests, 'we academic scribes are not always very sociable' (2007: 163).

This undoubtedly varies between people and across disciplines. But I think Back correctly identifies what is at least a tendency within academic life. Oddly for a profession so dominated by publishing, with its literal meaning of 'making public', practical questions concerning the visibility and circulation of the actual publications which ensue have rarely received the attention that an outsider might expect. Certainly, there are 'how to' guides, but these tend to be problem orientated or aimed at graduate students. We might ask: *how public are our publications?* Inevitably, the answer depends upon what we have published and where we have published it. A paper published by an open access journal is in one sense more public than a chapter included within an expensive edited book. But what if the edited book has been widely promoted, enjoying an enhanced prestige and visibility in virtue of the commentators assembled within it? Is a paper published in a high-impact journal, read and recognised throughout a discipline, more public than one published in a highly relevant sub-disciplinary journal with a narrow but focused readership pertinent to the paper's topic? The point here is not to give way to an extended philosophical digression about what it means for something to be 'public' but only to indicate some of the practical dimensions to this issue. Learning how to approach publication in journals is a key aspect of professional socialisation, in which an aspiring academic learns to understand the topography of an intellectual field, framing their work within it and (hopefully) learning to negotiate the relevant gatekeepers who control access to the relevant public forums necessary to establish a career (Agger 2000).

The opportunities social media provide to publicise our research and publications invite us to consider issues such as these in much greater depth. The considerations discussed above concern how to place a journal article to maximal effect. In reality, how public the published article would be is only likely to be one factor amongst many in shaping the decision as to where to send it, though perhaps one that will become more pertinent with the unfolding institutionalisation of open access. In fields where publication in high-impact journals is a requirement, it's possible that factors such as these won't enter into deliberation at all. What makes these questions of which journal to choose interesting from the perspective of social media for academics is how relatively limited the options available for ensuring the publicity of the article now seem. The account Daniels (2013) offers of going 'from tweet at an academic conference, to a blog post, to a series of blog posts to a paper that became an article' is just one of the many potential iterations that become possible through social media, potentially transforming the process of 'making public' into something radically different (Carrigan and Lockley 2011). For instance, the psychologist MJ Barker described to me how they were invited by a journal to extend a blog post they had written into a paper for that journal. The cultural policy academic Dave O'Brien told me how he saw blogging as something to ensure his papers were more widely read. My own experience has been that many of the ideas that end up in my formal publications were initially rehearsed, sometimes rather speculatively, on my own blog.

There are certainly risks, which we'll come to later in this chapter. For now, my intention is simply to highlight some examples of how publishing is changing as a practice. Authors' potential influence upon the process has largely been a matter of choosing a journal which could best ensure that the right people saw their article. With open access, it became a matter of weighing up the greater visibility that would ensue from publishing in an open journal versus the loss of prestige which it would likely have entailed until relatively recently. The emergence of social media complicates this situation by radically extending authors' options for publicising their own work. In a sense though, it's still a matter of announcing that work within existing networks. It's just that the possibilities of *how* to announce and the potential scope of that network have expanded dramatically.

Publicising scholarship in the digital academy

Social media raise questions about publicising academic work of a sort which simply did not make sense when much of this activity was unavoidably con-ducted by publishing houses and perhaps, more recently, by communications offices in the case of particularly consequential research (Weller 2011). Perhaps the relationship between the words 'publicising' and 'publishing' reflects this: the former means to make something well known, the latter to prepare and issue it to the market. Until recently the 'publisher' was responsible for both. Now, to use the fashionable term, we're beginning to see their unbundling. Increasingly academics collaborate with publishers on publicising their books, sometimes to a degree that would have once seemed remarkable (e.g. paying money to hire a publicist) and in some cases without much of the promised support from the publisher (Chen 2015). Sometimes they're also publishing the book themselves, though this is still a comparatively rare practice. The changing dynamic between 'publicising' and 'publishing' captures significant changes in scholarly publishing, albeit ones much more developed in the sphere of books than in journal articles.

Much of this chapter will concentrate on the *practical questions* entailed by this, but to draw the present discussion to a close we can consider what these new opportunities call into question. There's always a risk of caricature when trying to convey an established way of doing things, particularly when the intention is to contrast it to a newer (often by implication better) way of working. Nonetheless, it's hard not to see an element of truth in political scientist Patrick Dunleavy's (2014b) description of 'academic hermits, sitting alone on top of a pillar somewhere in academia and doing their level best to not communicate in any way with the outside world, or let any information about their work leak out'. While there's an obviously polemic dimension to this accusation, it's a claim made on the basis of a sophisticated piece of empirical research which sought to better understand the impact that academics do and don't have. As Dunleavy explains, his research team were unable to compile basic information on 35% of the academics they had initially targeted to be part of their random stratified sample. There was simply no information available about themselves and their work. Now these academics might not be working in solitude, in one sense of the term 'hermit', and, furthermore, any discussion to this end must recognise disciplinary differences in relation to working individually and in teams. But they surely are being reclusive in the other sense of the word, at least in relation to the proliferating opportunities for engagement which social media afford for academics.

While the motivations for seeking to publicise your work might seem obvious, it can nonetheless be helpful to take a moment to articulate precisely what these are. Here are some examples:

1. I want to increase the frequency with which my work is cited
2. I want to increase my visibility within my research area
3. I want to increase my visibility within my discipline
4. I want to disseminate my research to practitioners and others outside the academy
5. I want to generate media interest in my work

These reasons are neither exhaustive nor mutually exclusive, but being clear about *your* reasons can be immensely valuable in negotiating the practical questions encountered by anyone seeking to engage online: what service should I use? How should I use it? How should I combine multiple services? Being clear about your goals at the outset does not entail they must be set in stone, but it does give you a starting point without which engaging online can be a confusing and ambiguous experience.

However, such questions don't simply concern what you want *to get out of it*. How you choose to answer these questions also depends on what you are willing and able to *put into it*. How much time do you have? These themes will run through the next four chapters. The different purposes considered in each of these chapters (publicity, networking, engagement and managing information) all overlap to some degree and all of them entail similar issues. My hope is that considering similar issues from a variety of perspectives will help deepen your understanding of what's at stake in each of them.

Potential Pitfalls

The issue of sustainability is one we'll come back to at various points throughout this book, but in brief it is simply a reminder to *be realistic*. Consider how much time you have. Consider how much energy you have. Consider the viability of your goals in light of these constraints. It will help you more to have a basic personal home page that you update regularly on an ongoing basis than it will to have a Wordpress blog on which you post twice weekly for a month before other commitments push it out of the picture. It will help you more to have a Twitter account you use regularly than to have rarely updated profiles across the full range of social media platforms. As the cultural policy scholar Ele Belfiore put it when we discussed this, 'because there are only so many hours in the day, I tend to stick with what works for me and that I enjoy'. Once you find what works for you, stick with it. There's no need to be active on all platforms and doing so could easily detract from your capacity to derive any satisfaction or enjoyment from a single one of them. It might be that *guest blogging* is right for you: approaching established blogs with offers of posts on particular subjects. The experience Dave O'Brien recounted to me of soon building up helpful relationships with the editors of these blogs is becoming an increasingly common one. Alternatively, it might be that a group blog or Twitter feed is the best thing here, allowing you to split the workload between a group of collaborators.

What is 'publishing'?

What is 'publishing'? Most would see it as integral to what academics do and yet the nature of this centrality has changed over time, with 'publish or perish' now axiomatic in a way that would have previously been unthinkable (Carrigan 2015a). The practice of publishing changes with the institutions within and through which one publishes. This is a matter of new opportunities but also of new pressures, as Laura Brown and her co-authors stress in their helpful definition:

> By publishing we mean simply the communication and broad dissemination of knowledge, a function that has become both more complex and more important with the introduction and rapid evolution of digital and networking technologies. There is a seeming limitless range of opportunities for a faculty member to distribute his or her work, from setting up a web page or blog, to posting an article to a working paper website or institutional repository, to including it in a peer-reviewed journal or book. (Brown et al. 2007)

In this sense, we can see that the meaning of 'publishing' isn't fixed. So what is fundamental to it? What makes 'publishing' publishing beyond the particular forms of publications which might be involved? In an important way we can think of 'publishing' in terms of 'making public'. Exactly what can and should be 'made public' is partly a function of the technology available, and with the emergence of social media platforms the range of potential forms of publication has expanded greatly. This helps bridge the gap between 'publishing' and 'publicising': the former has always entailed the latter but in a way which usually entailed this being the publisher's responsibility rather than the author's. Social media complicate this longstanding state of affairs when offering many new opportunities for authors to publicise their own publications. Furthermore, academics are under a diverse range of pressures across international higher education systems to demonstrate the impact of their publications and establish their public relevance (Burrows 2012). It's for this reason that *publicising* will inevitably be a big part of how academics use social media, but hopefully as we go on it'll become clear that this needn't have its usual negative connotations when applied to publications.

Publicising your publications

An obvious question posed by an intention to 'publicise your publications' is how to make that work available in a way susceptible to promotion. While it is certainly possible to simply announce the existence of a piece of work, doing so is unlikely to encourage others to engage with it unless they have a strong pre-existing reason to do so. It will always be more effective to provide a URL where the work can be obtained online, or at the very least, details about where it can be found. However this can be easier said than done. Though most journals will be accessible online, this is by no means true of all. Chapters in edited books can be difficult to obtain, with a tendency for publishers to focus on purchases by institutional libraries leading to small print runs. Putting the effort into making your work *accessible* certainly represents an additional set of demands involved in online engagement. However, if you seriously intend to publicise your work online then putting some thought into ensuring accessibility can really enhance the effectiveness of your activity. How accessible are the publications you want to publicise online? Are there people in other fields who might be interested in your work? Are there people outside the academy who might be interested in your work?

Yet 'accessibility' is not a straightforward concept. Making pre-prints available, writing blog posts and sharing other resources might be 'accessible' relative to material that is published in a pay walled journal for which few have access. But there are issues of accessibility specific to social media: there are 'web accessibility barriers that people commonly encounter from poorly designed websites and web tools' which pose difficulties for those with auditory, cognitive, neurological, physical, speech and visual disabilities (W3C 2012a). Familiarising yourself with accessibility principles is necessary to avoid inadvertently creating new barriers around material which your intention is to make accessible (W3C 2012b). These include providing text alternatives for non-text content, for instance by using the option in blogging platforms to provide a text caption for images included within posts. Text transcripts of multimedia content can be difficult without funding but they ensure an accessibility which is otherwise denied. YouTube actually offer automatic captioning on videos that meet certain technical criteria. These can easily be edited to improve their accuracy, something which varies greatly depending on the quality of the video. WebAxe (2012a) offer a really helpful introduction to these issues, stressing how '[d]espite the web's great potential for people with disabilities, this potential is still largely unrealized'. They summarise potential design issues in order to highlight the perspective of the end user, for whom what might have seemed to be trivial issues relating to the design in fact render the content inaccessible (WebAxe 2012b). WebAxe (2011) provide 25 ways to help make your website accessible. In researching this topic for the book, with particular help from Sarah Lewthwaite, I realised how little I'd thought about these issues in my own online activity and the state of the web suggests that I'm far from being alone in this. Hopefully we'll see the emergence of an *expectation* that those engaging online take steps to this end, because without it academic social media will remain characterised by a pervasive inaccessibility.

Standing out from the crowd

Part of the pressure to publicise one's work comes from the sheer volume of publication. Arguably reflecting a much broader acceleration of the pace of social life (see Agger 2004 for an engaging overview of this idea), it seems that ever more publications are being released only to be read, we might pessimistically assume, by ever fewer people. The challenge posed by this proliferating stream of content is how to ensure your publications are recognised and read when there are so many other books, chapters and articles available to potential readers, as well as so many other demands on their time. Haunting discussions and debates about this challenge is the spectre of 'unread' and 'unloved' publications (see Back 2008), with ever more articles and chapters attracting ever fewer readers and often no citations whatsoever. Obviously the meaning of citation is a complex issue, however this chapter is being written from the assumption that if you're seeking to 'publicise your work' then you're seeking to increase its circulation and influence. All I'm suggesting here is that citation *fallibly* tracks influence, in so far as that someone choosing to cite your publication presumably indicates that they have encountered it and it has influenced them sufficiently to lead them to cite it, whether positively or negatively. As Bastow et al. put it, 'Within academia itself, the central form of such influence is for author B to cite an earlier author A's work, which implies that B has read the work and found it valuable in some respect'. Though critical citation certainly happens, this occurs much less frequently than many assume (2014: 37). So while we should avoid any simplistic assumption that citation rates track the value of publications, it seems necessary to recognise that they are measuring *something*. As will be discussed later in the book, social media provide many alternative ways of tracking the influence of publications, which can readily be seen to *complement* citation rather than *replacing* it, fleshing out what can sometimes be a simplistic measure. Non-citation rates vary widely across disciplines, but the rapidity with which inflated non-citation rates circulate as urban legends points towards an underlying anxiety (Remler 2014). This might confirm a personal fear ('no one cares about what I write') or it might license a self-aggrandising judgement ('obviously people will cite *my* work but most people's work isn't worth citing'). What seems clear is that being cited does matter to most people, to at least some degree. Nonetheless, a focus upon citation doesn't entail the view that citation is the only thing that matters (Biswas and Kirchherr 2015).

Leaving aside these questions concerning citation for now, we can turn to the question of how you can help increase the frequency with which your work is cited. For people to cite your work, they will (hopefully!) have engaged with it. For people to have engaged with it, they will have had to open it. For people to have opened it, they will have had to download it. For people to have downloaded it, they will have had to access it. For people to have accessed it, they will have had to find it (Wang 2014). So when this chapter discusses 'publicising your work', this actually amounts to a number of things: inventorying your publications, making them accessible and publicising them.

Google Scholar

The most common way in which academics inventory their work is a publications list. In such a list, sometimes though not always part of a CV, publications are itemised and ordered. However these lists are frequently far from accessible, providing (sometimes incomplete) bibliographical details but failing to help a potential reader gain access to the publications in question. One useful starting point for making your work accessible is Google Scholar. Establishing a Google Scholar profile is quick and easy. In fact, if you already have an existing Google account, for instance as a Gmail user, then you might be surprised to find that you already have a Google Scholar profile waiting to be activated.

Google Scholar offers a number of additional features which can be valuable beyond publicising your work online. It tracks citations of your work in a way which can help you understand the influence it is having. It alerts you to new publications which might be of interest, utilising your citation network to make what I at least have found to be very useful recommendations. Maintaining your

Google Scholar profile serves another important function: it helps make the 'grey literature' visible by allowing you to incorporate working papers and blog posts into your profile. I've discovered this way that I've frequently had my blog posts cited in journal articles. However the newfound visibility of such material is not always welcome. Occasionally pruning your profile, adding overlooked items and removing reconsidered ones, can help sustain a clear portfolio of the research that you're choosing to track and are presenting to the world as being worth tracking.

Institutional repositories

Much discussion of academic social media inevitably moves attention away from the institution, but one of the most valuable features of the landscape for digital scholarship might actually be at your institution itself. Many institutions run repositories for publications, in which you can file and index all your publications, often in a way that makes pre-prints accessible to a wider audience. As well as directly leading people towards your papers, using social network services can also increase their Google ranking because of the value that is assigned to links from high-ranking domains. Another useful feature is the capacity to track how many people find your articles and how many download them. Terras (2012) used this to track the influence of her social media engagement on the profile of her publications, once she had lodged them in her institution's repository. The results were certainly positive, though our understanding of the link between downloading papers and their being read remains imprecise (Wang 2014). As Terras (2012) observes, the real test will come with the growing citation, or lack thereof, further down the line after this initiative. Using institutional repositories can be the most immediate option for self-archiving your academic work, albeit restricted in most cases to pre-prints (and even then, it's important to check your copyright agreement with the publisher in question) (Lupton 2013b). But without some additional activity, such as that undertaken by Terras (2012), simply making it available online is not going to ensure people stumble across it.

Personal websites

Many academics will already have a university web page but using it effectively to publicise their work is a different matter. It is something which can too easily be overlooked in an age of social media. But a home page can be an effective way of integrating your social media activity into a coherent whole. Ele Belfiore explained to me how she felt her institutional web page had become *more* rather than less important as a result of her social media engagement, with the traffic she soon observed on the website motivating her to make a sustained effort to keep it regularly updated with a wide range of information about her work. As she put it, 'The people who want to find out more will go on my staff page'. However, this leads to issues of control and autonomy within the university as a drive towards the standardisation of the brand leads many universities to impose restrictions on staff web pages or even take away direct control of them altogether (Corbyn 2010). This was certainly MJ Barker's experience, who described to me how WordPress provided a degree of control over online publishing that simply wasn't available at their institution. Furthermore, given the insecurity of academic employment, in which a long-term presence at one institution is becoming the exception rather than the rule, it seems likely we'll see a drift away from voluntary affiliation with the university brand through websites. Nonetheless, many do keep a personal website as well as an institutional website, in spite of the additional workload this entails.

An often unanticipated benefit to time spent tweaking a personal website is the panoramic perspective this can help engender about your work as a whole. Though the risk that this becomes a powerful excuse for procrastination should not be underestimated! This issue is explored at length in a later chapter. The process of inventorying, sorting and presenting your work can help illuminate the interconnections within it. What can be particularly helpful here is identifying the themes within your research, in order to present your publications in an engaging and accessible way. Using your website to prominently display your publications frees them from the sequential and reductive ordering entailed by a list. It offers an opportunity to categorise your publications, defining your research agenda(s) and gifting a visibility to individual items which is impossible in a list. Using images of book covers or journal covers can help individual publications stand out, as can giving space to the relevant abstracts, blurbs and details about where a reader can gain access to the publication in question. These can be URLs to publishers' websites, journal websites or pre-print copies of an article in an institutional repository.

Social networks

Social networks designed specifically for academics are growing in popularity, with services like Academia.edu and ResearchGate effectively constituting a 'Facebook for academics'. These can play a specific role of allowing you to archive papers in a way, while categorising them and promoting them to others who share an interest in these topics. The Victorianist Charlotte Mathieson described to me how Academia.edu provided an online presence that she saw as having a more official feel than her Twitter profile. It also highlighted her research in a way other platforms didn't. She also told me how her experience of tagging her papers by topic on Academia.edu almost immediately led to a demonstrable increase of interest in them, leaving her with a clear sense of how easy it was to find people on there and how actively engaged other members were as researchers.

The functionality of these services is geared towards the specific professional needs of academics as opposed to simply being smaller and professionalised versions of 'mainstream' social networks. Nonetheless the two can be used in tandem, with engagement on Facebook and Twitter helping to increase the usefulness of these more specialised networks. One advantage to using social networks that only becomes apparent when joining a service like Academia.edu is the role played by the 'social graph'. This term was popularised by Facebook but it has meaning beyond that service, in essence referring to a map of the relations which exist between users. By accessing your social graph from another service (such as Facebook, Twitter or your e-mail contacts) a new social network you sign up to becomes immediately of use in a way that would not otherwise be the case, incorporating your existing connections into ones that can be used as part of the new service. As well as helping to abate the spiralling numbers of usernames and passwords most internet users will be forced to deal with (or the security problems that can ensue from using the same password for all services), the social graph helps underwrite the usefulness of other services by leveraging your existing network to your activity using this new tool.

The service LinkedIn usually gets included in discussions of social networks for professionals. While some people report finding the discussion groups on the sites useful, it is far from clear how widespread the uptake of LinkedIn has been within academia, with their incisive deployment of new users' social graphs (see above) perhaps going some way to explaining the spread of the service. The vast majority of readers have surely received an 'I'd like to add you to my professional network on LinkedIn' e-mail at some point. Undoubtedly, the value of LinkedIn varies between disciplines and it may serve a useful purpose for those seeking to build and sustain networks amongst practitioners and policy makers. Nonetheless, it's easy to fall into the trap of assuming that a lot of people being *signed up* to a service means a lot of people are *using it*. There's no need to join LinkedIn just because a lot of other people seem to be using it.

Social networks can be an extremely effective way of publicising your research. At the very least, announce your new publications and share a link for those who will be interested. It can also be fascinating to see 'ideas in motion', reading and talking to people *during* the research process. This is a theme we'll return to multiple times later in the book. But Dave O'Brien offered a prescient warning when I discussed his use of social media with him: 'imagine if you were in conversation with someone and all they did was robotically, every two or three hours, tell you they were speaking at a seminar or had a new book out … you wouldn't want to speak to those people would you?' In other words – don't overdo it.

New forms of academic publishing

Thus far in the chapter we've considered 'traditional' forms of academic publication: monographs, edited books, book chapters and journal articles. These are integral to scholarship and seem likely to remain so for the foreseeable future, though of course their relative importance varies across disciplines and will likely change over time. One of the key factors driving such a change will be the way in which 'new' forms of publishing reshape the visibility and influence of 'traditional' forms of publishing. But what are these 'new' forms of publishing we're referring to? These are things like:

- Tweets
- Blog posts
- Podcasts
- Videocasts
- Curated collections
- Shared files

While many of the new publishing opportunities which social media afford can be seen as 'free standing', it is likely that most will be connected in some way to your research process more broadly. An important part of using social media effectively as an academic involves reflecting on this connection and ensuring it is best suited to meeting your prior goals, tweaking it if this is not the case. Some instances of this can be very trivial – for example if you are using Twitter to try and connect with others in your field but rarely tweet about specialised issues relevant to that field then you're unlikely to get very far! But as we'll see, the new opportunities which social media present us with raise some very non-trivial questions which reward further reflection. For instance if you have a new book being released, how could you best use social media to raise awareness of it? The rest of this section will consider some of the ways in which 'old' and 'new' can be linked to maximal effect.

There are many ways in which these new forms of academic publishing can be associated with more traditional modes of scholarly communication. One running theme throughout this book is the importance of rejecting the view that there are 'right' and 'wrong' ways for academics to use social media. Certainly, the things we can do online are likely to elicit varying degrees of approval and disapproval from the professional communities and networks within which we are embedded. But it is important to remember that social media are not the source of these professional norms. While they can complicate them, in ways that have important implications for the future landscape of social media, this should not be a reason for seeing academic social media use as somehow cut off from everyday life in a 'virtual world' of Twitter, blogging and Facebook distinct from the 'real world' of seminars, lectures and meetings. While using Twitter as an academic for the first time can *feel* very different from, say, attending an academic conference, it is worth being critical of this feeling. How is it different precisely? There are other academics, some of whom are known to you but many probably are not. There are existing networks between them that can help and hinder you in different ways. There are differing identities and interests, different ways of conducting and discussing research. We'll discuss in the next chapter how social media can enhance your participation in academic events but the point here is simply to stress that the novelty of these tools doesn't render your existing ways of doing things and evaluating their worth irrelevant. In short, *go with what works for you* but also recognise that 'what works' may have to be thought out a little more explicitly than usual when it comes to social media because of the novelty of the subject matter.

It is for these reasons that it is worth thinking in detail about how to link up 'old' and 'new' media publications. Differing interests and standards will tend to manifest themselves in divergent senses of what would be an appropriate or inappropriate way to use social media to further the reach of your publications online. Go with these feelings! While it can be extremely useful to consider the things that other people are doing, it's too easy to infer from trends we can witness that this is the 'right' way for academics to use social media or that what we were considering is the 'wrong' way. The key thing is to figure out what works for you and pursue this strategy in an enthusiastic and sustainable way, while avoiding the small number of objective pitfalls, by which I mean things which are errors in virtue of the properties of a platform itself (and are signposted in the 'Potential Pitfalls' boxes throughout the book).

In the rest of this section we'll consider four possible ways in which 'old' and 'new' can be linked in publishing. What they all have in common is using social media to enhance the visibility of an academic publication. These connected publications can take on a life of their own, circulating across online networks and potentially leading to a vast increase in the number of people who stumble across your book or journal article. We tend not to think of how it is others find our publications, either because the publisher takes responsibility for promoting a book or we assume being in a journal ensures the capacity to be found, but social media invite us to take a much more active role in this process.

Publicising

The simplest relationship a social media publication can have to a traditional publication is to *publicise* it. On the most basic level this can just be a tweet or a short blog post to announce a new publication. This can sometimes feel like a slightly awkward thing to do, particularly for the first time, given the connotations sometimes attached to 'self-promotion'. But if you're an academic who is blogging or tweeting then it is par for the course that one of the things you will blog or tweet about will be your publications. So let people know when you have a new publication. Explain what it is, where it's been published, and how they can access it. If it's a book then share any discount codes your publisher has given you. There's absolutely nothing wrong with circulating this information more than once. Twitter in particular is a medium that moves at a fast pace and the fact you've posted the same announcement a few times is much more readily apparent to you than it will be to most of your followers. Ideally space out the announcements over a certain time period and vary the wording to highlight various aspects of the announcement.

It's important to remember that *other people* will be publicising your work as well, though it's rather unlikely they'll see it in those terms. By using curation tools, discussed later in the book, it's possible to collate and present engagements with your work. For a book this might involve searching for reviews and collating them into a package with a permanent URL which can then be linked to from your own website. For an article this might involve using altmetrics and social search to collate links to the URL and curating these references, as well as the associated discussions, into a Storify which can then be included alongside the article in your catalogue of publications.

Furthermore, if you find people talking about your work online, why not talk back? To feel a certain reticence here is understandable, particularly when you found the discussion through searching for yourself, but this is much more likely to be your reading of the situation than it is theirs. For instance, one of the most enjoyable aspects of Twitter can be to suddenly find yourself in dialogue with a person whose work you were discussing. After all, if someone cares enough about your work to discuss it online then why wouldn't they want to talk to you about it? Engaging them in conversation doesn't commit you to any sort of ongoing dialogue but it can sometimes prove an immensely valuable experience, offering new perspectives or new insights that can contribute towards your future work. I've written about my own experience of this in Carrigan (2014b) when encountering a community newsletter discussing my work prompted a dialogue on my blog, a host of comments from community members, and recognition on my part of a significant oversight in a previous publication.

Summarising

Summarising our work is a familiar challenge. In many cases the summary we are asked for will be brief and functional, for instance an abstract for a presentation or paper. But social media open up new possibilities for 'extended abstracts' which have their own aesthetic and intellectual qualities, circulating independent of the papers or chapters they are connected to and encouraging the reader who encounters them to explore more deeply. They could take the form of a blog post which lays out the key arguments of your paper or the key findings, referring readers to the paper itself for the necessary methodological or empirical detail. It might be tweets of your paper which attempt to summarise it in 140 characters or less – no doubt a challenge but it can be an interesting one. It might be a micro-podcast between yourself and your co-author, discussing the main points addressed in the paper, personalising yourselves as authors and inviting readers to explore it more deeply. There are many ways in which social media can be used to summarise scholarly work and doing this isn't repetition, even if it feels like it. It helps make your paper more accessible and gives it a parallel existence in a much more fast-moving space, while nonetheless retaining its own existence as documented scholarship.

Contextualising

Behind every publication is a story. It might not always be an interesting story, but it's a story nonetheless. Why has the author written *this* paper? Why have they written it in *that* way? Why does the topic *matter* to them? One way to approach the relationship between a traditional publication and supporting forms of digital engagement is to see the former as being contextualised by the latter. For instance a journal article could have a video abstract or an edited collection could have an accompanying blog post submitted to a multi-author blog (more on this later). To blog about the work while it's in progress can accomplish the same thing. The political theorist Stuart Elden described to me how he would blog *about* his work, but not blog *the* work. His posts would cover the process of writing, things like chasing down references and copy editing, as well sharing resources he'd compiled in the process of undertaking the research. In one case, he collated past posts which tracked an entire book project from inception to completion (Elden 2015).

Constituting

This might be the least intuitive but also the most interesting way in which social media activity can be connected to academic publications. The philosopher Daniel Little has described this as being an 'open-source philosopher'. After six years of maintaining his Understanding Society blog, he reflected on the way he had seen the project and how it had unfolded over time:

> The blog is an experiment in writing a book, one idea at a time. In order to provide a bit more coherence for the series of postings, I've organized a series of threads that link together the postings relevant to a particular topic. These can be looked at as virtual "chapters". This list of topics and readings can serve as the core of a semester-long discussion of the difficult philosophical issues that arise in the human sciences. It roughly parallels the topics I cover in the course I teach in the philosophy of social science at the University of Michigan. (Little 2013)

The blog allowed his readers to 'observe ideas in motion' long before they would have otherwise found expression in print. I talked to Daniel at length about his experiences, something which we'll return to more than once later in the book. For that matter, this book itself has been constructed, in part, through a series of postings in a category on my own blog. To a certain extent this was just a matter of habit, with the blog providing a useful place to collate research and ideas while I was in the process of working on them. But it's become habitual because I've found it such an enjoyable way to work, inviting dialogue and discussion far earlier in the research process than would otherwise be the case and enlivening it as a result. This sort of 'continual publishing' – namely doing as much of the research process as possible 'out in the open' – may not be for everyone, but it's an interesting possibility which social media have afforded (Carrigan 2013a).

What are the risks of publishing your work online?

Notoriously, as the adage goes, *the internet never forgets*. There's some truth to this and we discuss the potential implications for how you communicate online later in the book. Making copies of what you post online is integral to how search engines work and it is unlikely that the economics of online search would remain functioning if the burden was on Google and other search engines to proactively gain permission to produce these caches (Vaidhyanathan 2012: loc 1266). Some platforms make it possible to restrict access to search engines, for instance there is such an option buried away in the Wordpress settings, but doing so has obvious consequences for the functionality of the blog in question: it makes it much more difficult for people to find it. I had a reminder of how unnerving this can be during the process of writing, as I discovered that an open letter I wrote after a spat with my professional association was, seemingly uniformly, being returned as the third Google result when you searched for the name of the association. While I have no desire to rejoin the association, the sense of animus had long since dissipated and the discovery of how prominently the letter was displayed left me feeling as if I'd been egregiously and unnecessarily rude, albeit algorithmically so.

I immediately deleted the letter from my blog, while leaving an associated note (easily discoverable by anyone who searched for the name of the professional association on my site) in order to make sure that anyone searching for the letter was able to find it. However 24 hours later it has still not been de-indexed by Google, although my understanding is that it will be. The entry remains prominent, though anyone clicking on it now gets a 'page not found' error from my blog rather than an indignant tirade. This experience reminded me of another occasion, on which I'd written a post about the writing style of a philosopher I admire immensely upon reading that his composition method was to dictate his books and then have these transcribed. I was surprised to find this incorporated into a

Wikipedia article, cited as evidence in a section about criticisms of his writing style. This wasn't my intention at all. Both incidents were useful reminders of the dangers of making things public online. They might become much more prominent than you would expect or be comfortable with. They might also be misunderstood and/or deployed to bolster a case with which you might be immensely uncomfortable. In a sense these risks aren't new – the same things were possible, if rather unlikely, when academics published via journals. But the characteristics of social media make these risks much more likely.

In fact digital technology as a whole creates new risks for existing publications, as the astonishing case of Andrew Feldmar makes clear. This Vancouver psychotherapist was stopped at the US border by an agent who searched his name, soon discovering an academic paper he had written in which he spoke of having used LSD as a student in the 1960s. He was prevented from entering the United States, despite having no criminal convictions or being flagged as suspicious in any way, other that the border guard had found a piece of academic work from *half a decade* earlier that described personal experiences *four decades* earlier which were deemed to be problematic (Vaidhyanathan 2012: 177).

It's undoubtedly an extreme case, but as Vaidhyanathan observes 'Even ten years ago we did not consider that words written for a specific audience could easily reach beyond that group and harm us at the hands of an ignorant and malicious reader' (2012: loc 3153). In the case of academics, it was probably a safe assumption that readers would share at least some degree of intellectual orientation and socialisation which introduces a degree of predictability into how things would be interpreted. It is not so much that this has now gone but rather that it has been supplemented by an infinitely diverse range of *potential* readers, with all the unpredictability that implies. Dwelling on this could prove rather inhibiting, to say the least, leaving the online world appearing as replete with an endless array of unknowable threats. But making your work public without considering these changes would be every bit as problematic, as well as being much more risky. The crucial thing is being clear about what you take those risks to be, as related to what *you* are publishing online and the work *you* are doing more broadly. Lupton's (2014a) findings offer some really useful insights into the anxieties, some much more concrete than others, surrounding publicising (and publishing) one's work online.

Perhaps the issue foremost in academics' minds when discussing the risks of making work public online is *plagiarism*. Without wishing to minimise the real risks that can be attached to publishing your work online, there seems to be a tendency to focus much more on the risks of plagiarism than on how a well-established online identity can guard against it. If your research forms an important part of your online identity then it can actually help establish your ownership of particular topics. For regular bloggers, it becomes possible to point to a time and date-stamped trail of engagements with particular issues, dramatically extending the range of outputs that can be pointed to as evidence of one's work. The risks involved for someone writing so openly might be said to have increased, in that there are more pieces of work online which could be plagiarised, but so too has the scope of the evidence which can be invoked to identify and pursue claims of plagiarism. That said the risks *are* real. There have been a number of cases in which journalists have reproduced the work of researchers without meaningful citation. In one case I spoke to the researcher soon after she'd made this discovery and it left me newly aware of how upsetting this experience could be, as well as how eager the publication in question was to resolve the situation in order to avoid a controversy. In part this needs to be understood against a background of change in the interface between journalism and academia, as well as within each, something which we turn to in a later chapter. I think there's a danger of overestimating the risks, but I'd also encourage you to read the account offered by Williams (2013) of her experience in order to make up your own mind.

As with being clear about the risks that concern you, specificity will always help. In this case one response to these concerns would be to consider carefully what you're willing to share online. How might you differentiate between the following categories?

- Speculative thoughts relating to your research
- Analysis of current affairs in terms of your research
- Interpretations of scholarly literature relevant to your research

Of course sharing speculative thoughts opens up the parallel fear that people might hold you to them. As Stuart Elden put it to me, 'I hope nobody would think my blog posts were of the same status as a journal article'. But there's also less risk involved in Stuart's strategy of blogging *about* his research but not blogging the research itself. The key thing here is to come to a conclusion that you feel comfortable with, informed by an understanding of the potential risks.

Furthermore, breaking down the possible things you might share online like this can help with thinking through precisely *what* the risks are. In the case of plagiarism described above, the researcher drew upon their ongoing research in order to offer an astute analysis of a high profile case in the media, prompting the journalist to reproduce it and pass it off as her own. I have no idea what the motivations were in this case: it might simply be a matter of the journalist having been in a rush, searching for ideas to feed into an article, and failing to attribute ownership correctly. While norms about citation online are still in their infancy, it's nonetheless the case that there are established systems for citing social media sources and these should be adhered to in order that ideas can be properly attributed. Exactly what form this takes obviously varies between referencing systems but various standards have now been well established. The challenge emerges because it's much easier to recall a journal article you read six months ago than an interesting idea someone presented you with in a brief conversation on Twitter. This is one of the things we'll discuss in a later chapter – how to make best use of the many discoveries that can so easily be found on social media but can just as easily be forgotten.

Further reading

- *Tales from Facebook* by Daniel Miller (2011) is a fascinating ethnography which highlights the way social media intertwine with everyday life, rather than constituting some 'virtual' sphere opposed to it.
- *Digital Sociology* by Deborah Lupton (2014b) offers an expansive overview of interdisciplinary literature on a whole range of related issues, as well as an extensive discussion of her own research into use of social media by academics.
- *The Googlization of Everything* by Siva Vaidhynathan (2012) is an extremely insightful account of the changing information environment, dominated by Google, encountered by academics when using social media to publish and publicise their work.

3

Using social media to build your network

Chapter themes

This chapter will:

- Explore how you can use social media to build and expand an academic network
- Discuss how Twitter chats work and the value they offer
- Examine the possibilities and challenges of live tweeting at conferences
- Consider how online connections can develop into face-to-face meetings

Much as the previous chapter reluctantly adopted the word 'publicise', in this chapter we turn to 'networking'. It's a horrible term with unwelcome connotations. It nonetheless designates something important for which social media provide uniquely potent resources. There's also the real possibility that social media will bring about profound changes in how academic networks function. As Weller (2011) notes, it has usually been through meetings at conferences and comparable events that academics meet and extend their network of peers. Academic networks tended to be limited to those with whom one interacted recurrently, if not necessarily regularly. Yet as he explains, '[o]nline social networks allow interaction with a wide group of peers … often through relatively light tough mechanisms' and so '[w]ithout having to attend every conference in their field, it is possible for scholars to build up networks of peers who perform the same role in their scholarly activity as the networks founded on face-to-face contact' (Weller 2011: loc 172–179).

This has certainly been my own experience, and as this chapter will explain, social media make it easy to build and develop international connections within and beyond your field of a breadth and quality that would have formerly required vigorous participation in the 'conference circuit' over many years (with all the time, energy and funding that would require). But it would be mistaken to cast this in either/or terms, as if face-to-face meetings are being *replaced* by digital networks. It would also obscure the intersection between them, for instance the way in which institutional affiliation serves as a marker of privilege online (Nickel 2011).

Arguably the most prominent manifestation of social media within higher education in recent years has been the role of Twitter at conferences, but influences extend much more widely than this. In this chapter, we discuss academic networks in general and how these can be integrated with social networks. Then we discuss the ways in which social media can help you discover things through your networks, as well as how they can facilitate collaboration. The second half of the chapter focuses upon how social media can help you expand your networks and enhance your existing connections. Much of the focus here is on Twitter, simply because the way in which it is rapidly becoming mainstream at events has radical consequences for academic networking, many of them hugely exciting, but this is also creating numerous problems which remain contentious and have the potential to become ever more so.

So what is 'networking'?

To talk of 'networking' raises the inevitable question of what your 'network' is and why it matters. This is a theme which cuts through the book given that the network is so crucial to social media: without a certain critical mass of users, it's difficult for social media platforms to be useful to anyone. What's the point of sending 140-character messages, sharing audio clips or self-publishing articles if no one is going to find them? Social media offer endless opportunities to communicate with your network and expand it in the process. But this doesn't really answer the question of what the value of this actually is. In part, it can simply be a matter of the enjoyment of sharing things you've produced, something which the media scholar David Gauntlett (2011) conveys power-fully in his book on creative production, *Making is Connecting*, which situated this aspect of contemporary digital culture in terms of a much longer history of *craft*.

One of the difficulties with the notion of 'networking' is that it can seem to imply that such an activity is extrinsic to scholarly activity, such that one does one's real work and then (reluctantly) looks outwards towards their connections. What this leaves out is the vast majority of academic work that involves collabo-ration in one form or another. Gauntlett expresses this nicely, suggesting three ways in which 'making is connecting':

- Making is connecting because you have to connect things together (materials, ideas, or both) to make something new

- Making is connecting because acts of creativity usually involve, at some point, a social dimension and connect us with other people

- Making is connecting because through making things and sharing them in the world, we increase our engagement and connection with our social and physical environment

While Gauntlett is talking about creative production in general, the same points can be extended to scholarship. In fact his discussion of 'craft', a term not often used to apply to the work that goes on within the academy, offers a useful reminder of the genuinely creative work that is undertaken by academics (albeit frequently within conditions which frustrate that creativity or at least make it difficult to experience it as such). By this he means a process of discovery, often involving new ideas which emerge through acts of creation. This helps bring people together through their shared acts of creation, consolidating bonds between collaborators which take on a life of their own in the outcomes of this work together. This language of craft, which Sennett (2008) talks about in terms of *doing things well for their own sake*, provides a nice counterweight to some of the instrumentalising tendencies which the contemporary academy can give rise to.

Talk of 'networks' and 'networking' can be off-putting. I like Gauntlett's account because it captures how networks are integral to creative work: *making is connecting*. It follows from this that *connecting* can be a preliminary to *making*. As Weller (2011: loc 172) puts it, '[n]etworks of peers are important in scholarship – they represent the people who scholars share ideas with, collaborate with on research projects, review papers for, discuss ideas with and get feedback from'. Networks are integral to scholarship. The possibilities which social media open up for networking can have hugely important implications for your scholarship, though they also pose challenges which we'll discuss. But first, it's important not to forget your existing network when you begin to engage with social media.

How can I integrate social media into my existing networks?

One of the most obvious ways in which social media can be used by academics is simply to communicate with people they already know. This is so simple, it feels slightly silly to point it out. But if you want to enjoy using social media, ensure you connect with people you already know. For social networking sites, particularly those designed specifically for academics, identifying these existing connections can be a quick and easy way to get started. It will often give you immediate access to the archived publications of people you're interested in. In the case of Academia.edu, the platform has been designed to be very effective in helping people connect automatically to others within their institutions. If you're new to Twitter, following those people you already know can be a way of getting the hang of a notoriously confusing service: the point of Twitter becomes obvious as you begin to use it. But it might be time consuming to do all this manually. Some services are able to use your social graph, as described in the last chapter, in order to automatically invite your existing contracts to follow you on a network. This can of course be a rather blunt instrument: it doesn't follow that because someone once e-mailed you that you want to connect with them on social media. It's also easy to forget the effectiveness of an e-mail signature as a way of communicating information to people you're in contact with. If you're using a social media platform in a wholly or partially professional capacity then why not add these details to your e-mail signature?

There are lots of perhaps rather obvious ways of ensuring you integrate social media into your existing networks. But it's possible that the character of these relationships will change through being incorporated into your network in this way:

Twitter has enabled its users to become more aware of certain everyday aspects of fellow users' lives. For example, when someone follows the tweets of people met at conferences, s/he will most likely be exposed to some combination of their daily music listening habits, sports interests, current location, and shopping wish lists, amongst other things. (Murthy 2012: 16)

Murthy suggests that many people see this as a way to get to know others in a more 'multi-dimensional' way. However for some it might be uncomfortable. It's certainly a change. Twitter is changing conferences but it is also changing existing professional relationships within the academy as well as new relationships which form *through* conferences, in ways which could have surprising consequences in the long term, at least if current trends continue. I discuss these possibilities in the final chapter, suggesting that we might see a *new collegiality* arise in this way, beginning with diminishing the pluralistic ignorance which leads many in higher education to underestimate the difficulties peers face, simply because they do not discuss them (Becker 2008). My experience has been that what at points appears to be 'shop talk' – an inevitable function of intensive interaction within professional worlds – can on occasion come to look more like consciousness-raising, or something surprisingly close to it (Boden and Epstein 2011).

How can my networks help me discover relevant things?

The value of social media networks isn't just a matter of getting some of the upsides of regular conference going without the crushing costs. My own enthusiasm comes in part from the seemingly endless array of things I discover through social media that are personally and professionally relevant: I can, without fail, find any number of interesting items in a few minutes spent browsing my Twitter feed. This follows quite naturally from what scholars actually *do* on Twitter: perhaps unsurprisingly, they tend to be scholarly things (Veletsianos 2012). I'm certainly not alone in the extent to which Twitter has broadened my horizons as a scholar through the sheer range and diversity of material I've discovered through it (Stewart 2015). This obviously raises problems of what to do with the things you discover, something we'll come to in a later chapter. But the key thing is to *follow people who interest you in some way*. If you do this, perhaps rather indiscriminately as I do, you'll inevitably find that people who interest you tend to post things that interest you. They might also post things that don't interest you. Or even offend you. Alternatively, it might be that the stream becomes too fast, making it so impossible to keep up that it deprives Twitter of any enjoyment. In which case, it might be time to try and carefully reduce the number of people you're following. The point is that it's possible to exercise control over the quality of the material you encounter in this way, modulating your social networks in order to facilitate better discovery (Johnson 2012).

But discovery isn't something confined to Twitter. As Gregg (2006) suggests, we can see blogging as a form of 'conversational scholarship': opening up a space of interest-driven exchange that can often no longer be found in a stressed and stressful academy. Blogging in the style of Stuart Elden, who runs the popular Progressive Geographies blog, builds an audience through sharing interesting discoveries with readers, a dynamic which has been integral to blogging from its inception (Rosenberg 2010). If you encounter blogs that are pertinent to your work then seek out the bloggers themselves, who will usually link to their other social media accounts if they use them, as well as signing up to their blogs using RSS readers. There's a broader social aspect of blogging, sometimes overlooked, which can be helpful here as well. Many blogging platforms provide a place to link to other blogs. Following the success of Tumblr, WordPress introduced a 'follow' and 'reblog' function, allowing you to view updates from other people's blogs via the dashboard and automatically link to posts you liked via your own blog. This offers an easy way to begin to build a network around your blog. If you're a WordPress user then try to get into the habit of following other WordPress blogs you like when you come across them. These are all ways of building useful connections with people whose work is relevant to you. Other networks have the same potential. For instance, Ele Belfiore explained to me how she had regularly found the work of people who weren't on her radar by following research categories on Academia.edu.

How can social media help me expand my networks?

Earlier in this chapter, we discussed how social media can be integrated into your existing network. If you find yourself looking at Twitter, wondering 'who do I know?', it's inevitable that you'll look towards the people you already know well – friends, collaborators and colleagues. But your existing network will be broader than this, encompassing those you dimly recall having met, with whom it was formerly difficult to build connections unless you happened to meet again. Marwick (2014: 217) offers a helpful account of how social networks 'have created a semi-permanent address book of former co-workers, high school friends, ex-boyfriends and girlfriends, distant family members, and other acquaintances whom users may rarely see'. How you relate to your school friends and ex-partners is thankfully beyond the purview of this book. But your acquaintances, at least your academic ones, represent a group of people with whom you might develop very rewarding relationships. What makes Twitter such an effective tool for professional networking is how readily it lends itself to registering these sorts of connections, with no social constraint upon who you follow. To 'friend' someone on Facebook implies some degree of familiarity, but no such connection is implied by 'following' someone on Twitter (Murthy 2012). To follow someone in this sense is a minimal unit of social connection, implying nothing more than *some* degree of interest or concern with the other and what they are doing. In other words, follow everyone you know who you find at all interesting. The interactive character of Twitter discussed earlier, in which all manner of ephemera tend to get aggregated together into a stream, means you sometimes get better acquainted with someone through a process that is almost osmotic: picking up details not only about *what* they're doing but also about *who* they are, without making any effort to seek this information out. Charlotte Mathieson told me how positively this had impacted upon her experience of conferences, allowing networks to coalesce that might otherwise have developed very slowly between people who only saw each other at an annual conference. As Ele Belfiore described it, 'Once you start a conversation, you realise there's a lot more in common than you thought'. It's much easier to interact professionally with people, for instance inviting them to speak at an event, after interacting on Twitter.

Potential Pitfalls

There are many services which claim to address this problem by offering to sell you Twitter followers. Though this might prove superficially appealing, it's actually a rather pointless transaction that not only leaves you out of pocket but also might damage your reputation. Buying followers is generally frowned upon and, crucially, it's usually easy to see when someone has done this. Depending on the service in question, the followers acquired for your account will be conspicuous by their artificiality. They will have no profile

(Continued)

(Continued)

photo, no tweets, and little to no description. Even the more sophisticated services will have few tweets for each of these accounts and a window dressing for the profile which won't withstand even a moment's scrutiny. It might be that no one happens to skim through your Twitter followers, but it's possible to check this in other ways. Tools such as fakers.statuspeople.com offer an audit of any Twitter account to estimate a percentage of fake followers. For anyone familiar with Twitter, it's also possible to get a sense of this from the *follower* to *followed* ratio for a given account.

What's more important than this is that it's effectively pointless. The only outcome from handing over your money will be a superficial appearance of online popularity of a sort that will reflect extremely badly on you if anyone sees through the facade. The meaningful benefits of Twitter – the ability to communicate material quickly and effectively to an international audience – don't kick in if your followers are all fake accounts that you've purchased. They won't retweet or favourite your tweets. They won't care about your work. The only purpose they'll serve is to entrench you in a view of Twitter which misses the opportunities it offers for scholarly communication.

However the best way to extend your network is to help other people. To some this can be seen as an academic gift economy. To others it might look like free labour. No matter what your view is, written as someone who flips between the two, it undoubtedly works. Academic bloggers like Stuart Elden have accumulated what are vast audiences, at least in academic terms, through finding interesting material online and sharing it via their networks. As we'll see in later chapters, activity of this sort doesn't necessarily entail the time commitment which many would expect. But simply engaging, sharing your ideas and responding to those shared by others will inevitably help networks coalesce around you. I liked how Dave O'Brien phrased this in our discussion: 'It's just me having conversations about stuff that I find interesting'. Do this and the characteristics of social media described by boyd (2014) will mean people who share those interests will tend to congregate around you online, at least over time.

Nonetheless, there are some more structured activities which can help extend your network through social media. In the rest of this section, we'll discuss *Twitter chats* and *live tweeting*.

Twitter chats

Twitter chats are regular online 'meetings' at a specific time using a particular hashtag. For those familiar with the pre-social media internet, it's effectively using Twitter to host a chat room. For instance #phdchat meets every Wednesday evening GMT with participants voting in advance on which topic relevant to PhD students to discuss. When a hashtag chat becomes very well established, it can often encourage participants to post messages using the relevant hashtag outside of the agreed meeting time. So for instance I intermittently found myself tagging tweets about writing my thesis with #phdchat during the final stages, even though I wasn't a regular participant in the Twitter chat itself. I'd also occasionally tweet frustrations during what was, in the closing few months, an extremely frustrating process. Established hashtags such as this can be useful because they indicate a relevant audience which has gathered around a specific theme. For this very reason, it's important not to use a hashtag too indiscriminately and instead to think carefully about the relevance of what you're posting to the hashtag community. If you merely use that community for advertising, without participating in it or contributing to it, it's likely the people involved will soon become frustrated and start screening out your tweets.

There are established Twitter chats for a surprisingly diverse range of topics. This perhaps reflects their usefulness in helping to build networks online: connecting with others who share an interest with you and establishing yourself as someone who can offer insights about it. Perhaps for the same reason they seem particularly conducive to professional use, possibly because these are the people most inclined to use Twitter in order to build a relevant network online. There's no comprehensive and authoritative listing of Twitter chats that I know of, partly because they cover such a diverse range of topics and partly because it can be difficult to establish one to such a degree that it would merit inclusion on such a list. While it's possible to find them via Google, for instance searching for "Twitter chat" + your specialism (retaining the quotation marks around the former term to search for the exact phrase because there's an awful lot of pages on the internet which use the words 'Twitter' and 'chat'), it's also something you'll likely stumble across through reading your timeline if you are following people who work in the same area as you. If you stumble across interesting conversations that are marked with a hashtag, click on that hashtag in order to check out other tweets marked with it. If you encounter people talking about a Twitter chat that sounds interesting but are unsure of the details then just ask them for more information: it's inherent in the project of establishing a Twitter chat that you will be amenable to potential participants asking questions.

It's also possible to establish your own Twitter chat. Choosing an adequate hashtag is crucial and many of the same points apply here as when choosing one for an event: not too long, reasonably informative, and not already in use. It's also important to get the scope of the chat right: too narrow and it'll be hard to gather an audience, too diffuse and it'll be hard to get the chat established. It might be wise to recruit others at an early stage, at least if this is something you're considering in isolation rather than as part of a group, for instance by writing a blog post in which you put forward an idea for the chat and ask for potential collaborators to get in touch. If you're willing to expand a lot of energy on a project that is far from guaranteed to succeed, it may even be worth setting up a web page for the planned chat. This could also include points for discussion which you could draw upon to help you facilitate initial scheduled chats.

The challenge here is to ensure that enough people participate for the Twitter chat to have a purpose. This might take time and it's worth persisting even if the initial scheduled chats prove to be slightly dispiriting. After all, it'll only take a few participants to potentially get something off the ground because with each additional participant the visibility of the Twitter chat increases, and with it the potential draw for further participants. As well as carefully refining the intended topic and scope, it's worthwhile announcing the chat through as many channels as you have available to you: on a blog, Facebook, through your email signature, or even face to face! If you can ensure that those for whom the chat is potentially relevant both know about it and remember when it takes place, it's possible that numbers will increase over time through on-and-off participants who 'drop in' on occasion. Encouraging participation, for instance by polling to decide each week's topic in the manner of #phdchat, helps establish a community and a sense of belonging around the Twitter chat.

Live tweeting

While the discussion has been predominately about what you do *online,* many of the most exciting aspects of social media relate to how they are changing face-to-face interaction within the academy, as well as the relations that flow from it. The most conspicuous aspect of this is Twitter use at conferences. In some areas of the academy, live tweeting is becoming an increasingly significant aspect of conference culture. But what do we mean by 'live tweeting'?

In the most straightforward sense, it means participants at an event tweeting about it while that event is taking place. But there are a number of forms which this can take.

- Live tweeting can be an intermittent commentary or discussion about an event that is taking place. This 'back channel' might simply be friends or colleagues, already known to each other, using Twitter to discuss what is taking place without causing an interruption. Some events use 'Twitter walls' to bring this 'back channel' more into public view, though this is not without its problems, as discussed below.
- Live tweeting can be an attempt to summarise or offer an ongoing commentary upon an event, using Twitter to provide a running commentary of what is taking place. Increasingly, given the ubiquity of smartphones with high quality cameras, this might include taking pictures of the event. Some conferences now have designated live tweeters, representing the event in an official capacity, who aim to thoroughly summarise talks, often while avoiding personal commentary upon their content or quality.
- One of the more unexpected aspects of live tweeting can often be the meaningful participation of those who are not physically present at the event itself. It can be safely taken as a sign of successful live tweeting if those not in the room are able to indicate that they're watching the hashtag with interest ('Interesting stuff happening at #conference') or even discuss some of the material summarised on it.

It's important to recognise how contested this activity still is. For instance, Murthy (2012: 61–62) cites the example of the Cold Spring Harbor Laboratory (CSHL) Biology of Genomes conference which 'amended their conference rules and regulation to prohibit tweeting, blogging, and other Internet-based reporting during conferences unless express permission was obtained from the presenter being talked about'. As Murthy explains, all manner of concerns were expressed here: intellectual property, privacy, attacks upon presenters, dismissals of presentations. A few months before writing this, I found myself at a conference where having been happily tweeting away all morning, leading among other things to me meeting a political philosopher I had much in common with at the coffee break, the room was told at the start of an afternoon session that the speakers had requested there be no live tweeting for their roundtable. I found this slightly jarring, though this in turn gave me cause to recognise how rapidly live tweeting at conferences had become normalised to me to the extent that it didn't even occur to me for a second that anyone involved might have an objection to it. To have one person live tweeting inevitably encourages others to do so, even if there isn't an officially designated hashtag.

This is why it's becoming increasingly necessary for anyone organising an event to clarify their stance on Twitter in advance, including consulting with those presenting if necessary. After all, you'd presumably do this if you wanted to record their talks (at least I hope you would) so why is Twitter any different? But things can go wrong with Twitter at conferences. A few years ago this was the subject of an intense discussion on the #TwitterGate hashtag which has been helpfully archived using Storify (Koh 2012). Kolowich (2012) summarises these concerns:

> Scholars often present unpublished work at conferences. But while they may be willing to expose an unpolished set of ideas to a group of peers academics may be less eager to have those peers turn around and broadcast those ideas to the world.

It was once possible for conference organisers to exercise a degree of control over what leaves the room. This was *far* from absolute, something which can risk being forgotten in concerns about the ethics of live tweeting. How did you know what people did after they left the room? How did you know what they were *really* doing while they were in the room? Pursuing these questions too far would be silly. My only point is to stress that this is a matter of *degree,* or rather the likelihood of something inopportune taking place, rather than a sudden injection of risk into what was previously a risk-free environment. But what exactly *is* the risk here? In some circles, it might be a matter of corporate confidentiality. In others, a sense of provisional findings been circulated too early or data unsuitable for publication being exposed to a much wider audience than was intended. The more diffuse concern is that, as Fullick (2012) summarises, 'academics "use" other people's work in social media venues like blogs and Twitter to build their own reputation and academic "brand", and ultimately to benefit their own academic careers (ostensibly at the expense of others)'. As she goes on to note, many (including myself) would make the opposing argument – that live tweeting in fact brings exposure to other scholars and to what is being said. Furthermore, as MJ Barker put it to me, this issue can be seen in terms of accessibility: live tweeting allows those who cannot attend the event, for instance if they are unable to travel for financial or physical reasons, to nonetheless participate remotely.

But what form should live tweeting take? A useful perspective on this question comes from the eLearning team at the London School of Economics (Lingard 2010), who conducted an interesting analysis of hashtag contents at the LSE

Teaching Day 2010 for which they heavily promoted live tweeting. Twitter was still at an early stage in 2010 and 249 tweets were made on the hashtag, including 29 people: 17 LSE staff and students and 13 non-LSE participants. They found 43% of tweets to be descriptive reports of what was taking place in the room, 29% were evaluating the event and presentations, 16% introduced additional information which provided a context or background to the presentations that were taking place, 7% were assistance tweets providing announcements or answers to questions, and 6% of tweets were people asking questions (Lingard 2010). Though the activity on hashtags at many conferences now vastly outstrips that which occurred at the teaching day, this gives a really useful overview of the composition of a hashtag. The best way to gain a sense of what it might look like in practice though is to actually view a hashtag for an event, if you haven't already.

Underlying all this is the thorny question of consent. Should speakers at an event be asked to consent to live tweeting? If so what form should that take? These are extremely difficult questions which have, as yet, no clear answers. The most pressing aspect of them is the dissemination of the work being presented: should live tweeters ask for permission before tweeting material from a talk? The potential problems here are rather obvious. The activity of a live tweeter can radically change the proposition involved in speaking, with a talk to a room full of people expanding into a potentially global audience, sometimes even without the knowledge of the speaker. Obviously it's unlikely that live tweets from an academic conference would 'go viral', though the possibility of wide circulation should not be discounted, but the point is that a speaker has a right to know the potential scope of the audience they're addressing. These difficulties become particularly pronounced when you consider the possibility of misinterpretation and misattribution: it takes a lot of care to ensure you attribute ideas correctly when live tweeting, not least of all because of how easy it is to forget that most people will have no context for the tweet. While it's certainly possible, perhaps even likely, that the interpretation made by audience members of a talk might diverge from the intention of the speaker, live tweeting makes these misunderstandings peculiarly public, fixing in text an interpretation of a talk that the speaker might object to.

These are key issues but the risk is that we come to frame Twitter at conferences as a problem to be solved, whereas it offers some enormously exciting opportunities for expanding and transforming what participation entails (McGeeney 2015). This is why it is so important that those organising academic events take the lead in establishing ground rules. Given the proliferation of tweeting within higher education, it is becoming problematic for event organisers to avoid engaging with these questions. In doing so they leave the door open to problematic applications of this exciting though challenging technology, with the risk of detracting (potentially seriously) from the enjoyment of their participants. If the event in question is a 'work in progress' event where people are likely to be sharing material that they would wish to avoid being disseminated widely, then this is something with obvious implications for rules relating to live tweeting. So too if the event in question is a major event within a field, one in which participants are likely to be networking, in which case encouraging the use of Twitter is likely to be welcome. These are questions which can only be answered in response to the specific aims and objectives of a given event. It's important that organisers think about the practical steps they could take to establish guidelines for Twitter use which are appropriate to their event and will either encourage certain forms of use or discourage others. These might include:

- Providing delegates with guidelines for attribution, for example including a speaker's name in each tweet
- Circulating Twitter handles in a delegate pack, in the same way as many events include the e-mail addresses of delegates
- Curating Twitter lists (on the platform itself) for delegates and speakers, perhaps including both in the same list or separating them

In this sense encouraging Twitter use at a conference can be extremely inclusive, at least for those who are using it. An intriguing way of including those who don't use the service themselves is to include a *Twitter wall* – a visual display collecting the contents of the event's hashtag. The appeal of such tools is that they bring the 'back channel' out into the open, facilitating a kind of participation which has the potential to feel significantly more engaged than simply watching a talk. In a sense the commentary can then become part of the talk itself, given that a wall will presumably be visible to the audience. But will it be visible to the speaker? If so then it might prove distracting, or even distressing, in the event that, say, criticism or even rude comments were to be posted on the wall while they were speaking. If it is not visible then it creates the risk that the speaker will be subjected to potentially hostile commentary while they are speaking which they will not be able to see. Certainly it could be argued that this is inherent in live tweeting itself (and even that speakers have always been subject to criticism, it's just that Twitter makes this newly visible), but the point is that discomfort on the part of a speaker is perfectly reasonable. The issue here becomes even more pronounced when we consider the ways that things like gender, class and ethnicity can shape interaction and be the basis of prejudice, even if a commentator may not understand their own comment in this way. For this reason it is important that the ethics of the Twitter wall be seriously considered. Ronson (2015) cites the example of popular science journalist Jonah Lehrer's public apology lecture after his recurrent plagiarism came to light. The organisers of this live streamed event had, as Ronson describes it, 'decided to erect a giant screen live Twitter feed behind his head' and so '[a]nyone watching at home could tweet their ongoing opinions of Jonah's request for forgiveness using the hashtag #infoneeds and their comment would automatically appear, in real time and in gigantic letters, right next to Jonah's face' (Ronson 2015: 42–45). I won't repeat the tweets here but some of them were pretty unpleasant. Then again Lehrer's past actions had provoked widespread outrage and there were legitimate questions to be asked about how substantive his apology for them was. The fact he'd been paid $20,000 by a charity to give this speech didn't help either. This is obviously a rather extreme case. Even so, it's a story that sticks in my mind as an example of what can go wrong at conferences with Twitter walls.

Beyond the conference circuit

We've discussed using social networks to expand upon connections that you've made at conferences. But an inevitable corollary of engaging online like this is that you're going to end up meeting people with whom your connection had been purely digital up until that point of meeting. It can often be slightly strange meeting people from Twitter for the first time. Obviously in some cases on Twitter those with whom you communicate will be people you previously met face to face. But in many, if not most, cases they won't be, and this lends a certain strangeness to meeting in the flesh. Given how new such encounters are, there's a lack of any well-established norms about how to approach such an interaction, and these are circumstances under which awkwardness thrives. Perhaps as Twitter becomes an ever more integral part of the conference experience, at least for those who are attending a conference and already tweeting, this awkwardness will cease to be such a frequent occurrence. But until then, the best thing to do is to be friendly but treat the encounter as a meeting with someone new who you happen to know some things about in advance. Be approachable but don't make too many assumptions. Don't assume that someone's 'offline' self-presentation will cohere with their 'online' self-presentation. Don't assume that they interpreted your online interactions in the same way or have the same memory of these that you do. Don't assume also that just because you've talked on Twitter and are attending the same conference that they are necessarily keen to meet up. Try and signpost your attendance at a conference in advance (for example 'Looking forward to #BritSoc15, who else from my feed is going?') and see who responds, rather than inferring attendance from someone's tweets or simply recognising them from their profile picture at the event itself.

It's also necessary to remember here that no matter how engaging these connections can be at times they are constituted through interactions of 140 characters or less and don't translate into offline relationships in a straightforward way. Nonetheless, it's important not to dismiss them because it's such a powerful way of finding people who share your interests. Engaging on Twitter can make higher education feel more friendly and collegial, particularly when it comes to negotiating vast conferences that might otherwise feel faceless and impersonal. As Daniels and Feagin (2011) put it, 'While in another era, scholars may have identified strongly with their PhD-granting university, the college or university, or the academic department in which they are currently employed, the rise of social media allows for a new arrangement of colleagues'. Do this well and you can have the 'ideal academic department' that has been 'tailored to your interests'.

Further reading

- *Twitter: Social Communication in the Twitter Age* by Dhiraj Murthy (2012) is a really comprehensive study of Twitter that conveys a rich understanding of its social dimension, its technical dimension, and the relationship between the two.
- *Personal Connections in the Digital Age* by Nancy K. Baym (2010) is an immensely readable overview of how social relations are being reconfigured by digital technology, offering a lot of novel insights while also summarising research across a range of topics.
- *Networked: The New Social Operating System* by Lee Rainie and Barry Wellman (2014) is an impressive account of how social networks are being transformed in the digital age.

4

Using social media for public engagement

Chapter themes

This chapter will:

- Explore the opportunities and challenges of using social media for wider engagement with the public
- Discuss how social media can provide a useful space for academic engagement with traditional forms of journalism
- Provide guidance on using social media as an engagement tool within higher education, focusing on the use of departmental feeds

Increasingly academics are being encouraged to break out of the 'ivory tower' and engage with the wider world. Who is doing this encouraging? Much of this impetus comes from policy makers and managers within universities rather than academics themselves. In light of this we can see a concern for public engagement in terms of a project 'seeking to redefine the modus operandi and external image of the university from incubator and producer of knowledge for the sake of knowledge pursued for the purpose of national (and international) economic and societal prosperity and prestige' (Watermayer 2015). Critics like Holmwood (2010, 2011b) have argued this process is giving rise to an interdisciplinary social science increasingly purged of any critical perspective, suggesting that what we can see is an attempt to make the social sciences 'useful' (to outside interests) that might ultimately lead to much of what social scientists value about them being discarded. We will revisit this critical perspective throughout the chapter and these concerns will be addressed again in the final chapter. It is an important part of this landscape that we should not lose sight of and one of my motivations for writing this book is a belief that the uptake of social media can help produce a more autonomous social science that is better able to resist these trends. However, to see public engagement *entirely* in these terms risks obscuring the fact that this activity matters to those undertaking it (Carrigan and Mahoney 2013). In some cases it might even be a concern to engage with the public that motivates a career in the social sciences, even if the requirements of building a career in the academy subsequently stand in the way of *making a difference* to the wider world in the way that was originally hoped (Burawoy 2005).

This motivation has tended to find its most famous expression in terms of the notion of the *public intellectual*. This notion is far from new of course (Fuller 2005). Exactly how such a role should be defined has eluded clear agreement but we tend to know one when we see one. 'Total intellectuals' like Sartre who took a stand on any social issue they confronted clearly share something in common with the 'specific intellectuals' described by Foucault who engage only on issues within their domain of expertise (Sapiro 2010). Part of what they share might be sheer visibility. The figures we tend to think of as 'public intellectuals' enjoyed a remarkable degree of visibility as social scientists in the wider public sphere: Bourdieu's *On Television* sold 200,000 copies (Sapiro 2010); C Wright Mills' *Listen, Yankee* had sold 370,000 copies by 1961 in a cold war context that mitigated against the popularity of such a polemic (Geary 2009: 206–214); and the Nobel peace prize that Jean-Paul Sartre turned down was offered on the basis of his having 'exerted a far-reaching influence on our age' (Jeffries 2014). But there's much more to public engagement than public intellectualism.

One way to make sense of the distinction is to consider the association of the *public intellectual* with the capacity for *broadcasting* – one-to-many communication with potentially vast audiences. Though broadcasting retains an obvious appeal, it's far from clear whether trying to talk to *everyone* at once is what social media are best equipped to facilitate. Instead, we can usefully see the possibilities of social media in terms of a newfound capacity for *narrowcasting*. The historian Marshall Poe (2012), who also founded a popular online book-reviewing initiative called the *New Books Network*, offers a helpful account of this transition:

> The Internet, however, can make these connections because it permits economical, finely calibrated "narrowcasting," that is, the transmission of specific information to specific interest groups. Of course print and — to a much lesser extent — radio and television also allowed some narrowcasting. Academic journals and industry newsletters are perhaps the best examples. But the scale of narrowcasting on the Internet is orders of magnitude greater than anything known before. Take the blogosphere for example. Here tens of thousands of interest-specific public intellectuals talk to tens of thousands of interest-specific publics concerning every imaginable interest. If you want to know about it — beer brewing, Italian shoes, organic chemistry — you can probably find someone with considerable expertise blogging about it. That's truly remarkable. (Poe 2012)

This is a potentially transformative environment for academic research because it means that intense specialisation need not lead to cultural marginality. Even the most seemingly obscure topics have a potential audience outside the academy and these new communications technologies offer a newfound capacity to form these connections. This doesn't preclude a place for a broadcasting approach: the most obvious example of this in an era of social media would be writing accessible articles for general interest digital publications like *The Huffington Post* with the large audiences they command. A more contemporary spin on broadcasting can be seen in podcasting, something which I'd always thought of as social media until Dave O'Brien made the case to me that, reflecting on his own podcasting, it was an activity in which the listeners rarely *talk back*. Hence it's not *social* in the (very specific) sense in which we were discussing the term. It's not helpful to get too preoccupied by the distinction between broadcasting and narrowcasting but I think it's a useful way of conveying a key change that has taken place: we now need to talk about 'the public' in a much more specific way.

So which publics are we talking about exactly?

To talk of 'public engagement' can easily be seen to imply a unitary public: 'we' are in here, 'they' are out there. If we start from the assumption of a unified public then our public engagement is unlikely to be effective. This assumption of a unified public, *people in general*, seems more understandable under the conditions in which the famous public intellectuals engaged in their broadcasting. But using social media effectively for public engagement necessitates a much more nuanced conception of the publics that concern you. As the social media scholar danah boyd observes, 'people are a part of multiple publics …

and yet, publics often intersect and intertwine … Publics get tangled up in one another, challenging any effort to understand the boundaries and shape of any particular project' (boyd 2014: loc 201). It is because of this intersectionality that publics tend to be fluid, either in formation or having been recently formed. Part of what constitutes a public is a reciprocal recognition of a collective life in which each member shares. In this sense publics are 'imagined' and the media within society are one factor amongst others in shaping how different publics imagine their own existence within a wider social order.

This a lengthy and abstract preamble to an observation that might seem obvious but is nonetheless crucial to any attempt to engage with publics using social media: social media are reshaping how publics imagine themselves and hence the groups within society which academics might seek to address using these very same media. Social media are reshaping the groups which social scientists might investigate, as well as the relations between students and their universities that in turn become those between alumni and their alma mater. But the trend here is a much broader one, not least of all because as José van Dijck reminds us 'researchers are part of the same culture of connectivity that involves software developers, platform owners, user and regulators' (van Dijck 2012: loc 3766). How academics imagine *ourselves* as collectives and relate to each other is being reshaped by social media, much as we ourselves might contribute to the reshaping of other publics through our engagements online. One of the more optimistic messages of this book, which I develop fully in the final chapter, concerns the possibility that academics using social media might become a 'networked public' in boyd's definition – encompassing both the 'space constructed through networked technologies' and the 'imagined community that emerges as a result of the intersection of people, technology and practice' (boyd 2014: loc 197).

The novelty of social media and their rapid pace of change can risk a descent into *presentism,* such that we become so excited by new innovations that we fail to see how they fit into longer-term changes. In the rest of this section I'll attempt to set *public engagement by academics using social media* in terms of a longer-term trend of how social scientists have been marginalised within public debate. However, it's important to note that this isn't a uniform trend across disciplines. For instance, economists have been mentioned 4.7k times in the Congressional Record since 1989, compared to 2.6k for historians, 996 times for psychologists, 233 times for sociologists, 168 times for anthropologists, and 63 times for demographers. Furthermore, around one in one hundred *New York Times* articles mentions the term 'economist' (Wolmers 2015).

Drawing on the ideas of the pragmatist philosopher John Dewey, a leading social reformer in nineteenth- and twentieth-century American life, the sociologist John Holmwood (2011b) argues that expert knowledge becomes more significant than ever in a world in which such knowledge is increasingly embedded within corporate and governmental bodies seeking to influence and manage public opinion. What Engle (2001) denounces as 'neo-sophistry' has more recently been analysed as 'agnotology' – the intentional manufacture of ignorance and doubt in the public mind, driven by specific motives of forestalling political action by making the knowledge underlying them seen to be uncertain (Mirowski 2013). It's possible that a reader might contest the specific details of cases cited as examples of agnotology such as man-made climate change or the health risks of smoking. But this is rather the point of those postulating agnotology: discussion of courses of action shifts into contestation of the knowledge underlying the issue, meanwhile preserving a status quo in which powerful interests in the related spheres of commerce continue without potently costly restraints. Holmwood's (2011b) contention is that the public role of social scientists, through their participation in public universities, can help foster public debate and enable publics to articulate their own interests rather than being drawn into the machinations of others.

Another way of looking at this is provided by the sociologist Tom Medvetz (2012) in his insightful study of the rise of think tanks in the United States. These organisations are so familiar to any observer of contemporary politics that it can be startling to remember just how recent these are. Through a rigorous empirical analysis of the emergence of think tanks, Medvetz argues that social scientists have found themselves pushed to the margins of political debate:

> [T]he growth of think tanks over the past forty years has played a pivotal role in undermining the relevance of autonomously produced social scientific knowledge in the United States by fortifying a system of social relations that relegates its producers to the margins of public debate. To the degree that think tanks arrogate for themselves a central role in the policy-making process, they effectively limit the range of options available to more autonomous intellectuals, or those less willing to tailor their work to the demands of moneyed sponsors and politicians. (Medvetz 2012: 225–226)

His point is that what we might, perhaps reluctantly, call the 'marketplace of ideas' has been radically reshaped by the entry of think tanks into such a prominent role within public life. It's harder for social scientists to compete with organisations that have from their inception sought to negotiate the twin worlds of lobbying and the media with a skill that social scientists within universities have struggled to match.

Those public figures who have been trained within this sphere of think tanks (something which Medvetz argues exists at the intersections between politics, the media, universities and lobbying) thrive in the contemporary media marketplace and enjoy complete institutional support, in contrast to social scientists who are encumbered by a diverse range of professional responsibilities beyond their impact in public life. Medvetz (2012: 225) recognises that while senior scholars who have 'little left to prove in the academy can afford to reinvest their academic capital in public debate – and often do – rank-and-file scholars have little incentive to follow this route'. This claim concerns the American system of higher education and the tenure system which defines career trajectories within it, but it can be seen as an accurate characterisation of university life beyond this specific context. Under these conditions social scientists are subject to the twin temptations of a comfortable retreat into narrowly professional concerns (escaping to the 'ivory tower') and orientating themselves to the policy demands of elites on the other. Many manage to resist each but in doing so, argues Medvetz, they are subject to a double marginalisation 'from the mainstream of their disciplines, which are less likely to reward those who dedicate their work to the goal of enlightening public debate' and 'from a public debate increasingly dominated by policy experts operating in symbiotic partnership with politicians, political professionals and media specialists who can select from a wide range of intellectual products to bolster their pre-held views' (Medvetz 2012: 225).

His gloomy thesis shouldn't lead us to despair. My contention is that both forms of marginalisation are being undermined by the normalisation of social media within academic life. It's easier for social scientists to 'occupy debate' in a way that allows their voices to be heard in a competitive way. In doing so, we can see new possibilities for academics to contribute to the consolidation of publics: not through broadcasting to the public in general, assumed to be characterised by a deficit which expertise can help alleviate, but in dialogue with particular groups who might *become* publics (Maile and Griffiths 2014: 8–10). The next section of this chapter offers advice about how to engage with particular publics using social media, as well as some of the issues liable to be encountered when doing so. However this shouldn't be taken to imply that social media are anything other than a useful set of tools to be drawn upon while engaging in such activity. Through a discussion of how social media can be used to engage *collectively*, for instance as a central resource for an academic department, the final section of this chapter introduces ideas about how 'offline' engagement might be enhanced using 'online' means.

Engaging with different communities

Practitioners and policy makers

The use of social media to engage with practioners and policy makers was an issue that came up frequently in the extended conversations I had while preparing material for this book. Ele Belfiore explained to me how indispensible Twitter had been to this end, all the more so because it allowed her to undertake this activity at a time when she was unable to travel to London after the birth of her child. As she put it, 'all the interesting meetings happen in London and when you can't go that easily you feel really cut out'. Twitter allowed her to engage in this way but it also allowed her to connect with the artists who had typically been absent from the policy conversations about cultural value that she was participating in. A number of projects developed from these connections, as well as collaborative funding bids. Dave O'Brien saw his guest blogging as something that was, at least partially, orientated towards communicating his research to policy makers. Having been told on numerous occasions that academic papers were too long to be effective for these purposes, he saw blogging for high-profile sites as a way of communicating findings more effectively while nonetheless retaining the important grounding in his published and peer-reviewed research. MJ Barker's first engagements with social media had been motivated by a desire to help promote the *Bisexuality Report* which they had collaboratively produced, creating a WordPress site as a forum to host the report and help disseminate it through a channel beyond those more typically available. These are very different examples of using social media to engage with practitioners and policy makers. But this variety illustrates the range of possibilities inherent in social media.

Students

One way of engaging with your own students on social media can be via an official departmental Twitter feed. It might be counter-intuitive to see students as a public in this sense, but Burawoy (2005) convincingly argues that they are precisely this, particularly for disciplines. Another way to look at students in these terms is as a public within an institution: to what extent do students feel part of your department and university? This obviously raises the question of what the benefits are of engaging with students on Twitter. My own experience with managing a departmental Twitter feed was that undergraduate students, particularly those in the first few weeks of their first year, would tweet practical questions to the account. These were often ones which I wasn't sure how to answer, leaving me either failing to answer the question or consulting the departmental administrator in a process that was remarkably inefficient and left me with the concern that I was being irritating in the absence of an established procedure for dealing with such issues. This experience illustrates some of the limitations in having a precariously employed part-time student performing this role rather than an established member of stuff with it factored into their workload allocation. Nonetheless, it suggests the potential promise for Twitter as a still largely untapped internal communications tool for academic departments when engaging with their students. Pragmatic guidance on departmental Twitter feeds is discussed later on in this chapter. The key thing to avoid is what has been called the 'creepy treehouse effect': don't assume students will welcome your attempts at engagement on social media. They may in fact see it as an unnerving intrusion into what they perceive as a non-university space (O'Shea 2009).

Research communities

This is a less intuitive public but one that is likely to become more important with time. Particularly for those who conduct research with organised groups or communities, the ubiquity of social media has destabilised boundaries between 'inside' and outside' the university which could formerly be taken for granted (Cohen 1979). This poses ethical and methodological problems concerning anonymity and the risk of identification. It also opens up the possibility, perhaps even the likelihood, that interactions cannot be assumed to finish with the fieldwork. People from these communities might discuss your research in a way that's easily discoverable online. As I've written about in Carrigan (2014b) this can prove an enormously beneficial experience. But they might also take issue with what you're doing, perhaps even on the basis of a misunderstanding. Sustaining research connections becomes much more challenging in these circumstances but the possibility also invites a more active engagement – one in which you engage *with* and *for* the communities who are the concern of your research.

The media

Obviously the media have always looked to academics to provide expertise and opinions. This is most obviously true of the famous public intellectuals, discussed at the start of the chapter, whose public pronouncements did so much to shape culture, including the rejections of their work that these interventions provoked. Furthermore, for each of the most famous cases we can assume the existence of many more who, even if only on a single occasion and in a marginal way, engaged beyond the confines of the ivory tower. The internet in general, as well as social media in particular, make it radically easier for those working in the media to find relevant academics to make contact with. This changing relationship between the media and the academy isn't wholly driven by the internet. The need to make a case for the value of research creates pressure for academics, or at least some of them, to build relationships with the media. In the other direction, the value of research findings as a 'news hook' and the more diffuse cultural authority of data creates an incentive for those working in the media to engage with academic research and to build connections with individual academics.

This isn't an unambiguously positive thing. When I've raised the issue on Twitter I found many others who shared my experience of last minute e-mails from journalists who had discovered my website through Google, often showing little attempt to have actually read or understood what I worked on, asking for commentary (sometimes a particular viewpoint, specified in advance) with an imminent deadline, often leaving me confused about why they assumed their deadline was urgent for me. While academics might feel rushed, something which I've written about elsewhere (Carrigan 2015a, 2016), the time horizons of journalism are nonetheless radically more contracted. When I interviewed the criminologist Tim Newburn about his experience of the Reading The Riots project, a collaboration between the London School of Economics and the *Guardian* that sought to elucidate the underlying causes of the 2011 riots in England, he explained to me how challenging it had been when the temporalities of academia and journalism met for the first time (Carrigan and Brumley 2013). These divergent time horizons can easily give rise to misunderstandings and practical difficulties when working with the media. The instantaneity of communication, in which an unexpected e-mail can lead to a Skype interview in a matter of hours, creates the risk of jumping straight in without establishing ground rules or ensuring that mutual expectations are established. It doesn't help when the other party is forceful about the rush they're in and the necessity of an immediate decision. I've more than once rejected enticing invitations because I felt unable to commit within the time window I was offered. At worst these interactions can prove slightly depressing – I've occasionally felt like I was used for a quote by someone who didn't even bother to thank me afterwards – but at their best they can be exciting and thought-provoking, as unexpected invitations can lead to enjoyable engagements which leave you with a new understanding of what you work on and its wider relevance.

While there are risks here, it's often not recognised how this engagement with social media can mitigate against them. There's always the possibility, indeed perhaps the probability, that those searching for academic contacts will select names through the most cursory and superficial of online searches. But even then, expanding your digital footprint through online engagement helps to increase the chance that someone will contact you on the basis of *what you actually do* rather than what a glance at your university web page leads them to think that you do. When I've worked with the media, usually with journalists but occasionally with film makers and television producers, I've often been told by them that they've listened to a podcast or watched a YouTube video of mine. In these circumstances a non-specialist doing preliminary research is unlikely to read an academic paper, if they can even get access to it, but the prospect of reading a few blog posts or listening to a short podcast is much more likely to be amenable to them. This doesn't eliminate the possibility of misunderstanding but these forms of online content are likely to be much more substantive, or at the very least more accessible, than the contents of a typical university web page. Engaging with them in advance of any meeting helps give a sense of where you're coming from, how you relate to your topic, and will hopefully feed into how they prepare for their work with you. Rather than blurring the boundaries between the academy and journalism, I think that social media use by academics can constitute a 'third space' that mediates between them, helping those working in the media to find and make contact with academics in a way more likely to be mutually beneficial and informed throughout by an understanding of what the other does. Adkins and Dever (2015) suggest that initiatives like *The Conversation* can be seen in this light. Recognising the unique role such intermediaries play, between a changing media and a changing academy, underscores their importance for academic social media.

How do I act with and for publics, rather than act at them?

The language of 'public engagement' emerged from within science education, representing a shift from a deficit model in which experts were seen to 'fill the gaps' in public knowledge (Maile and Griffiths 2014: 9). Though aspects of the debate are specific to the natural sciences, the underlying transition here is interesting to note, motivated as it was by a sense of the elitist connotations of prior projects of 'public understanding' of science. It seems to me that this notion of a public lack remains remarkably pervasive. In my work on public sociology I have suggested we can understand this as the *amelioration fallacy* – the assumption that the amelioration of social problems requires nothing more than increasing the circulation of expert knowledge that's currently accumulated within the established social sciences (French 2012). In its crudest forms it essentially amounts to the self-regarding assumption that these social problems would be easy to fix, *if only people would listen to us*. In its more sophisticated variants it leads to a frustrated and technocratic mindset, seeing social problems as susceptible to expert-driven solutions but assuming that particular blockages stand in the way, for instance an excess of technical jargon in papers, paywalls imposed by commercial publishers, or a diffuse anti-intellectualism within the wider culture.

There can often be an element of truth to these claims. But they also reveal a particular kind of conceit, overestimating the finality of our knowledge and underestimating the durability of social problems, which supports an unhelpful view of how academics relate to wider publics. This leads to what Michael Burawoy describes as 'books written for but not with publics', produced by people who 'talk down to publics' and 'place [themselves] above publics'. Instead, he advocates that one 'steps out of the protected environment of the academy and reaches into the pockets of civil society' (Burawoy 2008: 372). His critical remarks here were directed at the radical sociologist C Wright Mills, who Burawoy nonetheless admired, but I think they're a valuably succinct statement of the mentality to which the amelioration fallacy can too easily give rise. Later in the book we will discuss some of the practical implications of this for academic communication online, such as how to position yourself as an expert in relation to non-experts. But the underlying necessity is that public engagement must entail acting *with* and *for* publics rather than *at* them. If this condition isn't achieved, it's worth considering whether what you're doing constitutes *engagement* in a meaningful sense. It may very well be valuable but *engagement* necessitates something more than dissemination.

To reiterate the earlier point: there is *much* more to public engagement than can be achieved through social media alone. Nonetheless, social media open up exciting opportunities for certain forms of it. Not least of all because, as Weller (2011: loc 1642) notes, a '[t]raditional broadcast requires a large team effort usually, whereas digital, networked and open approaches require relatively little effort and associated costs'. These technological capacities do not in themselves guarantee anything, but they open up possibilities which were once largely restricted to those established public intellectuals or people with significant resources supporting their activity. The previous section offered some substantive ideas about how this might be pursued with particular publics, as well as the issues liable to be confronted when doing so. But one of the overarching themes of this book concerns the possibility of being an 'open-source academic' through engaging in a mode of continual publishing. Weller (2011) talks about this in terms of *public engagement as collateral damage*. He goes so far as to argue that '[m]uch of what we currently aim to achieve through specific public engagement projects can be realised by producing digital artefacts as a by-product of scholarly activity' (Weller 2011: loc 1783). His point is that each individual item published (tweet, blog post, paper, slide deck, YouTube video or podcast) might have less impact than a particular project, but that the cumulative impact of such engagement may equal or exceed it.

I worry that this way of framing the issue risks slipping into an unhelpful dichotomy, so we see this *digital* public engagement as something distinct from, and potentially liable to replace, *analogue* public engagement. Nonetheless, Weller highlights something important when we consider public engagement in light of social media. Digital scholarship builds engagement into the core of scholarly life, constituted through the habitual sharing of artefacts produced as part of the research process. We could see it as a form of doing scholarship *in the open*. This is neither necessary nor sufficient for public engagement in the sense that we've discussed in this chapter but it's a very useful starting point for this additional activity, as well as being something valuable in its own right.

What are the risks involved in digital public engagement?

Recent research has found evidence that public engagement carries hidden costs for research careers (Watermeyer and Lewis 2015). It can lead the engagers to be seen as inclined towards administration rather than research, as public engagement fails to be recognised as a legitimate scholarly pursuit. Such activity also fails to find recognition in promotion criteria, leading to a situation where academics are both encouraged to engage yet do not win recognition when they do. Public engagement resists easily evaluation in terms of the metrics system through which performance is assessed (Burrows 2012, Watermeyer 2015). There are also perceived reputational risks for the university, an issue which is explored in greater depth in the section on academic freedom in the final chapter (NCCPE 2010).

While these findings are specific to the UK higher education system, Maynard (2015) points to 'a strongly hinted at cultural and institutional bias against engagement which decreased research productivity' that characterises attitudes in the United States. Much like Watermeyer's (2015) findings, he highlights a vibrant community of scholars in the USA who are highly engaged *despite*, rather than because of, their institutions. The obstacles to public engagement seem significant, in spite of what Beer (2013) plausibly identifies as a trend towards a much greater degree of engagement which is emerging across the social sciences.

It's obviously important that we recognise the possibility that public engagement might carry hidden costs for academic careers. But there are more pronounced as well as more immediate risks entailed by *digital public engagement*. For instance Lupton (2014b: loc 1774) cites instances of academics being found unacceptable for job positions, allegedly as a consequence of outspoken political views on blogs, as well academics being subject to libel actions because of comments made on social media. Crucially, not everyone is equally placed in relation to these risks. Grollman (2015b) observes that those within the academy from marginalised communities are more prone to imposter syndrome, 'feeling as though we do not belong and/or are not as good as our privileged colleagues' – something which is a 'symptom of systems of oppression that operate through academia, just as they do through every other important social institution'. The challenges of engagement will be more keenly felt under such circumstances, both in terms of anxieties surrounding the activity itself and the objective costs to careers discussed earlier in the chapter.

Yet there can be much more immediate and pronounced risks faced through engaging online. One of the most disturbing illustrations of this is offered by religious studies professor Anthea Butler, who created a Tumblr site, *The Things People Say*, collating the racist abuse she receives online (Butler 2015). As Cottom (2015a) notes Butler has close to 30,000 Twitter followers, suggesting a degree of visibility which many institutions would claim to admire and value immensely. It's worth noting that Cottom (2015a) herself has 'received 11 death threats' and '19 threats of what could be considered general bodily harm'. Grollman (2015b) points out that we can see countless instances in which 'scholars, particularly women and people of color, have been harassed, been subject to hate mail, or, worse, have received death threats in response to op-eds, blog posts, tweets, and other media appearances', concluding that there is little real institutional support for people attacked in these circumstances. In another piece McMillan Cottom (2015b) writes incisively of the potential for communications departments to overreact in the face of what may seem in the moment to be overwhelming public outrage:

In academia, where twenty readers is a big deal, 200 angry emails can feel like a tsunami of public opinion (it isn't). When three members of a committee can constitute a quorum, seeing 142 retweets of a negative opinion about your new assistant professor can feel like politics (it isn't). Five whole think pieces at the online verticals of legacy media organizations can feel like the powers-that-be are censuring your institution (they aren't; as my grandma would say, they ain't studdin' you except that right now you're filling empty space on a website). Basically, the scale of current media is so beyond anything academia can grasp that those with agendas get a leg up on pulling the levers of universities' inherent conservativism. (McMillan Cottom 2015b)

The novelty of such controversies compounds the underlying problem Grollman (2015b) diagnoses of what is often called 'academic freedom' being in fact a matter of 'academic tolerance', something which 'appears to be quite low for scholars of color who dare to critique racism and white privilege'. I return to this theme in the final chapter.

How can social media be used to engage as an academic department?

In the final section of this chapter, we'll discuss how engagement is something that can happen *within* institutions. The focus will be largely on Twitter but there are certainly many other ways in which social media can be used for communicating internally. In fact I've placed this section within the chapter because thinking in terms of *engagement* can be an extremely helpful way of getting beyond the slightly sterile language of 'internal communications': social media can be used to constitute publics within organisations, as well as *by* collectives. In other words, you can help consolidate a community through social media within your organisation, rather than just seeing it as a way of communicating pre-conceived messages to a pre-established group.

There are a number of ways to approach the maintenance of a departmental feed. Each has their strengths and weaknesses in terms of the quantity and quality of engagement likely to flow from them, but obviously these decisions will be much shaped by institutional circumstances. If funding is available then a postgraduate student could be employed on a part-time basis to maintain the Twitter feed. This is a role I performed early in my PhD and it's an enjoyable and interesting job. However it's obviously important to provide support, not only in the sense of technical training but also via guidance about what to post and how to frame it. It can also be tricky for PhD students to seek participation from established staff, even if they are inclined to do so. If the purpose of the Twitter feed is construed relatively narrowly then this may not be a problem (for example, if it is simply intended as a tool to disseminate news about the department), but departments will use Twitter most successfully when the account is seen as a public resource and members of a department are willing and able to use it to help raise the visibility of projects they're involved in.

Given that social media skills are increasingly valued within a sector committed to impact and public engagement, it's perfectly feasible that postgraduate students would be willing to perform the role in order to gain demonstrable experience of using social media for curriculum vitae purposes. In acknowledgment that this is a book about social media, rather than my political views, I'll simply observe that many would argue that unpaid labour is a growing problem within higher education, entrenching inequalities by restricting opportunities to those willing and able to work without pay.

The maintenance of the Twitter feed can be rotated amongst staff and students. This can help ensure that the content is fresh, with each curator taking charge for an allotted period of time, such as a week or a month. There will probably be a need to actively search for volunteers, though it's likely this will change in time, as the rotation of the feed becomes institutionalised as part of the department's activity. Perhaps more so than the other approaches, it will be necessary to offer detailed guidance to someone taking on this short-term role, given that long-term expertise won't be able to accumulate in the same way as would be the case if one person was taking responsibility for maintaining the Twitter feed in the medium or long term.

The Twitter feed could be included within the formal allocation of workloads within the department. This recognition of social media as administration that makes a key contribution to the life of the department represents an important statement about the organisation being open to digital engagement. It also offers an opportunity for staff, at any stage of their career, to learn new skills by managing a social media presence on an ongoing basis. However it's important to be realistic about how many hours will be required to do this effectively, so as to avoid underestimating or overestimating the amount of work involved.

Having addressed the 'why' and the 'how' question in relation to academic departments using Twitter, we're now left with one question remaining: *what* exactly should departments do with their Twitter feed? For example it could be announcements of new publications by faculty ('The Sociology of Twitter – new paper by @facultymember just released by @journal'), upcoming events ('Research

Seminar on Contrived Examples in Books – 4pm at S0.21') or student-focused announcements ('Remember all 3rd year dissertations due in 1 week').

Potential Pitfalls

Many of the possibilities mentioned above rely on the person updating the Twitter feed being informed about relevant news by colleagues within the department. Is this feasible? In many departments it probably won't be and this is a problem faced by academic departments when seeking to use social media to maximum effect. There are obvious ways around the problem: using Google Scholar and other services to track publications by faculty, or simply relying on what knowledge *is* available and updating the feed on this basis. However the latter option risks over-promoting certain people within the department at the expense of others (namely, those whose work the person updating the feed happens to be most familiar with). This is a broader point, applying in the case of those who publish most frequently, have the highest media profile, or are the most active online. Given that finding sufficient content to update the feed with any degree of regularity is likely to be the most immediate challenge facing the departmental tweeter (at least in the early stages), the obvious temptation here is to use all the relevant content that can be found. But the distribution takes on an obviously problematic dimension in this case, as the collective account increases the visibility of those who are already most visible at the expense of others within the faculty. In other words, it will likely irritate colleagues within the department if they access the feed only to find that a small number of staff members are dominating the content that is posted there.

As with all things, you need to be realistic about the resources available to you and the likely success of any undertaking. For instance, there's no reason to start a blog if your department is not in a position to maintain it and recognising this from the outset means that the time and energy invested in an infrequently updated blog can be utilised elsewhere. What makes Twitter somewhat different is the role it can play in assembling an audience which can be leveraged for other purposes. Any news published through a university website, announcements from staff within in the department, and multimedia projects undertaken on an ad hoc basis, can be distributed via a departmental Twitter feed. For this reason, Twitter should be at the heart of a department's social media strategy and building up an audience is crucial to reaping the benefits of this. Doing so probably requires that someone has overall responsibility for the feed because building an audience entails certain logistical demands which can't really be enacted on an ad hoc basis. These demands aren't particularly onerous, involving as little as a couple of hours a week, but they're crucial to ensure the visibility and popularity of the feed. In many ways, these are the same as the procedures for an individual feed described earlier in the book.

There's no reason *in principle* why finding sufficient content to keep the feed updated should be difficult because of the degree of activity undertaken within any academic department: publications, events, media coverage, multimedia featuring staff or students, recruitments and university-wide announcements are all things which could feature. In practice, it can be a bit trickier to overcome the lack of communication that can sometimes be found within a department in order to ensure you're aware of these activities. In part this depends upon who it is that's keeping the feed updated. In my own experience I found it hard to encourage staff to send me information to keep the site updated. This meant that I used a significant amount of the time I was paid for tracking staff down via Google and the main university website in order to find announcements to post. This might be easier for staff members but the difficulties in getting busy people locked into lone working patterns to update a central resource in this way shouldn't be underestimated. The obvious point to make to them is the efficacy of Twitter as a dissemination tool – for instance stressing the number of followers to whom their new paper could be publicised if only they send a brief e-mail to inform you of it. However people who aren't using Twitter tend to be sceptical of the benefits and without any frame of reference your invocation of follower numbers won't necessarily persuade them otherwise. Ideally, you want to establish this as a public resource which is habitually drawn upon by individual staff members. For instance, if someone promoting an event usually e-mails a flyer to a departmental administrator in order to circulate this internally, it makes sense for them to send it on to the relevant person for it to be circulated externally via the department's Twitter feed and perhaps blog or other platforms. This again points to the desirability of having one person with overall responsibility for the feed, even if this is perhaps something which rotates over time throughout the department.

This whole process becomes much easier if other staff members are using Twitter and one of the most effective ways for a new technology to spread is by colleagues seeing the benefits it offers through observation of someone working with them. This highlights how 'networking' takes on a slightly different role in this setting when the remit is for the department as a whole.

Group Twitter feeds

Managing group Twitter feeds poses some specific challenges which need to be considered. In part this depends upon precisely what this 'group' is: research network, study group, research centre and so on. It's important to discuss in advance with your collaborators how the management of the feed will be handled and to ensure that everyone is aware of this activity and feels able to comment upon it or offer suggestions. Tweeting on behalf of a group means that you are in effect speaking for that group. Even if you understand its internal structure it's extremely unlikely that even the most attentive follower will, and therefore you must be aware of how content will be attributed to the entire group. In many cases this might be fine, but the potential problems arising from, say, a controversial tweet which generates a negative reaction towards the group as a whole mean that it's necessary to discuss the content, as well as the tone, in advance. Furthermore, if you're sharing material produced by the group then ensure this is done in a fair way, as problems might arise if a communal feed for the group as a whole is seen to spend much more time promoting the work of some group members rather than others.

These challenges are far from insurmountable. One solution is simply to curtail what the group feed says and how it says it, for example by broadcasting updates about the group in purely descriptive language. This is the safest option but the end result can often be rather bland in a way that's far from conducive to consolidating a network on Twitter. Another is to sign off on individual tweets, at least when these are seen to reflect the opinions of an individual rather than a group, such as adding '- mc' at the end of a tweet to ensure that readers know that Mark Carrigan wrote the tweet rather than another group member. This could be complemented by a Twitter profile which introduces the group members and their signatures.

Further reading

- *Punk Sociology* by David Beer (2014) is a book with much more relevance to non-sociologists than would appear to be the case from the title. The author makes a compelling case for a *punk ethos* as something that can help us embrace the opportunities for engagement and communication offered by social media.
- *Think Tanks in America* by Tom Medvetz (2012) concerns a very specific topic but it has enormous relevance for the social sciences, diagnosing a root cause of their declining role within public debate.
- *You've Been Publicly Shamed* by Jon Ronson (2015) is an enormously readable book that offers a thoughtful perspective on the broader climate within which digital public engagement can be a risky activity.

5

Using social media to manage information

Chapter themes

This chapter will:

- Discuss the role of information management in scholarship
- Explore how blogging can be used as part of the research process
- Consider other software that can be used to manage information

Try searching Google for the phrase 'information overload' and it soon becomes apparent that reading even a small fraction of the results would be a vast undertaking. There's a pervasive sense that the internet has led to there being *too much stuff*: too many messages to answer, too many things to read, too many potentially relevant ideas to pursue. Whatever we're doing online, we're always liable to stumble across interesting avenues to pursue. As the technologist Alex Soojung-Kim Pang (2013: 47) describes the dilemma, '[i]t amazes me how often during a single (admittedly rather trivial) thought my mind wants to veer off onto these other paths, pick up this idea and that one, answer this or that question – and how easily the web lets me satisfy that curiosity'. The problem is that it's often the case that each of these avenues *could* be pursued, possibly in a way that's both quick and rewarding (Pang 2013). With each new avenue we consider, the time available for attending to the things that *really* matter diminishes, if we can even sustain a sense of our priorities in the face of the ever-growing array of alluring distractions (Rosa 2013).

In a sense this is a matter of managing *distraction*. In a later chapter, we'll discuss this in terms of finding time for social media. But as Todd Gitlin points out, '[d]istraction is one of those terms – like freedom, responsibility, and alienation – that requires an object to make sense' (Gitlin 2007: 32). This question might seem simple on the surface: all this stuff online is distracting us from work. But so much of it *is* relevant to work. The problem is working out what is relevant and what isn't, as well as exactly *how* it is relevant. The torrents of information to which we are exposed of course predated social media, but with this new social layer opening up, the challenge of coping with what Gitlin (2002) calls 'supersaturation' becomes ever more pronounced. If I scroll through my Twitter timeline for five minutes, I'll inevitably encounter many things that catch my attention. I'll often find things that are directly relevant to my work. In the first case, the challenge is to decide which ones I'd like to pursue and which ones I wouldn't. In the second case, my existing work on the topic makes it easier to identify them but it becomes a matter of clarifying *what* they are and *how* to relate them to what I'm doing.

The danger is that we get lost in these leads, exploring indefinitely in the face of the seemingly endless array of *potentially* relevant material and never getting round to doing anything with it. For this reason, I'd like to suggest that the answer to Gitlin's query is that 'distraction', in this case, refers to *distraction from relevant information*. In previous chapters, we've seen how social media can provide a tremendously powerful discovery engine, facilitating our encounter with all manner of resources that might otherwise be difficult to find. But this in turn poses the aforementioned challenge of working out what to do with all this material. It is easy to find our attention pulled in many different directions, fracturing the sustained immersion upon which many difficult activities depend (Crawford 2015, Pang 2013). We can increase our capacity to manage these distractions, becoming more efficient in how we respond to and process them, but the problem escalates as we try and find some solution to it (Rosa 2013). The more we read, the more ideas we're confronted with about what we haven't read but *should*. The more blogs we follow, the more links to other interesting blogs we encounter. The better we become at keeping track of new journal issues, the more we feel we should keep track of.

Our expectations and standards have a tendency to inflate alongside our technological capacities (Wajcman 2015). Not only is there much out there, we're also much more likely to encounter relevant things we're missing.

In this context *managing information* comes to entail something much more than record keeping. In the next section, we'll discuss scholarly practices of *managing information* and how social media can be incorporated into them. The following section will consider how to keep track of the discoveries made through social media in a way that allows you to put them to good use at a later date. We then look at some trends in social media and recent tools which have emerged to meet these needs.

How can social media help you manage information?

It can be easy for already busy academics to see social media as an additional and unwelcome labour in an already demanding life. The *practical* challenges of finding the time for social media are discussed later in the book. But before we get there, it's important to consider how this view of social media as *intrinsically* draining on time might be slightly misleading. While social media can certainly be distracting, they can also be clarifying. They can offer more things to think about but they can also help with the process of clarifying what you think about them. In this sense, using social media is much like interactions through other channels. Sometimes going to a conference might prove distracting, taking up time and energy in a way that is challenging to getting things done. But sometimes going to a conference can prove immensely clarifying, helping to generate a much clearer idea of where you stand on a particular issue or how you intend to pursue a specific project. I don't wish for a second to deny that social media can prove distracting. In fact I'm writing this at the end of a day in which I lost an amount of time to the hashtag #sociologicaldesks that seems rather absurd upon reflection. I'm only trying to balance out the usually pretty negative treatment of social media and time pressures by stressing that social media *can* help you do some things more effectively.

One way of thinking about this is to see social media in terms of giving shape to, and perhaps actually increasing the effectiveness of, work you already have to engage in. This is immaterial work which often escapes our notice and which we rarely categorise as a discrete activity constituting 'work'. But it's still work in an important way and integral to scholarship. The sociologist C Wright Mills talked about this in terms of learning 'to use your life experience in your intellectual work: continually to examine and interpret it'. This mysterious immaterial work which I'm talking so elliptically about is working out *what you think about things*, the imperative to 'capture what you experience and sort it out' in the way necessary to 'guide and test your reflections'. He talks about this in terms of keeping a 'file', suggesting that it

> encourages you to capture 'fringe-thoughts', various ideas which may be by-products of everyday life, snatches of conversation overheard on the street, or, for that matter, dreams. Once noted, these may lead to more systematic thinking, as well as lend intellectual relevance to more directed experience. (Mills 2000: 196).

The labour involved in engaging with social media begins to look rather different if we see it as an alternative to the formerly private process of keeping a file. Mills advised that '[w]henever you feel strongly about events or ideas you must try not to let them pass from your mind, but instead to formulate them for your files and in doing so draw out their implications, show yourself either how foolish these feelings or ideas are, or how they might be articulated into productive shape' (Mills 2000: 196). His point is that we need to evaluate the information to which we're exposed, as well as our day-to-day experiences, in order to clarify where we stand in relation to them. His contention is that clarifying what we think about things is an integral part of scholarly practice. If we accept this then it's not much of a stretch to recognise that social media offer us ample opportunity to talk and write about matters which concern us with likeminded others who understand those concerns and are similarly inclined to talk to us about them. The trick is to do this in a way which is, as Bozarth (2014: loc 288) puts it, 'an organic activity in everyday workflow, not some separate over-engineered process that eventually proves to be nothing but more work'.

There are many other ways in which we can do this. The most obvious are actually keeping a file or notebook, in the sense in which Mills originally discussed, and going to research events in order to have face-to-face discussions with others working on the issues which concern us. Many academics do the former and all will surely do the latter.

Prior to adopting a blog as a research journal, I used a seemingly endless sequence of ornate notebooks to record my developing ideas. In some cases this proved very useful and consulting one of these books during the writing-up stage of my PhD was far more helpful than I ever would have expected it to be. But mostly I ended up with scribbled notes that weren't categorised in any meaningful way, reflecting the fact that I just picked up the notebook and started writing when an idea struck me. Perhaps the problem was simply my handwriting.

When I spoke to Daniel Little, the philosopher who writes Understanding Society who is also Chancellor for the University of Michigan-Dearborn, he vividly conveyed how blogging allowed him to combine sustained scholarship with a crowded schedule filled with administrative responsibilities: 'If the only way that I could be involved in research as a chancellor of a university was by blocking out the time necessary to write an article on scholarly mechanisms, I would never get to it because it isn't possible for me to avoid meetings because of major research work'. But his research blogging means he 'can grab 30 minutes here, another hour there – that can be fitted in. It's more granular'. The result has been a 'body of knowledge' that is 'more threaded and less sequential'. He explained to me how the practice of research blogging had enriched his scholarship, facilitating 'lateral connections' following from the ever-present opportunity of contributing to the blog. As he put it, 'When I read something new, I almost immediately think "What do I think about this? What is my reaction to this? How does this fit into a larger theoretical issue?"'. The ensuing project has grown immensely. The downloadable version of the site as PDF which Little (2013) compiled, up to and including July 2013, runs to 1793 pages and Understanding Society has only grown since then.

Stuart Elden described a similar experience of his Progressive Geographies blog. As he put it, 'If I find it interesting, chances are other people will find it interesting' and uses the blog as a 'public notebook' and 'public set of bookmarks'. The advantage of the blog is that it's largely a matter of doing things he would be doing anyway. But using the blog imposes a helpful structure on the material he shares while encouraging reflection upon it. Each individual entry can be a matter of seconds: 'If I see something, click "reblog", write a quick comment and post'. But the cumulative result is a fully searchable archive of a vast range of material that he's found relevant to his work, indexed and with contextualising comments attached. It's also built a vast audience in the process, without representing any major time commitment. As he explained to me, 'It's quite nice to be able to do a quick search and ask "What did I write about this two years ago? What did I link to? What was I reading?'. It also allows 'writing for which there is no forum', always offering a reason to elaborate upon nascent thoughts that may later be put to more extended use. This habitual use of the 'public notebook', accessible from anywhere, allows a comprehensiveness which would otherwise be difficult to achieve. As he put it, without the blog 'I'd either probably forget. Or read it and not record the link, then if I ever wanted to find it, it would be really laborious'.

I found my conversations with Daniel and Stuart extremely interesting because they have such similar experiences of blogging, in spite of the different forms their blogs take. Whilst Understanding Society is largely filled with short essays, extended reflections on a particular topic or text, Progressive Geographies is what has often been referred to as a *filter blog*: filtering the contents of the web through the interests of the author, sometimes taking a form as simple as lists of links but more often with some commentary (Rettberg 2008:13–17). Academic filter blogs can involve a continuous sharing of useful materials, often with expert commentary that places them within a broader context. There's a great degree of influence that operates within the peer networks of bloggers, as the most visible within the network shape the behaviour of others, up to and including the decision to cease blogging (Pedersen et al. 2014). But there's no reason to copy the actions of other bloggers, other than with norms like attributing other people's work, unless you like what they're doing.

The best way to get a sense of how blogs can be used academically is simply to read academic blogs. Reflect on examples that appeal to you. What is it about it that you like? Is there anything you would do differently? How much time do you think it will take? Do you think it would sustain your enthusiasm? In their extremely insightful analysis of 100 academic blogs, Mewburn and Thomson (2013) identified a wide range of functions that were served: *self-help, descriptions of academic practice, technical advice, academic cultural critique, personal reflections, research dissemination, career advice, information* and *teaching advice*. They also identified a range of styles in which blogs were written: *reportage, journalistic, informal essay, formal essay, pedagogic, confidential* and *satirical*. Recognising this diversity can be a really useful way to overcome any residual sense of their being a 'right' or 'wrong' way to blog as an academic.

For instance there's no reason why *everything* has to be shared. The suggestion so far has been that a blog can provide a useful platform for the kinds of *information management* activity that are an unavoidable part of scholarship. There are particular characteristics which leave it well-suited to this task. But there are other tools which can be utilised to this end. The next section discusses the challenge of how to keep track of things that you've discovered on social media. Many of the tools people use for this purpose can also be used in exactly the same *virtual notebook* manner as some have done with a blog. My own experience has been that blogging forces me to elaborate upon the meaning of each item, challenging me to say what I think about something rather than just posting it online. But if you're a more disciplined writer than I am, it's worth considering whether some of the tools discussed in the following section might usefully serve as your electronic file.

How can I keep track of things I discover on social media?

Elsewhere in this book we have considered the way in which social media can act as a vastly productive 'discovery engine', unearthing all manner of relevant material through the collective filtering that emerges from a diverse and dispersed online network. However this in turn can pose an important problem: how do you record this material and store it in a way susceptible to convenient retrieval at a later date? This is a practical challenge inherent in scholarship, encountered most obviously in engaging with scholarly literature, which nonetheless intensifies through social media engagement, with the plethora of fascinating material that begins to serendipitously cross one's path potentially proving overwhelming. People respond to this in different ways: some find it immensely distracting and conducive to procrastination, others find it overwhelming and seek to avoid the potential distractions, while more still simply engage sporadically, inculcating an awareness of the intellectual resources that are available but failing to make the most of them. The material in question here can be incredibly diverse (for instance books, journal articles, chapters, podcasts, videocasts, magazine articles, YouTube videos) and encompass a diverse range of formats (such as URLs, PDFs, Docs, MP3s) to an extent that piles technical complications on top of the underlying question of knowing what to engage with and deciding when to do it.

The difficulty here can be usefully seen in terms of managing your attention (a finite resource) and negotiating competing demands (an unavoidable aspect of academic life). Immediately reading interesting discoveries will likely prove untenable most of the time, at least if you wish to avoid continual distraction from whatever task is at hand. Adding 'to read' entries to what is likely an already overloaded to-do list can prove overwhelming, risking that urgent tasks get drowned out by potentially important but manifestly non-urgent self-imposed reading assignments. There's a sense in which keeping these lists might still constitute *managing information*. But it probably isn't managing information effectively. To return to the themes of the previous section, recording the details does not in itself help elucidate how this particular item relates to other things that are important to you. It doesn't offer any guidelines for how you will work on it in future. Once the excitement of discovery has faded away, it will just be a title or a URL, with little context and little likely value.

Potentially the most common way of recording interesting material is emailing links to oneself. I must admit I still do this, with the 'blogging/Twitter' folder in my email account providing a repository for relevant material I might want to come back to. The remit of the various blogs and Twitter feeds I mention is extremely broad and I keep them very frequently updated (with around 60 tweets a day scheduled between them, not including my personal Twitter feed which I don't schedule). This means that I'm always on the lookout for potentially interesting material and have a pretty expansive sense of what is relevant in each case. If I wasn't casting my net so wide, it's possible I would be inclined towards a more structured approach. But it works for me. If this works for you too, then there's no reason why you should feel the need to abandon it in the face of a more sophisticated solution. If your e-mail provider has an effective search function and lots of space, it's possible that the material could be just as easy to search and retrieve as if you'd used a more high-tech solution.

The most obvious such solution would be software like Evernote. This note-taking and archiving tool, more recently branded as a 'virtual workspace', launched in 2008 and has become ever more popular since then. Advocates of its use by academics argue that it helps improve efficiency in all manner of solitary and collaborative scholarly activities, through the provision of a reliable system through which any kind of information that might be of potential relevance can be stored and later retrieved (Bergen et al. 2013). It's easy to see how this can be so and the plausibility of its fans has led me to try and use Evernote on multiple occasions. It's never quite worked for me though, partly because between my 'blogging/Twitter' e-mail folder and my research blogging, I already have a preferred repository for much of the information I'd like to archive. I also struggle with the notion of 'notebooks' and 'stacks': the metaphor has never made complete sense to me and I've encountered others who've had a similar experience. Allan Johnson (2013) wisely cautions against creating notebooks too readily because of the risk that the 'number of notebooks will quickly get out of hand, relegating the most important notes to the background and making digital note taking less effective'. This is certainly my experience of Evernote when I have tried to use it on a regular basis in the past. These categories inscribed in the software that are supposed to provide context can actually erode it, leaving me with masses of information sorted into a taxonomy that makes little sense to me.

When we discussed this, Stuart Elden offered a helpful explanation of how he uses Evernote. He has a main notebook which he tries to keep to less than 20 things: commitments, deadlines, things he's ordered, important addresses and other action-orientated information. Then he has notebooks for research projects and just throws material into them which he can then refer to when he's using them. He also uses the e-mail to Evernote function a lot, explaining how he lays the groundwork for future projects by sending relevant links as and when he encounters them, as well as using the associated e-mail address to have alerts of relevant literature automatically sent into the notebook for the upcoming project. The system allows him to call up a lot of information, immediately and easily, from whichever device he is using and wherever he is at the time. In this sense it's not unlike his blog and he has described the relationship between them as being akin to a 'queuing system': he uses Evernote to store the material which would have to be filtered and contextualised (however briefly) before being published on the blog (or used for any research purpose). He cited the example of an annotated bibliography he had recently produced on Boko Haram as part of a new project. He set up a Google Scholar alert for any new literature referring to Boko Haram, using the e-mail to Evernote function to have this automatically sent to the relevant folder. These accumulated in Evernote before he would go through them, downloading the articles, updating the bibliography and then clearing the folder. The annotated bibliography would be shared on the blog but he wouldn't post every time he encountered a new article that was relevant to the project.

This description of his workflow certainly conveyed the appeal of Evernote to me, though after one recent attempt to get used to the software that led to the same result as all those that went previously, I think my engagement with it is at an end. There are nonetheless alternatives. Centrallo is an effective application that uses the overarching structure of a to-do list to structure information contained within it. This resonates with how I tend to think in a way which Evernote never has and it's a well-designed piece of software once you negotiate some slightly counterintuitive aspects of the interface. However, unlike many of the players within this sphere it lacks substantial funding and organisation behind it. Therefore, it's probably not safe to assume that it could be a sustained presence in your life. Obviously Evernote was once in this position as well. But in the winner-takes-all marketplaces that social media tend to generate, it's much harder to enter the competition at a later date. The same fear would be unwarranted in the case of OneNote, Microsoft's surprisingly accomplished virtual notebook system that has developed continuously since its launch in 2003. It has a more free-form interface than Evernote and is built around, what I've found to be, a more flexible and intuitive framework of clusters of notebooks, notebooks and notes. This may simply be a matter of personal preference however. As well as applications like Evernote and OneNote, there are all manner of journal and notebook applications available for mobile devices which could prove useful as a research notebook. At the simplest end of the spectrum is the appropriately named Simplenote. It offers a plain text editor which allows you to quickly and easily record thoughts, tag them and synch between devices. There are *many* others though. Many of the minimalist writing environments which have become increasingly popular, as part of a movement towards what Pang (2013) calls *contemplative computing*, have introduced cloud synching that in effect means they can serve this purpose. My particular favourites are WriteRoom, iWriter and Daedalus. But there many others. In the case of the latter, it synchronises with the writing environment Ulysses III, offering an integrated environment for writing and research which functions across devices. There are also extremely functional journal apps, such as Day One Journal, which can be used for similar purposes. The options are endless, writing as someone who has gone out of my way to try as many of them as I can over the course of writing this book. The key is to find one that works for you. Some of this is practical but in other aspects it can be as much about aesthetics and sensibility. For instance there's something about the 'terminal' environment offered by WriteRoom, in which a black screen contains nothing more than my writing and a charmingly retro blinking green cursor, that I find immensely satisfying – for reasons I can't quite articulate.

What many of these applications share is the use of tagging as a basis to organise material you have collected and to facilitate discovery. In a helpful account Allan Johnson (2013) describes how he applies four categories of tags to every piece of information he enters into Evernote and his task manager: *context, output*, *topic* and *x-ref*. The first refers to the general areas of responsibility into which information falls such as doctoral research, teaching notes and his blog. The second refers to the kind of output to which each entry might ultimately contribute, such as lectures, seminars, conferences or publications. The third category encompasses a descriptive summary of the content. The fourth category constitutes cross-cutting themes which allow cross referencing between the disparate entries he makes into these organisational tools. This might seem an unnecessarily complex way of utilising an electronic tool but it's something worth considering, at least if the experience I described earlier of confronting a pile of information with no context is something you recognise. It's only by providing this information that the context can be preserved and unexpected convergences identified between seemingly discrete pieces of information recorded over time.

Part of the difficulty with these apps is how much they rest on what you happen to find intuitive. Personally, I find the notion of the bundle (discussed later in the chapter) immensely obvious, reflecting my very familiar tendency to pile relevant material up into heaps (or bundles) that are grouped around a shared theme. This is what I always did offline (my filing cabinet is a mess once you look beneath the surface) and it comes naturally to me to do it online. In this sense, it seems obviously worthwhile to experiment with different services if no one particular app appears immediately attractive. Nonetheless, if you're struggling to find a *virtual notebook* that works for you, it might be that you simply don't work in a way that makes one a requirement. There are other solutions which might serve the purpose of saving material in an organised way so you can read it later. While reference management systems are largely beyond the scope of this book, these are one type of utility likely to become ever more relevant to the concerns of this chapter. There are some basic social capacities built into newer reference management systems and this only seems likely to grow with time. It seems likely that a greater capacity to share annotations and reflections upon literature *within* a reference management system might lead them to develop into a type of software that could be used as a specifically academic equivalent to applications like OneNote and Evernote.

Then there are the *curation* tools which are the focus of the next section. Before that, however, we must not overlook the *read later* apps and *bookmarking services* which record links to online material without necessitating the cumbersome process of e-mailing links. One of the most popular, Pocket, allows me to save anything seemingly interesting that I don't wish to read at that moment in time, usually only opening the app to read on my iPad or iPhone when on public transport. It never fails to be enjoyable to suddenly discover how much interesting material is archived in there. I rarely, if ever, exhaust the material I have saved, and once declared 'bankruptcy' because the sheer quantity of archived pages was so great that in some subtle but nonetheless noticeable way it detracted from my enjoyment of the app. While these apps make it easy to register material that you have discovered, they do not in themselves ensure that it is put to effective use. Apple's Safari now has a similar feature built into it which works across devices. Other popular read later apps include Readability and Instapaper. To a certain extent the slightly older category of social bookmarking tools has been eclipsed by micro-blogging on the one hand and read later apps on the other. The former is an easier way of sharing and discovering links, while the latter has incorporated the categories which are so crucial to social bookmarking. Nonetheless, Reddit has gone from strength to strength (though some people would dispute its categorisation as a social bookmarking service) despite being a perpetual locus of controversy. But along with Digg, these have tended to foreground their role as news aggregators in recent years, facilitating a 'curated front page' that is shaped by users.

What is curation and why is it becoming so important?

From the early days of blogging, the tendency of bloggers to filter the vastness of the web by selecting and presenting items they've found interesting has been a crucial driver of their popularity. This is something that the bloggers themselves found enormously helpful. As Cory Doctorow (2002) explains, in words that echo those of Daniel Little earlier, '[w]riting a blog entry about a useful and/or interesting subject forces me to extract the salient features of the link into a two- or three-sentence elevator pitch to my readers, whose decision to follow a link is predicated on my ability to convey its interestingness'. Describing himself as 'in the business of locating and connecting interesting things', he identifies a particular role increasingly referred to in terms of curation. Doctorow is literally 'in this business' – as well as being a successful author and highly influential activist, the blog he co-edits (Boing Boing) is amongst the most popular on the internet and provides a substantial income for all those involved (Rosenberg 2010: 198–206). Rosenbaum (2011: 4) draws an important distinction between 'aggregation' and 'curation': 'aggregation without curation is just a big lot of stuff that seems related but lacks a qualitative organisation'. The point is that the curator 'adds value', to use a cringeworthy buzzword, in the sense of the collated materials coming to have an additional worth in virtue of the manner in which they have been collected and arranged.

So for instance we might say that one of BuzzFeed's notorious lists is curated while a Google News search result for a particular topic is merely aggregated. The former becomes something more than the sum of its parts, while the latter is merely a list of potentially relevant sources that leaves the process of selection entirely to the end user, at least within the remit of the search term they initially provided. There's still filtering in the latter case but it's entirely algorithmic. Another way of expressing Rosenbaum's distinction might be to ask when *collating* materials amounts to *curating* them. The former is a necessary but insufficient condition for the latter: all curation involves collation but not all collation constitutes curation. The point is that curation is a matter of 'selection, organisation, presentation' and that this involves a qualitative aspect which necessitates human involvement, though it's interesting and important to recognise the extent to which algorithms do shape the material we're presented with online, usually through the analysis of patterns in choices made by other users (Beer 2013), constituting a 'filter bubble' which risks perpetual entrenchment in a situation where widespread awareness of it is still relatively lacking (Pariser 2011).

Many popular tools have emerged which aim to facilitate online curation. Many of these are framed around the idea of a magazine or newspaper, such as Flipboard. They vary a lot in spite of this though and one way of making sense of the differences between them is in terms of how active a process of curation they're intended to facilitate. Some are quasi-automatic, proceeding autonomously from the series of initial criteria you provide, for instance paper.li and RebelMouse. Others are intended to collate material for you in a way that makes sharing it in an appealing format effortless, for example Pearltrees. Then there are those which are intend to facilitate a real engagement with the information you're curating, inviting you to add commentary upon it and in some cases not really working very effectively if you don't. Scoop.it and to a lesser extent Bundlr would be examples of this category. But others still, most famously Pinterest, revolve around images. This range can make it difficult to know which curation tool might be most useful for your purposes. One solution is to simply experiment, playing around with them until you find one that works for you. An alternative strategy would be to try and clarify exactly what you want to use them for. Getting a grip on the potential uses of curation tools for you requires an identification of those points in your day-to-day working life when you find yourself finding, collating and filtering information. It's possible this won't be immediately obvious simply because activity of this sort is so ingrained in the work that academics do that we don't always recognise it as the very specific form of activity it is. Here are some examples:

- Producing a reading list for an upcoming writing project
- Compiling relevant material for a research project
- Producing a reading list for a module or course
- Collating articles you might like to blog about or share on Twitter

- Collecting academic resources for external groups
- Keeping track of media coverage of your work
- Keeping track of engagements with your work
- Maintaining a list of your publications

Further reading

- *The Information Diet* by Clay A. Johnson (2012) is an insightful and practical reflection on the challenge of coping with an over-abundance of information.
- *The Distraction Addiction* by Alex Soojung-Kim Pang (2013) is a thoughtful exploration of how to sustain your focus under conditions where distraction is ubiquitous.
- *The World Beyond Your Head* by Matthew B. Crawford (2015) is a strange and impressive work of philosophy, shedding light on the changing nature of human experience in a distracted world.

6

Professional identity in an age of social media

Chapter themes

This chapter will:

- Explore the dilemmas and challenges associated with putting aspects of ourselves on social media
- Discuss the implications of social media engagement within higher education
- Offer some practical tips on crafting an online identity

As a teenager I was captivated by Harper Lee's *To Kill a Mockingbird*. I'd enjoyed fiction prior to this but there was a certain quality to the story that left it lodged in my mind long after I read it. Looking back on this much later, it's hard to pinpoint exactly what that quality was, though I think one of the features that resonated so strongly with me was the intensely memorable character of Atticus Finch. One particular line that stuck in my mind for years has been Miss Maudie's praise for Atticus Finch as being 'the same in his house as he is on the public streets' (Lee 1960/1997: 51). The plausibility of the politics underlying this seems less obvious to me in hindsight, but I can easily see how this characterisation captured the attention of my impressionable teenage self. It's such a clear account of what's taken to be a virtuous character trait, treating all people the same in all circumstances, and presenting a consistent identity to the world under all conditions. My ageing copy proclaims over 30 million sales, a number which has presumably only grown since I bought it as a high school student. Coupled with the fact that it was required reading in UK high schools, as well as I imagine in the United States, it seems likely there were many others similarly taken with this portrayal of integrity as a matter of being 'the same in the house as on the public streets'. But was Mark Zuckerberg, Facebook founder and CEO, among them? After all he famously claimed that '[h]aving two identities for yourself is an example of a lack of integrity' when defending Facebook's restriction of users to their real identities. Leaving aside the evidence that neither Facebook, nor Zuckerberg himself, live up to these lofty standards of integrity (Helft 2011), it's worth contemplating this particular view of identity which has been proving so influential within the digital sphere, to the extent that it is built into many of the platforms themselves.

If 'having two identities' constitutes a 'lack of integrity', it must be important to act in ways which ensure consistency between your behaviour 'in your house' and 'on the public street'. But in practice this takes work. As the ethnographer Alice Marwick points out, the practical requirement of 'being authentic' is emotional labour and a lot of it (Marwick 2014: 16–17). As she goes on to write, 'authenticity is judged over time, in that people's authenticity is determined by comparing their current actions against their past for consistency' (Marwick 2014: 120). This already begins to sound rather tiring, not least of all because there are particular qualities of social media (the persistence, visibility and searchability of online content) that make it much easier for people to compare past actions and present behaviour to evaluate your integrity than would have been the case for Atticus Finch (boyd 2014). Imagine the same dynamic playing out in the present day and Miss Maudie's dismay upon, say, discovering that Atticus Finch has an additional existence as a prolific troll on YouTube comments threads.

When considered in personal and political terms, the desirability of Zuckerberg's ideal soon appears questionable. As the sociologist Nathan Jurgenson observes, 'we know that anonymity is also used by the most vulnerable and least powerful'. It is easy for people to have integrity in Zuckerberg's sense when they're in a position of power and their 'real' identity enjoys widespread social acceptance (Jurgenson 2011). Particularly when we consider how authoritarian governments around the world are coming to use social media, the peculiarly self-righteous way in which this policy of real identities is enforced begins to look rather unseemly (Morozov 2012). Even within a more liberal climate, this policy causes profound problems for anyone who needs to keep part of their life from those around them, leading PJ Rey (2010) to ask if social media have led us to build a society without closets? As someone who has studied the sociology of sexuality, the implications for queer youth are the most obvious to me (Driver 2008), but it's not hard to think of other groups for whom the need to maintain two identities can be a necessity of getting by as opposed to what Zuckerberg sees as a lack of integrity.

But what about in the professional sphere? Marwick's (2014) ethnography of the tech scene in Silicon Valley shone a spotlight on the exhausting labour necessary to ensure the appearance of 'integrity' in such a media-dominated world. Entire careers and vast libraries have been built to cater to the anxieties created by this demand, with the LinkedIn founder Reed Hoffman's (2012) *The Start-Up of You* representing one of the most prominent expressions of this trend. It's a fascinating and strange book, which I began to read out of a sense of morbid curiosity but was unable to persist with, providing a jarring insight into the developing norms of the professional world within which it has been studied intensively. Unfortunately what was once limited to Silicon Valley has long since spread beyond it – something which Marwick attributes in part to the capacity of social media to facilitate such branding because it simply wasn't possible in any meaningful sense until there was widespread access to the communicative possibilities it affords (Marwick 2014: 166). As she writes, '[b]efore the internet, a prospective self-brander was limited to putting up fliers at grocery stores, knocking on neighbours' doors, buying advertisements in the local paper, or attending potentially inaccessible industry-only events' (Marwick 2014: 185). The other part of the story is the growing armies of freelancers, contractors and consultants for whom this self-promotional activity is a necessary step for winning clients (Marwick 2014: 186). While some have seen this in an optimistic light, heralding the dawn of a Free Agent Nation (Pink 2001), the reality is considerably more ambivalent. This self-branding activity can involve vast amounts of unpaid work (Marwick 2014: 194) likely motivated by the desire to escape economic redundancy, current or potential (Bauman 2015).

Unfortunately higher education is not immune from this trend. The growth of precarious labour within higher education, as increasingly large swathes of the academic workforce move between multiple institutions and from one fixed term contract to another (if that), represents an environment within which the expectation of self-branding will thrive, even if the inane rhetoric is (thankfully) disowned by most. These pressures are likely most pronounced for precarious staff who 'teach at more than one place, have other paid work outside academia, or have serious unpaid responsibilities equivalent to another job' (Berry 2005: 13). But it's a broader trend, in which declining job security creates a risk of being invisible for those who move between jobs, as institutional markers of identity become decreasingly central to professional identity, simply because for most people they don't last (Gratton 2011: 238–242). The challenge of being 'heard above the din', as 'unread and unloved' publications proliferate due to the intensifying demand to demonstrate your 'productivity' as a scholar, creates incentives for self-branding as a way of ensuring visibility and standing out in some way (Back 2008, Beer 2012). Plus many universities are coming to be dominated by a managerialism that's likely to see the rhetoric emanating from the titans of digital capitalism as the cutting edge in organisational life (Ginsberg 2011), creating a risk that these norms will simply be imposed anyway, even if there were no 'bottom-up' trend in which academics seek new ways of managing their professional identity. If those in power have the expectation of entrepreneurialism, and self-branding is what this is part of and what this is taken to mean in practice, this stuff is unlikely to go away. A particularly poignant sense of what this is coming to look like came from the President of Imperial College London's recent description of professors as 'really like small business owners' (Carrigan 2015b). Perhaps the next step will be handing out Reed Hoffman's book to Imperial's professors. Nonetheless, I want to argue that there are some key practical questions about professional identity posed by social media which we need to retain while rejecting much of the vacuity surrounding 'self-branding'.

What is it about social media that creates a problem?

Before we get into the more practical questions, it's worth stopping to consider what exactly it is that's the problem here. Even the literature on identity I'm familiar with is vast, to say nothing of the literature I'm sure exists within other disciplines, so I won't try and review it here. Instead I'll make a simple proposal to serve as a basis for the ensuing discussion: the problem of identity goes hand in hand with the problem of information. Most discussions of 'self-branding' and 'online identity' ultimately hinge on the information available about us online, how others make sense of this information and the control we seek to exercise over these processes. What do we want others to know about us? What *don't* we want others to know about us? In the abstract these questions are not intrinsically complex, even if the matter of 'us' and 'others' might very well be (Verhaeghe 2014). The difficulty arises when we begin to think about how this varies between different groups in our lives, for instance our employers, students, colleagues, friends and family. It becomes more complex still when we consider that the information control techniques, in which we try and shape *who* knows *what* about us under *which* circumstances, themselves change as the media we use for communications do.

What control can we exercise over the information others have collected concerning us? What control can we exercise over how that information is linked together? To what extent can we ourselves retain control over what we have voluntarily made public? Part of the challenge here is intrinsic to digital technology because information that has been digitised is reproducable in a way that analogue information is not (Mayer-Schönberger 2011). For instance, it takes time and money to copy a physical book and information is lost in the process because mistakes are always made. In contrast, I can duplicate a PDF document of a book manuscript instantaneously at zero cost, at least once I have a computer upon which I can open and duplicate the file, with the certainty that no information will be lost in the process. Digital storage for information has long been cheaper than the analogue alternative – as costs continue to fall, it creates a situation where it's more economically rational to store everything by default than to take the time to filter out that which can be deleted (Mayer-Schönberger 2011: loc 947–989). These generic characteristics of digital data manifest themselves in specific ways on social media platforms.

These are the particular features of social media we discussed in the first chapter, what boyd (2014) describes as *persistence, visibility, spreadability* and *searchability*. But when we look at them in the context of professional identity, the exciting opportunities they offer for academics can begin to seem rather threatening. They hold out the prospect of losing control over what we have made public, risking that statements we might once have been confident would be understood correctly could be picked up by unexpected others at some indefinite point of time. This represents a challenge to academic authority because suddenly our utterances are competing for attention and their value is unlikely to be assumed by those engaging with them (Savage and Burrows 2007). In the face of this unpredictability, there's a risk of feeling unable to say anything substantive. Mayer-Schönberger suggests that 'If one does not know how one's utterances will be used and by whom, one must assume the worst, namely that any criticism will end up where it will cause the most damage' (2011: loc 1549).

Potential Pitfalls

Social media and academic expertise

Much of the challenge posed by new forms of publication stems from the way in which their novelty precludes the establishment of recognised norms concerning their use and interpretation. This leaves academics facing important challenges of *managing online identity* when using social media. One important aspect of this concerns the question of *expertise*. Given how readily these new forms of publication lend themselves to experimentation, with their instantaneity encouraging users to range beyond their familiar topics and styles, it is important to consider how the ensuing publications will be received, particularly by those outside the academy. The Public Policy academic Alex Marsh (2013) framed this issue succinctly by describing himself as an *academic who blogs* rather than an *academic blogger*. His point was that these were 'two separate but overlapping identities' which he was forced to negotiate, often finding that the topics he was inclined towards discussing as a blogger fell outside those he felt qualified to discuss as an academic. We need not accept Alex's conclusions to recognise that he raises an important point. Being clear about the extent to which one is engaging in a professional capacity online is a key aspect of managing online identity and much of it is connected in one way or another to professional identity, which in the case of academics has complex associations with the notion of expertise.

Through digital engagement, we leave information circulating in the world about *who we are* and *what we do*. To talk of online identity is simply a matter of trying to be aware of this information, how it might be interpreted and how we can exercise control over it. At its most practical level, this involves reflecting on how to present yourself on social media and how this presentation coheres with the expectations which the groups you're engaging with will have about self-presentation online. There's a wide range of ways in which it's possible to present yourself on social media. But in practice there are obvious patterns in how we actually choose to do so on a day-to-day basis. One of the reasons for this, Marwick (2014: 227) notes, is because users learn a sense of what it is to use technologies appropriately from friends and peers, often in a way that alters their behaviour. It might not be a case of straight-forwardly restricting oneself in accordance with the norm, but coming to the conclusion that there does *seem* to be one will inevitably have an impact on behaviour. You may think the way people do things is stupid, but in thinking that you've already been influenced by your sense of the norms concerning how people do things. Twitter is a particularly interesting case for this because of the enthusiasm within which so many professional groups have embraced Twitter. If these networks are as closed as they often appear to be, constituting the 'echo-chamber' which is an occasional source of speculation within them, it seems plausible that a sense of 'how one is supposed to behave' will develop more quickly than amongst a diverse group with contrasting aims and objectives. This point can be over-stated, not least of all because trying to break out of those echo-chambers is an individual practice that can be easily accomplished, for instance by follow-ing a user very different to oneself after reading an interesting tweet that was retweeted (Murthy 2012: 36). But when considering the question of what con-stitutes 'appropriate behaviour' on any social media, it's crucial to consider the reference group implied here, particularly when it might be more closed than commonly assumed.

However it would miss the point to leave things here. How you relate to your peers on Twitter and the expectations they have of you might very well be the easiest aspect of online identity. The more challenging questions emerge when we think about other groups (employers, students, friends, family) and how your interactions with them on social media might pose dilemmas in their own terms, not to mention how each of these dilemmas might further complicate the other situations. The second half of this chapter turns to the more practical question of the steps you can take to craft an online identity through profiles and about pages. These tasks are mundane and easy. At least they are if you're clear about how you understand your online identity and what you want to convey in rela-tion to the different groups you interact with. Without such clarity, misunderstanding is inevitable. These might prove inconsequential. But it's also possible that they won't. We can overstate the risks, but those risks are real.

In the final chapter I discuss some recent cases and what they suggest about the future landscape of academic social media. The key thing to remember here is that people won't stop telling a story *about you* simply because you've chosen not to tell a story about yourself. I'd hate higher education to descend into the depths of inanity which Marwick (2014) so expertly analyses in the Silicon Valley tech scene, but if we can abstract away from the irritating rhetoric there's a crucial issue underlying it all. Information about you is out there and people are drawing conclusions on the basis of it. You *can* exercise control over the information you share and tell a story about it to the different groups you engage with online. But this does require a bit of thought if it's likely to succeed.

Identity dilemma #1: Your employers

Universities are changing, as are the employment relations within them (Holmwood 2011b, McGettigan 2013). This book isn't really about these changes but it's hard not to refer to them because they have such obvious implications for how universities *as employers* orientate themselves to the social media activities of academics *as employees*. From the perspective of modern management trends, universities appear to be 'dumb organisations' (Fuller 2003) in the sense that managers at all levels often struggle to keep up with the activities of their highly individualised workforces. If managers are concerned with efficiently managing the human resources of the university, it would be understandable that they might see social media as a distraction from work. After all, as Ele Belfiore observed to me, 'There's still the perception that colleagues will see you as skiving'. I know of at least one case in which university managers raised the possibility of counting tweets in order to measure time spent away from work. At the very least, social media pose obvious questions of how they can be incorporated into the time management practices adopted by universities (Vostal 2015). The answer is not straightforward, and at least if the managers in question are sceptical about the value of social media, it's easy to see how this might prove extremely worrying.

There's also the issue of what Marwick (2014: 238) describes as 'the intrinsic conflict between self-branding and corporate employment': what's best for the self-branding employee might not be what's best for the company and vice versa. In this case you can't have academics running around the internet offering 'outspoken opinions' without feeling that your carefully worked-out plans for the corporate brand are potentially at risk. The institutional brand has cachet on social media, in fact a stated affiliation could be shaping people's perceptions of you to an extent far beyond what you imagine to be the case (Nickel 2011). In turn, the personal brands academics are developing – in some cases having drawn audiences via an online engagement that has vastly exceeded anything that could be imagined through traditional forms of scholarly publishing (Pearce et al. 2012) – risk being seen ambivalently as both an opportunity and threat to the university. As Cottom (2015) puts it, 'public engagement leverages attention into brand awareness which, in turn, somehow contributes to greater prestige in the competition for prestigious students'. But that brand awareness also carries risks. How this might be construed and then acted upon will likely vary immensely, but the risk is inherent in the relationship between employers and employees within a digitised environment and any reflection on your online identity as an academic needs to begin by recognising this. The fact that academics are embracing social media at precisely the time when most universities are imposing a standardisation upon the web presences they provide for their staff, suggests diverging priorities and the potential for growing conflict.

What compounds the problem is the potential instability in how management respond to a strategic question like this, as well as how the ensuing shifts are imposed on academics within the institution (Ginsberg 2012). One academic with a deep commitment to public engagement, digital and otherwise, described to me the difficulties this created with their institution. The institution initially saw their online activity as a threat, invoking the possibility of disciplinary action upon the discovery that they'd been critical of research assessment practices on their blog. After some negotiation, an agreement was reached that they would remove references to their work from the blog and keep it entirely distinct from their academic work. However the growing prominence of Twitter within higher education led them to change tack entirely, actually pushing them into more engagement online at a time when various unpleasant events had meant that they wanted exactly the opposite. As I discuss in the final chapter, there's a real risk that social media are becoming mandated by institutions in a way that risks squeezing out the potential scholarly and personal value to be found in their use. At least superficially, it might appear that negotiating this identity dilemma is likely to be a simple matter of familiarising yourself with a code of practice and ensuring that your conduct stays within what it defines as acceptable behaviour. However the reality is likely more complex, or at least it will become so over time. At present social media guidelines are intensely liable to revision, likely introduced either as a form of retrospective crisis management or in a non-binding way as an initiative of social media managers. This is not universally true though and it's important to familiarise yourself with the policy at your institution.

Though as Mewburn and Thomson (2013) suggest, 'An academic blogger could make the argument that they are operating as a private individual who blogs in their own time'. But how would this be received? Trends in other sectors do not give cause for optimism. In an overview of how employers are using social media for recruitment, McDonald and Thompson (2015) suggest the two main benefits this offers to employers: helping them to select 'enterprising' candidates and screen out those deemed to be undesirable in some way, particularly on the basis of criteria which are difficult to act on as part of the formal recruitment process. Exactly how widespread such a practice is remains difficult to ascertain reliably. There are polls of employers which suggest the figure could be over 50% but it's a difficult phenomenon to measure reliably. For instance, it's hard to imagine that any employer would ever record figures on 'people we would have hired but didn't when we check their Facebook profile', and the causality would remain elusive even if this were not the case.

We might assume that higher education, as well as the professions more broadly, will tend to be somewhat unique simply because there's a greater likelihood that candidate and recruiters might already have encountered each other in a professional setting. This might seem unnerving: someone reading an ill-judged tweet you sent when travelling home from a party on a Friday night might one day be charged with assessing whether or not to give you a job. But is it really so different from the situation which already applies in the academy? The person you're making small talk with at a conference might one day be a future colleague. The presenter to whom you are addressing an ill-tempered intervention (perhaps a 'comment rather than a question') might one day be your manager. These possibilities are inherent in academic life and we rarely find ourselves socially inhibited in light of them, so is there any reason why social media should be any different? I don't think there is. However it's perhaps easier to lose sight of this on social media than it is when physically attending an event. The prospect of being surreptitiously judged and found wanting by potential employers is obviously worrying. What makes it so unnerving is the likely opacity of the criteria involved: being judged in private upon standards to which you are not privy violates many of our intuitions about fairness. While it may be difficult to know how widespread this screening is within higher education, as well as the potential impact it has on any particular case or on recruitment processes more generally, it nonetheless points to what I think can be taken as a general rule of professional identity in a digital age. The more you tell your own story on social media, the more difficult it is for other people to tell a story about you based on the fragments of material they find about you online (Thompson 2015). Plus a disclaimer would never hurt, if for no other reason than to placate your employers in the event that something does go wrong.

Potential Pitfalls

Social media and disclaimers

One way to make clear your own understanding of your activity is to add a disclaimer to your relevant accounts. Obviously the appropriate form for such a disclaimer varies across platforms. The most familiar form of such a disclaimer can be found in the countless academic Twitter profiles which make clear that 'all views my own' or 'tweeting in a personal capacity etc.'. However these need not be confined to Twitter. For instance my own blog featured the following disclaimer:

> *The views on this blog are my own and are not connected to my institution. Pretty much everything on here is a work in progress. I also use it to record thoughts which haven't yet reached even this status. Please note the date stamp on anything you read and consult my academic publications for a reliable record of my considered thoughts on the topics which feature on this blog.*

My intention here is to make clear that I often work out provisional ideas on my blog. Anyone who reads it on a regular basis has probably already realised this, but adding the disclaimer reassures me that those stumbling across it will (hopefully) refrain from taking anything they encounter as a definitive statement of my views. Other people's disclaimers can be a useful template but it's important that you're clear about what it is you're trying to express through the disclaimer and that you do this effectively.

Identity dilemma #2: Your students

As if all of the above weren't bad enough, we're then faced with the question of students. Using social media for communication has 'the potential to engage audiences to which the communications may not be specifically targeted', and as Sugimoto et al. (2015: 6) go on to observe, this may create problems for academics because the personas we adopt in relation to different audiences within our lives take on a newly problematic character beyond what might once have been the relatively discrete contexts within which we interacted. In this sense the problem of context collapse is far from unique to academics. But there is one particular kind of relationship which renders context collapse problematic within higher education: faculty/student relations. Even this isn't unique to higher education, as any number of widely reported cases regarding teachers at a primary and secondary school level being judged to have been using social media inappropriately makes clear. However, while the interactions between student and faculty may be easier in one sense because these are relations between adults, this also introduces a greater degree of ambiguity into the process. Furthermore, there is a general lack of agreement about what constitutes appropriate behaviour in how students and staff interact online (Malesky and Peters 2012). Cultural boundaries may be less obvious and dual relations, in which one is a graduate advisor and a friend or a lecturer and an employer, become possible (and even likely) in a way which is certainly not the case at prior stages in the educational system. The relationships themselves are more complex and so are the potential impacts that social media have upon them. As Sugimoto et al. (2015) identify:

> Informal interactions between faculty and students in physical spaces are nothing new, such as while at the grocery, a café, or out to dinner and drinks. The informal interactions that may occur in these physical spaces do not typically leave evidentiary traces nor are they broadcast. A quick chat, or a subtle avoidance, is temporal, happening in the moment at the checkout line or sitting adjacent in a restaurant. Awareness of audience presents itself through an immediate sensory experience through sight and sound. While the interaction may not be forgotten, though it probably is, it is captured, for the most part, by only the memories of those involved and is not purposefully broadcast. Interactions via SNSs, such as Facebook, however, fundamentally change and challenge the norms of these interactions.

The potential for awkward moments and ambiguous interactions inherent in student/faculty interactions is multiplied by social media in a manner that renders these susceptible to scrutiny in a way that some fleeting small talk while waiting for public transport or an evaded interaction at a social event simply is not. This also works in both directions, with students talking about their teacher online, either in what are understood to be private conversations or in increasingly organised forums for evaluation: the online forums of student societies, university-wide Facebook groups and dedicated sites for rating professors are becoming a pervasive part of the higher education landscape (Beer and Burrows 2007). It's a great experience to stumble across non-academics discussing your research online, but I imagine it's a much less pleasant one to accidentally encounter students attacking your teaching, denigrating your views or commenting on your attractiveness. Such reactions by students are not limited to these forums and there are many reports of sexist and otherwise unacceptable comments on student feedback forms (Garden 2015). But what makes social media different is that students who would never dream of mocking the physical appearance of a lecturer in person may nonetheless make such a comment in an online context on the assumption that the lecturer in question will never see it. Hopefully they're right! But while ignorance is bliss, simply ignoring the fact students are using social media to talk about their teachers doesn't make this go away, and prevents us better understanding the issues raised by it in a way that might help those who accidentally stumble across this as a consequence of context collapse.

The obvious question this raises is how much of your self are you willing to share with your students? Reflecting on your teaching, it's possible this might be more than you initially think, given the tendency Sugimoto et al. (2015) discuss for self-disclosure to be drawn upon as a strategy to humanise oneself as a teacher. Not everyone does this by any means, but the possibility that you may be sharing more than you realise in face-to-face interactions with students is an important one to consider when beginning to think through these issues. Perhaps the more pressing question is this: *are you sharing more about yourself with your students through your online activity than you realise?* What makes context collapse so pernicious is the ease with which it is possible for communication that was perfectly appropriate to a particular context (such as an ironic conversation about politics conducted over Twitter with a personal friend) to escape the boundary of that context and be received in a way that calls its appropriateness into question (for example a student reading and being offended by a remark that presupposed a shared knowledge of reciprocal facetiousness). At the risk of inducing paranoia, it's worth taking a look through your Twitter feed or blog and considering how things you've posted *could* be interpreted by someone with little to no knowledge about yourself, regardless of how unlikely that interpretation might seem to you. If you find nothing that might *potentially* seem worrying when viewed in this way then that's great. But for others this can give a new perspective on how you risk being interpreted. It's possible to extend this auditing exercise further by googling for your own name (both with and without quotation marks around it) in order to see what turns up. Assuming you lack the funds to hire one of the online reputation management companies who now cater for the rich and famous (Ronson 2015) there is a limited amount you can do about anything you may find, but a thorough trawl through Google results in this way can help you begin to see how your online self may appear in the absence of the familiarity which we all take for granted when considering our own lives. It's important to remember that your online footprint contains more than what you have deliberately published, given the avowed commitment of many social media companies to 'frictionless sharing' and sharing your online activity on a real-time basis.

Their insightful analysis leads Sugimoto et al. (2015) to the conclusion that 'where faculty and students are connected via SNSs, the lowest common denominator applies: that is, if anyone in your social network would find a message problematic, you should not send it'. However it's not always obvious when this condition is met. I remember being taken aback when I discovered my students were following me on Twitter and then feeling ridiculous for being surprised by this given my Twitter username is included in my email signature. The fact I felt silly for not having realised this was likely did nothing to mitigate against how disconcerting I found it to realise that my students had been an (unintended) audience for every tweet I had sent over the course of the academic year.

Identity dilemma #3: Your friends and family

This dilemma might be less pernicious, but it's worth thinking about nonetheless. It might be that you're using social media in a way that sharply differentiates between 'private' and 'public'. This works for some people but it's hard to sustain unless you do it deliberately from the outset. Plus my experience has been that this terminology, with all the baggage it implies, can complicate these issues unnecessarily. We often talk about 'public' and 'private' as if these are two discrete sectors of our life that can be unproblematically delineated. In practice, the reality is much more complex: we work with our friends, encounter our students outside of the university, or find that information from our 'private' life is relevant to work in our 'public' life. In practice, it takes work to keep public and private distinct, in ways we've touched on in this chapter and will discuss more practically in the next one. If we want to keep 'public' and 'private' distinct in this way then it has significant implications for how we use social media. For instance, we might seek to use Facebook's closed networks for our private life and use Twitter open networks for our public life. Another way to look at this is to consider what you're not willing to share with everyone. Information about your relationship? Your friends? What you do at the weekend? Everyone's answers to these questions will be different and asking them can help with finding a private/public balance that works for you. It can be easier to think in these specific terms than to treat 'public' and 'private' as general categories.

We might see the dilemma here as operating in two directions. The first is when your 'public' life intrudes upon your 'private' life. For instance once I began to use Twitter with my present degree of enthusiasm, I soon found that my non-academic friends began to be frustrated by the sheer quantity of academic material I was publishing on my feed. In most cases they were already familiar with what I was doing and we had on many occasions discussed my research interests, but the continual exposure to my academic persona and activity sat uneasily with how I had tended to relate to them in the past and how they expected me to relate to them in the present. The popularity of Twitter with certain professions creates an intrinsic tendency towards context collapse of this sort, as friends outside the profession suddenly find themselves bombarded with material that much of the time represents 'shop talk'. This can present a useful opportunity to see how non-academics perceive academic communication. But it can also irritate your friends and lead them to unfollow you on Twitter (as a couple of mine in fact did). I assume they didn't hold it against me but I realise writing this that I never asked so perhaps I should check.

The other direction through which the dilemma operates is when 'private life' intrudes upon 'public' life. This might be completely trivial – for instance with the risk discussed earlier that 'frictionless sharing' leads the music you listen to and the videos you watch to be shared with your professional networks without you realising it. More serious issues might emerge if there are aspects of your private life which could create difficulties for your public life. One example is provided by Morozov (2013) who discusses the experiences of law professor James Gardener whose donations to various political campaigns were publicised via a data journalism feature on *The Huffington Post*. As Morozov (2013: 74) observes, Gardener had put time and energy into cultivating an identity as politically neutral with his students, something which he saw as a matter of necessity to teach constitutional law. While some might see this as a lack of integrity necessitating adjustment to the digital age, it seems more obviously understandable as one of the identity dilemmas that inevitably emerges once you start looking more closely at the different institutional worlds in which we move. Presumably Gardener's friends and family were entirely aware of his political views but he had legitimate reasons to keep them from his students, an ambition which was undermined by the *HuffPo*'s data feature. This might not be an issue for everyone. As the sociologist Gurminder K. Bhambra put it to me when I talked to her about this, 'what's the point of a private opinion?'. Though individual circumstances differ, perhaps it's actually easier to be upfront about all your opinions in this climate than it is to try and demarcate them as something 'private'. Will social media turn us all into Atticus Finch after all?

Crafting an online identity

The prospect of laboriously crafting an online image is probably somewhat off-putting. It's certainly a recurrent theme in critiques of social media and the digital narcissism it is said to engender. However it doesn't have to be a time-consuming process. Reflecting on how to present yourself online is helpful because it's the most immediate way of addressing the issues discussed in this chapter. While there's more to online identity than what you happen to put in your social media profile, it's nonetheless the case that this is the aspect of your online identity over which you have the most control. Hopefully the first half of this chapter, considering three kinds of dilemma which academics using social media are likely to face, helped provide a useful context for the more practical part of the discussion. However having said all this, it's certainly possible to find yourself wasting time cultivating a profile when you're supposed to be doing something else. So be wary.

The choices available to you largely function within parameters defined by the services you're using. In other words, there are only so many things you can customise. But the clearer you are about the story you're trying to tell, the easier it will be to do something interesting within these limitations. For instance, consider Twitter. Obviously there's a limit to how much information it's possible to fit in a Twitter profile. That's why it's necessary to decide what information is most important for you to present. For instance, if you're primarily concerned with meeting others working within your area then foregrounding your research interests makes sense, being much more specific about them than might otherwise be the case. For example 'interested in sociological accounts of asexual identity' as opposed to 'interested in asexuality'. Furthermore, it's hard to tell a story in 160 characters. But it is possible. My favourite example of this comes from Yanis Varoufakis, the economist who is Finance Minister of Greece's SYRIZA government at the time of writing. As he describes himself to the world, 'Economics professor, quietly writing obscure academic texts for years, until thrust onto the public scene by Europe's inane handling of an inevitable crisis'. He literally tells a story with his Twitter bio, introducing himself as a thoughtful man happily toiling away in relative obscurity until circumstances conspired to draw him into the public sphere in order to deal with the self-evident failings of the political class. Many of his 506k followers as of 3 July 2015 will, no doubt, reject this analysis of the political scene in Europe. But he leaves them in no doubt about where he stands. Of course, it's much easier to tell a vivid story if your work has carried you into the epicentre of the unfolding history of Europe. But this isn't a reason not to try anyway.

The powerful thing about telling a story is that it gets beyond the level of simply listing facts about yourself. Not that there's anything wrong with this; in a way it's like a story because you choose which facts you present and the order in which you present them. But telling a story places them in a wider context, giving meaning and direction to things which people come to know about you. Nonetheless, listing facts is important. Yet what sort of facts are likely to be relevant for these purposes? Here are some suggestions:

- Your institutional affiliation
- Your research interests
- Other accounts you're involved with
- Your personal interests
- Hashtags you contribute to
- An institutional disclaimer
- An additional website

We discussed personal websites earlier in the book. These are more challenging because websites are obviously more text-orientated, though the importance of images should not be overlooked in a digital culture which, as we'll discuss in the next chapter, has clearly taken a visual turn in recent years. Personal websites provide more of an opportunity to tell a story about yourself and what you're doing. This opportunity can itself be challenging though and perhaps that goes some way to explaining why the branding consultants Marwick (2014) examines thrive in the way that they do. Even though I sneer, a suggestion offered by one of them that Marwick (2014: 194) discusses could prove potentially useful if you're struggling to know what to write. As an exercise, here's the suggestion offered by Julia Allison, or rather five exercises:

- Longer biography written in the third person
- One-page biography written in the first person

- 30-second elevator pitch
- 140-character Twitter bio
- 2–3 word tagline, intended as a pithy summary of yourself

The final exercise might be taking this too far. But the others could prove useful if you're struggling to get started on presenting yourself on a website bio. Another way to approach this is to search the websites of academics you know or know of. How do they present themselves online? What do you like about this? What do you dislike? Are there things that surprise you? Are there things that you suspect may be misinterpreted? What do you think they're trying to convey? These are all useful questions to develop a sense of what sort of self-presentation online feels right for you. By trying to articulate your reactions to other people's online identities, it's much easier to develop a sense of how you want to enact your own.

However the visual element to these matters is important. It can be tricky to get a social media profile to *look* right and the effort involved in doing so can be a potent source of procrastination. Many people have tried to capitalise on the concern people have with the aesthetics of their social media presence, though this can actually create a new problem because there's so much unsuitable material to sort through in order to find something useful. Search for 'Twitter headers' and you'll see what I mean. But within this range of material you'll find websites offering free images that can be used in your profile. The quality of these varies, to put it mildly, though it will likely be possible to find suitable images if you look through a selection of those available. However this obviously raises the question of what would constitute a 'suitable' image. To a certain extent, it could just be one you like. If you find an image that pleases you to look at then why not use this as your header photo? For instance, for a long time I had a Tetris-style image as my header photo which I liked because it reminded me of, unsurprisingly, Tetris. It didn't have any academic significance and to the best of my knowledge it didn't reflect some aspect of myself which I felt was key to my identity. It was just an image that I stumbled across which I thought looked appealing as a header on my Twitter profile. That said, it's possible that some of the things you think look appealing might not be similarly regarded as such by others, so while I'm suggesting that you should just choose something that you like, it's worth being cautious about anything that could possibly cause offence.

There's no obligation to use a profile picture of yourself on Twitter, or any other social media platform for that matter. However it's worth considering what practical purposes such a picture could serve. It makes it easier for people to identify you at conferences (though perhaps this could be a reason not to have one) and helps someone you're already acquainted with to confirm it's you when encountering you online. It also creates an impression of you in ways that might prove important for all the reasons we've discussed in this chapter. Unfortunately, as with everything else, its absence might create an impression. It's just much harder to know what this would be.

Further reading

- *Status Update: Celebrity, Policy and Branding in the Social Media Age* by Alice Marwick (2014) is a fascinating ethnographic study of self-branding in the San Francisco technology scene which sheds light on social media more generally.
- *Delete: The Virtue of Forgetting in the Digital Age* by Viktor Mayer Schönberger (2011) is a thoughtful reflection on the move towards a state of perfect remembering and what it means for human identity.
- *What about Me? The Struggle for Identity in a Market-Based Society* by Paul Verhaeghe (2014) is a provocative and wide-ranging reflection on identity in contemporary society.

Communicating
effectively online

7

Chapter themes

This chapter will:

- Examine the different audiences you may be reaching on social media and how to engage with them effectively
- Discuss how to respond when social media communication turns nasty
- Offer pragmatic advice on effective online writing including the use of titles and images
- Explore how to measure the effectiveness of online communication including Twitter analytics and article altmetrics

The earlier chapters of this book focused on activities academics engage in for which social media can prove useful. Underlying much of this though is something quite basic: *communication*. Talking and listening. Sharing ideas. It's something scholarship depends upon, even in its most hermetic forms (Dunleavy 2014b). But it's also so basic that, not unlike the process of 'keeping a file' discussed in Chapter 5, it can fail to be a matter of public discussion. This is a problem for many reasons. The most pressing one, at least for present purposes, concerns how academics communicate *online*. The novelty of online communication poses a plethora of challenges, calling into question all manner of taken-for-granted assumptions concerning scholarly communication. These assumptions can also creep into online communication in ways that can prove problematic, often compounded by going unrecognised.

In part we could see this as a matter of etiquette. As Douglas Porpora notes (2016), a longstanding manual of manners, by now in its 18th addition, includes advice on defriending someone on Facebook and how to approach online dating. We may be sceptical of the notion of an etiquette handbook, specifically that there is one 'right' way to behave, but these guides to manners are one response to a practical question of knowing how to comport oneself in particular situations. New technologies create novel situations, leading to dilemmas which actors must negotiate. This isn't something that began with social media. In our excitement about the transition from 'a culture dominated by mass media, using one-to-many communication, to one where participatory media, using many-to-many communications, is becoming the norm' (Rettberg 2008: 31) it can be easy to lose sight of how engrained comparable technologies like e-mail become during the transition between the two.

Nonetheless, something *has* changed in our present circumstances. Digital anthropologists describe our contemporary communication environment as polymedia. Whereas we once had a limited number of channels through which to communicate, we are now faced with a plurality and few intrinsic criteria to guide us in our choice of which one to use and for which purpose (Miller and Sinanan 2014). This can create a real challenge for how to avoid communication becoming something into which we sink ever greater amounts of time. Much of the problem comes from the fact that academics don't stop using e-mail when they start using Twitter. We don't stop writing journal articles when we start blogging. Even if we wanted to, something which I must admit has appealed to me on more than one occasion, we can't see this as either/or if we want to remain employable within a university. But if it becomes a straightforward matter of both/and, the demands upon our time risk continually escalating, not least of all because there's no reason to assume that this process of innovation has now ended and no new channels are on the horizon (Carrigan 2016).

There are extremely specific communication challenges posed by each social media platform. For instance, as Lee (2015) observes, '[e]ach tweet is only seen by a small percentage of your followers—in some cases, a *super* small percentage'. If this seems surprising then consider how you relate to Twitter. Do you read everything that's posted by every one of your followers? Unless you're following an extremely small number of people in an extremely committed way it's unlikely that you do. It's much more likely that you dip in and out of the stream. There's no one right answer about how we should respond to this. For some people, it seems like a reason to continually recirculate content because only a fraction of the followers will have seen it on each occasion. But if someone is following you in an engaged way, it's possible they may see it repeatedly. If so, it could become extremely annoying and do you really want to irritate your most engaged followers? On the other hand, without this kind of repetition, it's possible that things won't find the audience they otherwise would, potentially depriving people of something they might find useful and interesting. The right answer here depends on you, your audience and what you're trying to share with them. This knowledge itself requires prior communication, actual engagement with them, in order to understand their interest in what you're doing and their views on how you're doing it. Or you could just guess. But the point I'm trying to get across is that there's no *correct* answer, at least not one that is correct across all contexts. This is why it's necessary to grasp the dilemmas of communicating effectively online. Nonetheless, it's important that we don't get too preoccupied by the tools we're using to communicate. As the philosopher Steve Fuller puts it, 'there would be little point in being an intellectual if you did not believe that ideas, in one sense, always transcend their mode of communication' (Fuller 2003: 3) The constraints and obstacles will always be there. What matters is finding a way of communicating effectively in spite of them.

Who am I communicating with?

A key aspect of communicating effectively is being clear about *who* you intend to communicate with. Here are some potential answers:

- Colleagues working within your field
- Colleagues working within your discipline
- Other academics
- Students
- Journalists
- Policy makers
- Practitioners
- The general public

There are particular issues raised by many of these categories which we've discussed elsewhere in the book. But these audiences are an important thing to keep in mind when reflecting on communicating online. Who is your intended audience? Who is your actual audience? What can you assume about them? What can't you assume about them? In many cases, it might be relatively easy to answer these questions if we are talking about *one* audience. For instance, a familiarity with a research literature can be assumed when talking with people working within your field. But the problems emerge when, as will often be the case, multiple audiences collide. What if you're trying to talk to the general public and specialists at the same time? What if you're trying to talk to journalists and practitioners? In each case, it's necessary to have an idea about the group in question and what factors would help you communicate effectively with them. Alongside this is the additional problem of having to manage potentially contradictory imperatives when communicating with multiple audiences on the same platform.

For instance, engaging with multiple audiences on the same blog can certainly be a challenge but it is by no means impossible. Economics bloggers have led the way in this respect and there are many examples which show how it is possible to host technical posts for a specialised audience and non-technical posts for a wider audience on the same blog. The Nobel Prize-winning economist Paul Krugman, whose *New York Times*' blog Conscience of a Liberal could arguably lay claim to being the world's most popular academic blog, simply flags up technical posts by including the word 'wonkish' in the title. This works rather effectively and as a regular reader of his blog I've occasionally dipped into one of these posts out of curiosity, sometimes gaining some sense of the discussion but more usually being baffled by material far beyond the grasp of my rather primitive quantitative skills. He also marks content as personal which allows those solely interested in his academic or political reflections to skip over the occasional personal musings which inevitably seem to emerge in even the most serious blogger once it becomes a regular habit. This strategy might be more difficult for a blogger less prolific than Krugman who regularly publishes multiple posts in a day in spite of his peripatetic lifestyle and intense speaking schedule. If you were a non-specialist browsing the blog of someone who posts a few times a week or a few times a month, regularly encountering content labelled 'wonkish' or 'technical' might prove off-putting as you might easily scroll through a few months' worth of writing and find little of it to be directed at you. But in general it's a strategy that works well, as can be seen in the tendency of other economics bloggers to use a similar technique. For instance the Oxford economist Simon Wren-Lewis (2013) describes how he approaches the problem of multiple audiences:

I try and make what I write accessible to non-economists, but I know that I often fail, in part because jargon comes so naturally. There are a large number of non-economists out there who are genuinely curious about economic issues, and know that the stuff they get from the conventional media is either simplistic or just wrong. If you do try to write for that audience, but also want to write something more technical, you can flag that at the beginning of the post, as Paul Krugman and others do.

Consider the other people in your life who aren't academics. How do you explain your work to them? We all explain what we do to non-specialists with varying degrees of success. It's just that we often don't recognise this is what we are doing at the time. Instead, it's simply talking to partners, friends and family about our work. Obviously there are obstacles here. Specialised vocabulary gets in the way, we can't assume prior knowledge, and there are conceptual leaps which seem obvious after the fact but can be a real challenge to those who haven't yet made them. But the ways in which we negotiate these constraints in everyday communication can usefully inform how we write online. Part of the problem is that *simplicity* and *simplification* are often confused. To a certain extent this is understandable because the two often go hand-in-hand. Writing can exhibit simplicity precisely because it has simplified a complex issue. But there's no intrinsic reason why this need to be the case. It's possible to aim for simplicity in academic writing while nonetheless being aware of the dangers of simplification: avoiding the overly elaborate constructions found in academic writing while retaining its analytical rigour.

In other words, clarity and complexity aren't really antipathetic, it just takes a bit of work to reconcile them when we are writing. The proposal that academics render themselves unreadable through overuse of jargon is repeated so frequently that it has almost attained the status of cliché. The point can certainly be overstated and it's worth stopping to consider whether those who berate the jargon of social scientists reliably make similar criticisms of the technical terminology used by natural scientists in their communications. If they don't then we might wonder if there's some unstated assumption that because social scientists talk about *the social world* (and therefore things that we all encounter) then their work should be straightforward in a way that wouldn't be expected of the natural sciences. Would mathematical notation be attacked by some people because it makes the work in question unreadable for those for whom the symbols lack meaning? It worries me how readily some social scientists can flip into berating their own disciplines in a way that is sometimes suggestive of a striking lack of confidence in their own expertise and the specialisation which they've committed themselves to contributing to. Technical terminology often serves a useful purpose and I'm not sure a generalised distaste for it serves any purpose other than soothing anxieties about public status which have their origins elsewhere.

Technical terms often allow us to talk in ways that are simultaneously more nuanced *and* concise, working with precise meanings and taking understanding for granted without feeling it necessary to elaborate at length upon the meaning of each term we use. If you're writing a blog for other specialists or using Twitter to exchange information with them then what purpose would prohibiting technical jargon serve other than to place an artificial restraint upon the conversation? However, if you're trying to communicate with a broader audience – even with others within your discipline but outside your field – then technical terminology can rapidly become unhelpful. Its use as a matter of reflex, above and beyond any practical requirements, perhaps suggests underlying anxieties about speaking to a wider audience without the protective cloak of esoteric terminology. In one of my favourite passages by any sociologist, the radical intellectual C Wright Mills suggests that the '[d]esire for status is one reason why academic men slip so readily into unintelligibility. And that, in turn, is one reason why they do not have the status they desire'. This status anxiety mitigates against writing in an open way, amenable to being engaged with by those outside one's field, because doing so comes to feel as if it calls into question one's own status as an authority:

> In many academic circles today anyone who tries to write in a widely intelligible way is liable to be condemned as a 'mere literary man' or, worse still, 'a mere journalist'. Perhaps you have already learned that these phrases, as commonly used, only indicate the spurious inference: superficial because readable. The academic man in America is trying to carry on a serious intellectual life in a context that often seems quite set against it. His prestige must make up for many of the dominant values he has sacrificed by choosing an academic career. His claims for prestige readily become tied to his self-image as a 'scientist'. To be called a 'mere journalist' makes him feel undignified and shallow. It is this situation, I think, that is often at the bottom of the elaborate vocabulary and involved manner of speaking and writing. It is less difficult to learn this manner than not. It has become a convention – those who do not use it are subject to moral disapproval. It may be that it is the result of an academic closing of ranks on the part of the mediocre, who understandably wish to exclude those who win the attention of intelligent people, academic and otherwise. (Mills 2000: 218)

The point Mills is making extends beyond writing. He suggests that seeking to engage in the affairs of social and political life is too often construed as in some way vulgar, unfitting for someone who has undergone an extensive education and been recognised as a scholar. Given he was writing over fifty years ago, it's easy to wonder if this judgement is an artefact of his time. But if he's correct that status anxiety is at the root of this tendency to 'slip so readily into unintelligibility' then there's no reason to believe his analysis has a sell-by date, at least as long as social scientists remain in some way threatened and their cultural esteem lacks the secure foundations widely taken to characterise the natural sciences.

These issues often come to the fore when we speak to different audiences or across multiple audiences. When we switch from our usual audience to one which is unfamiliar, it can increase our awareness of things we take for granted at other times: ways of speaking, items of knowledge, limitations on the scope of what we're saying. Sometimes these experiences only increase our awareness in retrospect. The first time I was ever interviewed about my research, I was asked by a journalist whether I believed asexuality was 'nature or nurture'. I responded with a lengthy digression in which I used the term 'ontological stratification' and tried to explain in a cumbersome philosophical language that I rejected the terms of the question. Suffice to say, the intended nuance of my answer was not captured in the printed interview.

Another instance of this can frequently be seen with academic blog posts discussing specialised issues: is the likelihood that a reader leaving a comment may have misunderstood the discussion. On one level, this is indicative of the power of blogging for academics, as what are often niche discussions can often gain a broader audience inclined to comment on then, even in the absence of any particular attempt to promote the post outside of the ivory tower. On another level however it can be slightly awkward because depending on the tenor of the comment it can be difficult to know how to respond. Do you aim to correct someone who agrees with you effusively on the basis of a misunderstanding? If so how do you address the misapprehension without lapsing into a didactic style likely to be off-putting to your readers? What if the misunderstanding has led to an abrasive attack upon your post? How much time and energy is it worth spending engaging with someone who is attacking you on the basis of a misunderstanding?

I imagine the problem is worse if you embrace social media as a well-established authority in your field, your confidence buttressed by a career spent accumulating academic capital. It may be that you are well known but this doesn't necessarily translate into immediate prominence when engaging online. For instance, people may know who you are but this doesn't necessarily mean they're going to read your blog. It's important to avoid the assumption that people will be familiar with your work and to resist instructing them to familiarise themselves with it in lieu of engagement with the substantive content of what someone is saying to you. Most of all – don't simply broadcast. This is an injunction which has almost reached the point of cliché when it comes to Twitter, but it is repeated to this extent because of the inarguable truth of the proposition. Watching someone announce their latest achievements from on high to a (sometimes imagined) crowd of adoring followers while ignoring attempts to engage can be a rather unedifying spectacle to say the least. It's the digital equivalent of an invited speaker turning up to an event 10 minutes before they're due to speak, giving their lecture, and then cutting questions short immediately afterwards. In short, it's rude and it irritates people. But whereas the aforementioned conference speaker has power in virtue of their role as an invited speaker, digital communications are at least in a superficial way more democratic, insofar that people feel under no compulsion to listen to you, no matter how esteemed you may be in reality. This doesn't mean you have to patiently engage with every person who begins a conversation with you but it does mean you should avoid being perceived as someone who *never* does this, if for no other reason than the instrumental one that it will impede your online profile building and lead to you being seen in a negative light. Obviously this point applies most directly to Twitter, but it's true of other services as well. For instance, it would be similarly rude to never acknowledge comments on the blog posts you write, even if the quantity or quality of these is such that detailed engagement seems neither possible nor desirable. To put it bluntly – your expertise might not carry the weight you expect it to online, and you need to avoid performing it belligerently in the absence of expected (and hoped for) recognition.

All that said, if you're already prominent within your field then you will have an obvious advantage when beginning to engage online. It's just important to recognise that your latent audience might be more circumscribed then you expect and that academic capital doesn't inexorably translate into online attention. Even if you're an extremely well-known figure in your discipline, over and above whatever esteemed contributions you've made to particular fields within or cutting across it, this is not in itself a draw to people outside that discipline. It may lead you to say very interesting things and share extremely valuable resources – in short to 'add value' as 'social media gurus' are prone to saying – but these are what will lead people to engage with you online, as opposed to the disciplinary expertise upon which they are built. This shouldn't discount the relevance of your existing networks though, as well as the broader audience likely to be familiar with your work. If you are well established within a field or the discipline as a whole then build upon this: seek out people you already know, those working within the areas you work in, and people talking about issues you've worked on. As with the earlier suggestions, avoid the temptation to breeze into conversations, instruct people to read your work and then leave again, without ever explaining precisely what it is that they will find in your work and why it might be relevant to the discussion at hand. But by all means, refer to what you've done, just be aware of how these referrals might come across to others. For instance, say 'I think X is mistaken on this issue, for reason Y. I wrote about this in Z' rather than 'read Z to find out why you're wrong'. While your existing academic capital might not automatically translate into online promi-nence, it's nonetheless something which others might be aware of and hence this will factor into their interpretation of your online behaviour. In other words, the reputational costs incurred through online rudeness are likely to be more pro-nounced for those who already have a well-established reputation.

What should I do when online communication turns nasty?

If you find yourself in such a situation, it would be entirely understandable if it puts you off social media. While technology doesn't determine how people use it, the particular characteristics of media can often contribute to certain ways of interacting which can be less than compelling when scrutinised from the outside. Nonetheless, as Kathleen Fitzpatrick, Director of Scholarly Communication at the Modern Language Association, advises, junior faculty should not 'let dust-ups such as these stop you from blogging/tweeting/whatever' because '[t]hese modes of direct scholar-to-scholar communication are increasingly important, and if you've found community in them, you should work to maintain it' (Fitzpatrick 2012). Sometimes, persisting may simply make things worse. When a misunderstanding turns nasty, it can often be likely that trying to fix this through further discussion will in fact serve to entrench it. My favourite xkcd cartoon, *Duty Calls*, captures the dynamics which can creep in under such circumstances: the stick-figure pro-tagonist refuses to come to bed because there is important business to attend to: *somebody is wrong on the internet!* My enthusiasm for this cartoon reflects how perfectly it captures a feeling I know all too well from many years of engaging online: a frustration with how obviously wrong someone is online and a determi-nation to correct them through sustained argument. In practice it's usually a rather fruitless activity which can waste vast amounts of time in the pernicious sort of way that leaves you distracted and drained. There will *always* be people who are wrong on the internet. Sometimes they'll even be commenting on your blog. If it starts to feel really important to you to demonstrate that someone is wrong on the internet then it's almost certainly time for you to shut down your computer and walk away for a while. Learning to do this can be a really valuable way to save time and avoid pointless conflicts which undermine the effectiveness of your communication: if you end up in the 'someone is WRONG on the internet' state of mind you're much more likely to be inadvertently rude and offensive (or maybe deliberately so) in a way that will almost certainly undermine the point you were trying to make.

However this argument might be something you've neither sought nor contributed to. The evident fact of online harassment has been discussed elsewhere in the book. Under such circumstances Grollman's (2014) astute advice is to talk to friends and colleagues, to not read the comments where you can avoid them, and to consider informing trusted senior colleagues to be on the safe side. It's not necessary to look at attacks on you that you find on the internet. Furthermore, don't hesitate to block people on social media. It can be an enormously helpful tool for putting things out of your mind.

Potential Pitfalls

If you've said something on a social network that you later regret, it's unlikely that retrospectively deleting the post will leave you feeling better about it. While a seemingly questionable post left unretracted might be ascribed to misinterpretation, the act of deleting a post that was notable for its questionableness seems to indicate pretty clearly that you recognise it was a mistake. In fact from 2012 until Twitter rescinded its developer permission in 2015, on grounds which suggest it is rolling back on its commitment to journalism, there was a project called Politwoops (run by open-government group The Sunlight Foundation) which identified tweets that politicians had deleted after posting. In responding to Twitter's decision, The Sunlight Foundation's president reflected that their project had provided 'a unique lens to reveal how the messages from elected officials can change without notice or explanation – because Politiwoops did not allow for such reversal of messaging to quietly be swept under the rug' (Benton 2015).

It may be an overstretch to imagine academics, or even their institutions, being subject to this level of scrutiny, but looking to the political sphere helps illustrate how social media are changing what 'effective communication' means in practice. The fact that messages endure means that communicative missteps remain visible after the mistake in question has been made, but the inevitable temptation to try and hide these errors, by neatening up the stream of communications, can itself be more revealing than the original mistake. It may be difficult to imagine anyone establishing an Academiwoops, not least of all because Twitter seem to have made it clear that they don't want deleted content to be publicly reproduced, even when there are sound journalistic reasons for doing so. That doesn't mean that academics should be any less aware of how the act of trying to suppress something online can inadvertently draw attention to the information in question.

What are practical steps I can take to communicate effectively online?

Choosing effective titles

One of the most overlooked aspects of communicating effectively online is the way in which things like titles serve to provide a useful context. They help a piece of writing stand out to a potential reader, as well as orientate that reader towards what they can expect to find in the post. Even the most charitable observer would admit that most academics fail to give their writing catchy titles. It's inevitable that this would seep into social media but it can be much more important than might initially appear to be the case. Patrick Dunleavy, Director of the LSE's Public Policy Group which runs their popular range of blogs, advocates what he calls 'narrative titles' that 'make completely clear what your argument, conclusions or findings are'. Having worked for Patrick and received occasionally intemperate e-mails whenever my titles on the LSE British Politics and Policy blog deviated from this standard, I can truly agree with him when he recognises that 'titles take practice to write well' (Dunleavy 2014b). But while truly narrative titles can be tricky, at least while ensuring that they remain reasonably Twitter-friendly, it nonetheless seems to me that Patrick is on to something important. In the same article he suggests that in the absence of a full narrative title, it's still valuable to provide 'some narrative cues in your title, some helpful hints or signs for readers about the conclusions you have reached or the line of argument you are making' (Dunleavy 2014a).

Another way to look at effectiveness, though one we should perhaps be cautious about, is to use the metrics we have available. In a discussion of what makes for a successful title on Twitter, the team at Buffer shared a list of those which regularly attain 200+ clicks compared to their usual 100–150 (Lee 2015).

- Twitter Tips for Beginners: Everything I Wish I Knew When I Started
- How I Got 4x Faster Writing Blogposts
- The Origin of the 8-Hour Work Day and Why We Should Rethink It
- 59 Free Twitter Tools and Apps That Do Pretty Much Everything
- Shave 20 Hours Off Your Work Week With This Email Template
- How to Get Your First 1,000 Followers on Twitter — A Step-by-Step Guide!
- 30 Little-Known Features of the #SocialMedia Sites You Use Every Day
- How to Easily Save 60 Minutes Every Day on the Internet
- 7 Ways I Accidentally Got More Twitter Followers (and How You Can on Purpose!)
- 53+ Free Image Sources For Your Blog and Social Media Posts

Using images online

Another overlooked aspect of communicating effectively online concerns the role of *images*. In recent years there has been a visual turn in social media facilitated by smart phones with cameras and broadband connections with sufficient capacity to download images (Rettberg 2014: 3). This can be seen across the full range of social media: images and video now tend to feature heavily on Facebook, Twitter and blogs. In fact heavily visual interfaces are becoming the norm, with a striking trend towards the use of large high quality images as a central component of the aesthetics on new services like Medium. This intensifies an existing trend towards the use of featured images and carousels, particularly though not exclusively on magazine-style blogs. The most obvious driver of this visual turn at the level of social media services however has been the enormous success of Pinterest and Instagram.

Among American adults aged 18+, 22% used Pinterest and 21% used Instagram. Strikingly this was more than the 19% who used Twitter. The figure rises amongst internet-using adults, with 28% using Pinterest and 26% using Instagram in 2014. Perhaps most crucially 53% of 18–29 year old internet users in 2014 were Instagram users and 49% of these used Instagram on a daily basis (Duggan et al. 2015).

Seen in this light, the $1 billion Facebook paid to purchase it in 2012 immediately begins to make a lot of sense. As of May 2015, Instagram's press pages report 300 million active users of which over 70% are outside the USA. Between them they posted 70 million average photos per day and 2.5 billion likes per day (Instagram 2015).

Finding images that are licensed for use can be immensely time consuming but it's essential that you have the right to reproduce any content which you use on social media. One of the most important options is Creative Commons, something which can quickly and easily be used to license your own work through a process described on the CC website, with numerous platforms offering the possibility to search for images that are licensed for reuse. It's necessary to check the *precise* licenses on such images, as these do tend to vary. Many, if not most, prohibit modification or commercial use. Most necessitate attribution. But there's a wide range of high quality images that people have made available for reuse, at least under certain conditions. The Wikimedia Commons project falls into a similar category, and once you get the hang of a slightly counter-intuitive interface it can be a powerful tool for quickly locating images for use on the web, although the selection of such images is rather uneven. Unsplash hosts a continually updated stock of royalty-free images that do not require any attribution and can be used entirely at your discretion. Furthermore, if none of these options prove helpful, stock photography has declined in cost and increasingly constitutes a viable option, at least if you have a budget and want to ensure high quality images for a site. This can be particularly important for WordPress blog themes that rely heavily upon images, as many 'magazine'-style themes now do. Getty Images offer a WordPress plug-in which allows a library of royalty-free images to be easily searched and embedded within blog posts. This necessitates that you have a self-hosted site but it can be a tremendously useful resource if you do have one and greatly simplifies the process of finding and embedding images. Unfortunately the format in which they are inserted precludes their use as featured images, for example as images used to feature posts on the front page of a blog. It's also possible that the terms of the license could be changed at a later date – something which could prove remarkably inconvenient to anyone who has frequently embedded free images on their blog using this method, only to find that the licence for free use is withdrawn at a later date and these images have to be replaced.

Developing a voice when communicating

If you're tweeting from an institutional rather than a personal account, it can be more difficult to engage effectively, even if the same principles still apply. Who are your audience? What assumptions can you make about them? What does this mean for how you communicate with them? My own experience has been that it's hard to develop any sense of voice when tweeting on behalf of an organisation or group. My instinctual approach to this is reserved, erring on the side of caution. On the other hand, it's possible to try too hard to be engaging from a corporate account. On one of my far too frequent breaks to social media while writing this chapter, I was presented with a KitKat advert on Facebook consisting of an animated GIF of a kitten and the text 'Crazy cats or epic fails, have a LOL YouTube break with KitKat'. I'm sure I can't be the only one who finds this awkwardly affected at best and mildly creepy at worst. Perhaps it's worse when the vernacular lacks this awkward feel. For instance, Losse (2014) describes how she 'feel[s] unsettled, even usurped or displaced, by corporations' perfectly on-point social-media voices'. Her insightful analysis suggests that this mastery of the vernacular is a consequence of the constraints of marketing which any brand confronts on social media:

> It is a fact of marketing that brands can't ask for business too directly. People tend to recoil from requests that feel too direct, and this is why social-media accounts explicitly selling anything seem like spam, triggering disinterest. Brands have to make us want them by giving us something: in branding terms, providing #value. This is how humor, or the gift of laughs, becomes the universal gift that any Twitter account can provide to its followers, as #weirdtwitter proved in its universe of thousands of anonymous accounts tweeting nonsensical humor at each other. (Losse 2014)

What makes this so unnerving is the fact that the corporate brand suddenly has a voice in a way that was previously unimaginable. While KitKat might lack voice when its social media advertising consists of a mindless regurgitation of social media clichés, brands that display a complete mastery of a rapidly changing vernacular affect the appearance of personhood. As Losse (2014) recognises, it is a social media manager, often someone young and immersed in digital culture, speaking rather than the brand itself, but when 'brands speak anonymously and yet so intimately through the voices of unnamed social-media managers, we like them more than we can like any individual tweeter'.

How do I evaluate the effectiveness of my online communication?

What would constitute 'success'? This depends in large part upon what your goals were at the outset and how they have changed over time. However there are some basic measures which can be drawn upon concerning the effectiveness of publicity. For instance, if you're seeking to publicise your publications then the obvious question to ask is how much more widely known they are, if at all, after this activity. Analysing the effectiveness of your promotional activity in this way can sometimes be dismissed as narcissistic. From personal experience, it can also sometimes *feel* a little narcissistic. Many of the popular tropes which are used to dismiss social media (individualism, narcissism, self-obsession) can feel obviously relevant here. Tracking these activities can also risk being a potent means of procrastination. But it's worth doing, if only to see if the activity you're engaging in is actually having any discernible effect. This may include questions like:

- How many people have clicked on a link to my publication?
- How many people have downloaded my publication?
- How many people have shared my publication?

It's important to remember the limitations of these measures. Bastow et al. (2014) offer a useful analogy here when discussing how to measure the influence of academic publications:

> An occasion of influence arises when we can show that an outside decision-maker or actor was in contact with or aware of academic work or of research. But we can go no further than that up the causal chain. The analogy is with showing that someone has viewed a TV programme or read an item in a newspaper. In these cases, as for academic work, we cannot go further in construing (for instance) whether the reader or viewer agreed with what they saw, let alone acted upon it, let alone acted solely or decisively upon it. (Bastow et al. 2014: 53)

Though their focus with the analogy is upon 'outside decision-makers' the point applies more broadly. If you want to gauge the success of what you're doing then metrics matter. But it's important to remember a qualitative dimension which such metrics don't capture, for example many people might have tweeted a link to your article after you tried to promote it but what did they actually say about the article? It's also important to remember what they don't measure, even on their own terms. They can establish that someone clicked on a link to a post but not that they read it. They can tell you that someone downloaded a paper but not that they engaged with it. They can inform you that someone retweeted a link but not that they actually clicked it or even thought about it. This last case in particular can be an instructive lesson for many who are exploring Twitter analytics for the first time. It's surprising (and perhaps dismaying) how frequently a large number people can press 'retweet' but not, as the analytics reveal, actually click on the link itself.

One of the most significant developments concerning how to measure the effectiveness of your communication online has been the growth of article level metrics. The Altmetric score measures the quality and quantity of online attention a given article has received, using this to rank it in terms of:

- All articles in the journal
- All articles of a similar age
- Other articles of a similar age in the journal
- All articles tracked by Altmetrics

The score is generated using a weighted count intended to reflect the varying importance of the different sources citing the article. This allows all manner of sources to be included (encompassing social media, discussion forums and print media) while still retaining a balanced sense of their relative significance.

It is easy to get too caught up with metrics when you begin to think about evaluating the effectiveness of your use of social media. After all, we're working within higher education systems in which increasingly large swathes of academic life are governed by metrics. For instance, as Roger Burrows (2012) points out, academics at UK universities are potentially subject to over 100 metrics, encompassing every aspect of academic life. This is a climate in which measuring effectiveness in numbers can feel like the most obviously effective way to make a case for what you're doing. But making the point in this way invites an obvious question: who are you making your case to and why? If it's a matter of accounting for your time and making a case to an institution about the value of what you're doing, metrics might be a useful resource to be drawn upon rhetorically. But it's necessary to be clear about the value you place upon them and why. Consider a Twitter feed: it can be superficially impressive to have a high follower count, but what does it really mean?

If those followers have been accumulated mechanically through bulk following others and unfollowing those who fail to follow back, it's unlikely they'll be engaged with the material that's being shared. The average page impressions for a blog per month might seem remarkable, but do we know how many of those represent engaged readers? The problem is not that the metrics are meaningless, as much as that their meaning is not clear, particularly when taken in isolation.

However, if your interest in this is wholly or partly a matter of placating your institution there's no point in dwelling upon the limitations of these metrics. Instead you should think about how to tell effective stories with them. What is the case you're trying to make and how can the available metrics support you in making it? The most frequent case I've found myself making about this is that using social media as an academic will help ensure your publications are read and cited much more than might otherwise be the case. As discussed earlier in the book, the non-citation rate for academic papers is much mythologised and varies across disciplines (Remler 2014), but it's a widespread source of concern and the possibility that social media might help ensure that the papers and chapters upon which people work so hard avoid the fate of sinking without a trace is inevitably going to prove attractive. To make this case, I'd tend to point to my own publications as an example of how social media can help early career academics. My Google Scholar profile shows that, at the time of writing, my first paper has been cited 48 times and my first book chapter has been cited 11 times. I also have a co-authored article and an edited book that have been cited a smaller number of times (6 and 2 times respectively). There are also a few blog posts which have been cited, as well as a recent paper in an obscure journal that has heretofore only been cited by myself.

It would certainly be possible to make the case that my social media activity has contributed to a significant but far from unprecedented citation rate for someone still at an early career stage. But the picture starts to look more interesting when article level metrics are brought into the picture. For instance my paper that has been cited 48 times has an Altmetric score of 24, placing it in the top 5% of all articles scored by Altmetric. It's also the fifth highest-scoring article from the journal in question and has a high score (97th percentile) compared to articles of the same age. This still doesn't straightforwardly demonstrate that my social media activity led to a relatively high citation rate but the Altmetric scores suggest that it is circulating on social media, particularly through retweets of occasions on which I've shared the article from my own account, which we can take as something likely to increase the possibility that people will download and read the article, even if we can't be entirely clear about the extent of this influence. But the point is to use the available metrics to tell a convincing and useful story about the impact of your activity. The comparable data aren't available for the book chapter that is my second most highly-cited publication, though the tendency of publishers to 'unbundle' edited books – treating them as an aggregate of individual chapters with their own digital identity – suggests this will soon be a thing of the past in most cases.

The Altmetric scores for my co-authored article again prove promising, placing it in the top 5% of all articles scored by Altmetric and in the 96% percentile compared to articles of the same age. It has as yet been cited much less frequently (6 times, as opposed to 48 times) but at least to some extent this probably reflects the fact that it was published almost two years later. The additional data provided by the journal prove interesting here as well, informing me of 2131 views at the time of writing and that it's the third most-read article in the journal, despite having been published relatively recently (and the second most-read article is from the same special issue). In fact the journal had previously provided download data as well, the impressiveness of which I had used in the months after our co-edited special issue had been published to persuade them to offer a substantial open access period on parts of the issue (without any payment being required), that in turn meant that media citations of the journal were able to link back to an accessible paper, presumably contributing to these viewing figures.

My intention here is not to go on about my own publications. All I'm trying to do is illustrate how you might begin to tell a story about how your use of social media has had an impact. If you haven't already, set up a Google Scholar profile, add your papers, and remember to check the listings every now and again (I found an erroneous result while writing the previous paragraph which I'd managed to miss last time around). Install the Altmetric browser button (available at www.altmetric.com) and use it to examine the article level metrics for your own work.

Further reading

- *Web Cam* by Daniel Miller and Jolynna Sinanan (2014) is a fascinating study of how human communication is reshaped by new technologies.

- *The Impact of The Social Sciences* by Simon Bastow, Patrick Dunleavy and Jane Tinkler (2014) is an impressive and comprehensive account of the current state of play regarding metrics, measurement and impact in scholarly communication.
- *Seeing Ourselves Through Technology* by Jill Walker Rettberg (2014) is an engaging account of how technology shapes how we see ourselves, placing the visual turn in social media in a much broader context.

[illegible]

8

Finding the time for social media

Chapter themes

This chapter will:

- Discuss how we can sensibly fit social media into busy academic lives
- Explore how mobile devices offer opportunities to engage on-the-go
- Offer pragmatic guidance on time-efficient social media use

One of the most common questions which people who use social media regularly get asked is 'how do you find the time?'. In circumstances where half of academics report finding their workload unmanageable (Shaw and Ratcliffe 2015), it's understandable that this question is asked but it can still be a hard one to know how to answer. The subdued awkwardness which pervades these interactions can get in the way of actually understanding the broader questions of how people do fit social media into their academic and personal lives. An obvious way to approach this question is to take it literally and ask *when* do people find the time for social media? At least it seems obvious to me but it might not be for others given how rarely it seems to be asked. Concerns about the time potentially liable to be taken up by social media often assume that these will displace other more meaningful activities. There's no obvious reason why this needs to be the case and many prominent academics illustrate much more agreeable ways in which blogging can be integrated into their daily lives. For instance the Oxford economist Simon Wren-Lewis (2013), author of the popular Mainly Macro blog, describes how '[t]he main activity that blogging has displaced for me is watching TV' and that he writes 'the initial drafts of most of my blogs between 9pm and midnight'. Alex Marsh (2013), Professor of Public Policy at the University of Bristol, tends to write late at night or at the weekend. He raises the important point that, for him, it would be misleading to see academic blogging as 'work' in any narrow sense:

> Blogging is, for me at least, nothing like academic writing. Academic writing, while it can undoubtedly be enjoyable and rewarding, is most definitely work. It can be hard intellectual labour. Blogging, on the other hand, is a way to relax. It requires thought, of course. But it is a completely different quality of thought. It is nowhere near as taxing. Putting your view out there for others to agree or disagree with as they see fit can be quite a relaxing way to finish the day. (Marsh 2013)

For Alex blogging is a hobby but it's one which visibly overlaps with his professional life. As he puts it, 'because my hobby happens to be writing stuff that is made public (aka "ranting on the internet") rather than talking about the same stuff with my mates down the pub it is rather more clearly visible'. This raises many professional identity issues, including Alex's thought-provoking description of himself as an 'academic who blogs rather than an academic blogger', but for now I think it's worth considering what significance this has for the question of the time taken up by social media. For many, Twitter is an interesting diversion during a commute. Or it facilitates, as Charlotte Mathieson put it to me, the kinds of conversations 'you wouldn't have time for in the working day' and that keep you connected to a broader research community in an ongoing but low-key way. For those who do it regularly blogging is often a hobby, at least in the dictionary sense of '[a]n activity or interest pursued outside one's regular occupation and engaged in primarily for pleasure', even if they don't use that term themselves (Wordnik 2015). As much as he chronically overstates his point, I do believe there's a kernel of truth to Clay Shirky's (2011) notion of *cognitive surplus*: we're moving from a situation where '[w]atching sitcoms – and soap operas, costume dramas, and the host of other amusements offered by TV – has absorbed the lion's share of the free time available to the citizens of the developed world' to one in which cultural production becomes a mainstream activity. The social tendency inherent in the former really comes to the fore with the advent of social media because, as David Gauntlett (2011) puts it in his book of the same name, making is connecting. In Shirky's view, questions of 'finding the time' entirely miss the point, failing to grasp the sheer cultural significance of the changes we are seeing:

> People who ask 'Where do they find the time?' about those who work on Wikipedia don't understand how tiny that entire project is, relative to the aggregate free time we all possess. One thing that makes the current age remarkable is that we can now treat free time as a general social asset that can be harnessed for large, communally created projects, rather than as a set of individual minutes to be whiled away one person at a time.

Leaving aside his overestimation of how isolated cultural life used to be, I take his point to be that social media greatly increases the capacity to connect with others in creative and satisfying ways during time that would have formerly been isolated downtime. It seems difficult to disagree with this but it does raise questions about work/life balance that are far from unique to academics. For those for whom social media is effectively a hobby, it could be argued that these questions don't apply. As Alex Marsh (2013) observes in the account cited above,

> If my hobby were playing squash, growing bonsai or dabbling in oils then it would attract no comment. I could be addicted to soap operas or spend all my spare time baking cakes. I could even spend every evening in my local nursing a pint and engaging anyone who would listen in merry badinage about the latest idiocy emanating from the Westminster village. In all cases I would be flying below the radar. (Marsh 2013)

Beyond those like Alex for whom something like blogging is clearly a hobby, we're still left with the question of how social media fit into people's lives. To describe it as a 'hobby' and leave it at that perhaps misses the potential value that social media can have for professional development and academic careers. After all, if you were *purely* interested in this as a hobby, would you have ended up reading a book about it? Perhaps you might have but nonetheless it seems likely that anyone reading a book called *Social Media for Academics* will have an interest in the professional value of, well, social media for academics.

The point of this introduction has been to stress that for many people social media are something they enjoy and which they come back to largely because of this enjoyment. They fit into their lives quite easily and don't necessarily displace more important or worthwhile activities. The chapter itself discusses the many further questions which are left about time management and social media once we recognise this point.

Time for social media and time for scholarship

When someone asks 'where do you find the time?' in response to social media use by academics, it's often predicated on the unspoken assumption that this is a distraction from the much more important business of serious scholarship with which they themselves are occupied. What these debates ultimately hinge upon is the relationship between *social media* and *scholarship*. If using social media become an additional item on your to-do list, over and above the many other demands on your time, it's unlikely that you'll engage online in a sustained way (or that you'll enjoy it when you do). As Stuart Elden put it to me, 'if I had to budget time to do it, it would be something that got cut', but as a habitual part of his working routines, it's not something that would ever figure on a to-do list. If on the other hand you are able to incorporate social media into your existing working practices then it becomes much easier to find the time and much more enjoyable when you do. In part this is because it is no longer a matter of 'finding the time' but rather something that you do, serving an immediate purpose in a habitual way, as opposed to being something that you feel you need to do and find space for in relation to the other things competing for your attention. This is a slightly long-winded way of saying that sometimes social media use by academics *is* scholarship.

The activist and author Cory Doctorow, co-editor of Boing Boing, describes blogging as 'my major way of thinking through the stuff that matters to me', with the blog itself representing a 'repository of all my thoughts and inspirations, my public notebook and my soapbox' (Doctorow 2014: 67). Obviously blogging isn't the *only* way one could do this, but my suggestion here is that it's a peculiarly potent one with specific characteristics that make it well adapted for this function, all the more so when the material which one is thinking through tends to exist in a digital form. As discussed earlier in the book, there are many other ways to 'think things through': write them down in a notebook, record them in a Word document, jot them down on file cards organised into a system, annotate printed papers and so on. Blogging about your research should be seen in these terms, as a way of *doing* scholarship rather than an additional activity tacked onto the end of it. Not only should you not assume your research blog will cost you time, it's entirely possible it may actually *save* you time.

I began the chapter by observing that 'how do you find the time?' is one of the most common questions facing those academics who are active on Twitter. Implicit within this is usually an assumption about the value of different activities: how can you allow (trivial) social media to distract you from (important) scholarship? In response I've tried to show how many of the ways academics use social media either contribute to or are actually constitutive of scholarship. But it's also often the case that the time for social media doesn't detract from the time for scholarship because people do the former at times when they would rarely, if ever, do the latter. This was true of those people I quoted at the start of the chapter for whom social media are effectively a hobby they undertake at night or at weekends. We can see a similar tendency in the behaviour of those for whom social media are primarily something which they do when they travel.

Social media and mobile computing

Smart phones and tablets have transformed how people use the internet. Long gone are the days when this necessitated logging on to a computer, waiting for a modem to dial up and patiently browsing the web page-to-page. First wireless networks and laptops liberated us from our desks and then smart phones and tablets meant that the internet became something we carried around in our pockets, no longer a virtual space which we occasionally access but instead a continual feature of our environments. The omnipresence of smart phones and tablets can be overstated but the extent of their diffusion is nonetheless remarkable. Looking back to the recent past, it's interesting how anachronistic talk of 'cyberspace' and 'the information superhighway' now seems despite being less than a couple of decades old in many cases. We can see this amongst those social scientists who directly study digital change for whom what was once a matter of 'cyber' studies is increasingly expressed in terms of 'the digital' (Lupton 2014b).

Mobile computing has played a key role in the rise of social media. This may seem like an obvious observation to make but it's worth reflecting on how much the former has shaped the latter. Next time you're on public transport during commuting hours, it's worth having a look round to see how many people are glued to tablets or smart phones. Even if you suspect this might be a negative trend, perhaps longing for the days when people were glued to their newspapers instead, it's an important one to consider if you're engaging with social media as an academic. If you have access to the internet during a commute on public transport (a possibility obviously denied to drivers who wish to reliably reach their destination intact) it offers a great opportunity to let social media distract you from what's likely to be the most tedious part of your day. All the social media tools discussed in this book have mobile apps. In a few cases these aren't great but they're the most fully functional alternatives to logging in via a browser on your computer. In fact Twitter has spawned a whole ecosystem of apps, orientated towards different kinds of user, for example if you manage multiple accounts then TweetBot is the app for you.

In a way, it feels a little superfluous to include this in the book because it's likely that you're already using an app like this if you both have a smart phone and use Twitter. But my point is to stress how valuable this commuting time can be when trying to find the time for social media. For instance a bit of time on your smart phone when commuting can be sufficient for sustaining a presence on Twitter. It's also worth exploring some of the other apps that are available if those you've tried initially haven't quite worked for you. Given that Facebook has the most active users in the United States and United Kingdom of any app (outside games) for both iPhone and Android, with only marginally lower popularity in other markets (App Annie 2015), it's probably too obvious to be worth pointing out that the Facebook app is a useful way to engage online at points in the day when you don't mind being distracted. But have you thought about blogging on a mobile device? Blogging apps don't register amongst the most popular top apps for active users, though Pinterest and Instagram do, suggesting mobile blogging has not yet taken off to the extent that other social media tools have (App Annie 2015). It changes the experience by separating you from the keyboard which for many, including myself, long seemed intrinsically tied up with blogging as an activity. This isn't necessarily a negative feature though. My own experience has been that it leads me to write shorter and more concise posts, as well as making the inclusion of photos I've taken on my phone a seamless experience rather than the still surprisingly cumbersome operation of moving them from one device to another.

Could it all just be a waste of time … ?

While I genuinely believe that social media can help enhance scholarship, the thought has nonetheless occurred to me that advocates of academic social media such as myself are both directly and indirectly contributing to what the comedian Charlie Brooker (2013) describes as the 'sheer amount of jabber in the world', even if we might think that our particular style of jabber is well informed and culturally valuable. That's why being clear about *why* you're using social media is so important: it helps ensure that you aren't just wasting your time and it also helps me reassure myself that I haven't spent the last few years enthusiastically contributing to the collapse of human culture under the weight of our own verbiage.

Potential Pitfalls

Recognising that what academics do with social media might sometimes be 'jabber' doesn't mean we should forget some of the existing problems with scholarly publishing that often lead people to embrace social media in the first place. Under conditions where 'publish or perish' is taking on a new intensity for most, we can see the proliferation of academic books that are written to be counted rather than read or loved (Back 2008). The rapidly diminishing start-up costs associated with journals is contributing to a dizzying proliferation of new journals and a similar spiral of publications in spite of the lack of the shockingly low citation rates for the average paper in most disciplines. Increasingly these problems are being compounded by a new frontier of open access publishers concerned solely with revenue generation and exhibiting little to no commitment to academic standards. For instance Bohannon (2013) submitted 304 versions of a fabricated paper about a new wonder drug to open access journals. Over half accepted the paper in spite of the 'fatal flaws' the author had deliberately written into it before submitting under a pseudonym.

My point is not that 'traditional' scholarly publishing is awful and that we should embrace social media but rather that the entire landscape is changing. Instead of counterposing the 'new' and the 'old', regardless of which we evaluate positively and negatively, we should see how social media and scholarly publishing are key vectors in some profound changes in how academics communicate. We should be realistic about the strengths and weaknesses attached to each, as well as how they seem likely to change over time.

Any attempt to determine whether or not social media are a waste of your time will probably be helped by an accurate assessment of exactly how much time you are spending on social media. It might be that you already have an idea of how much time this is but there's a lot evidence that we are generally quite poor at making estimates about time. This is particularly pernicious when it comes to estimating how long work will take us. As the behavioural scientist Paul Dolan explains, 'our memories do not accurately recall the duration of post events, and so we will project these errors into the future' so that 'when it comes to longer tasks, we believe they will take less time than they actually do'. This manifests itself most emphatically in our tendency to believe we'll get things finished days before a deadline but it's more broadly true of how we evaluate the time we believe a task will take us (Dolan 2015: loc 2832–2851). If we underestimate how long work will take then it could be rather fatal to our productivity if we also underestimate how much of a distraction social media represent. That's why it might be worth using a tool such as Rescue Time to audit how much time you spend using various functions on your computer, even if it such an exercise might initially seem rather self-obsessed. Obviously, it's possible to record these data manually but the advantage of a digital tool is that it sits unobtrusively in the background over time, as opposed to working with a continual necessity to record when you switch tasks (itself rather distracting) or with the continual risk that you will get distracted in a way that doesn't show up in the data you're recording.

Talking of task-switching raises another important point. Many of us tend to believe that we're good at multi-tasking but an emerging consensus amongst behavioural scientists argues that this is founded upon a myth. In reality, what we experience as multi-tasking is a process of continually switching between tasks at a speed which might be imperceptible, but nonetheless constitutes a drain upon our energy. Once you begin scrutinising your own experience for evidence of this, it's easy to recognise a cognitive lag that results when you switch from one task to another and back again (for instance by going from writing a book about social media to checking your Twitter feed before return-ing to the book again) because of the necessity of reorienting yourself to the task at hand after you interrupted your immersion in it (Altmann and Trafton 2007, Ratwani and Trafton 2008). This might be insignificant in and of itself (such as forgetting the focus of the sentence you were in the middle of writing) but it can sometimes be more disruptive, such as when you struggle to regain your immersion in the theme of the chapter you were working on and wonder if you should go back to the much easier chapter on networking, or better yet give yourself a break and go talk to people on Twitter for a bit. Auditing the amount of time you spend on social media can be immensely helpful because, as Paul Dolan describes, '[w]hen you interrupt yourself to text, tweet, or e-mail you are using attentional energy to switch tasks' and when we do this frequently our 'attention reserves quickly become diminished, making it even harder for you to focus' (Dolan 2015: loc 2617).

The risk is that we blame social media for the habits they facilitate. Earlier in this chapter I argued that we shouldn't see the relationship between social media and scholarship as a zero-sum game in terms of our use of time. The former can often constitute the latter or at the very least contribute to it, as opposed to being something that inevitably takes us away from time we would be spending on serious scholarly work. Later in this chapter I introduce a variety of ways in which it is possible to reduce the amount of time it takes to maintain a social media profile. Nonetheless it's possible that our use of social media in itself doesn't take up a great deal of time but that it is embedded in our lives in a way which nonetheless undermines our productivity. For this purpose, the next section discusses ways to sustain your focus throughout the day and to cope with the many interruptions, digital or otherwise, unavoidably encountered in contemporary academic life.

Evidence from time-use surveys suggests that time pressure doesn't work in the way we tend to think it does. This can be seen in the fact that while the 'long-term growth in leisure for the working-age population is evident in nearly every country for which we have appropriate evidence' there is nonetheless a 'widespread perception that life has become more rushed' (Wajcman 2015: 64–66). The insightful analysis of Judy Wajcman (2015) suggests this is more a matter of increasing 'temporal density' than a reduction in the time available to us. The growing tendency to do more activities at once, these pervasive 'experiences of juggling and multitasking', leads us to feel harried and constantly under time pressure (Wajcman 2015: 104–105). The exact reasons for this have been the focus of an increasingly vast literature, for which Vostal (2014) provides a helpful overview and Rosa (2013) offers my personal favourite, but we could crudely gloss the implications of this for present purposes: our focus fragments as temporal density increases. As we saw earlier, we actually *can't* multitask no matter how convinced we are that we can (Levitin 2014, Wajcman 2015: 104).

The feeling of being continually pushed for time understandably leads us into temporal accounting: weighing up how much time we spend on X and Y and Z in order to allocate what we see as a fixed quantity of time to go round. There are obviously vast time pressures that characterise academic life, ones which are arguably increasing for reasons rooted in the university itself, which I'm not trying to minimise. But an important implication of findings in the sociology of time and behavioural science research into our experience of time is that the *quality* of a unit of time matters as well. This is why it's essential to consider ways in which you can help sustain your focus in an environment that is distracting – the technological reality that Wajcman (2015) describes as 'constant connectivity'.

Underlying all this though is the more profound question of what *is* distraction? What is it to *waste time*? As an ex-philosopher I perhaps find such ruminations more gripping than might be the case for many of the people reading this book, so I'll confine myself to the practical aspects of this when I discuss *prioritisation* at the end of the chapter. To talk of wasting time implies time not being spent in a way you value and this in turn raises the question of what it is you value. This question of what your goals are when engaging with social media has been a running theme through the book and at the end of this chapter I draw these considerations together to ask *what should you prioritise?* But first let's discuss the difficulty of sustaining your focus under conditions of constant connectivity.

Sustaining your focus throughout the day

In recent years we've seen the notion of 'internet addiction' enter the popular consciousness. As a self-description it's sometimes invoked facetiously, sometimes desperately and occasionally in a way which combines the two. It would be silly for me to try and take a stance on such a complex subject here. So I'll restrict myself to suggesting that we should be cautious about this term given a wider context in which the medicalisation of everyday life is rapidly intensifying (Rose 2007). Having got that out of the way, let's turn to an experience which will be familiar to most: finding yourself lost in a repetitive cycle of clicking from web page to web page, checking your e-mail every couple of minutes or passively skimming through a Twitter feed while paying little attention to what you're reading in it. These are those times when what social media companies describe as 'thumb stopping' (ceasing your endless scroll in order to focus on something you've chosen as worthy of attention) becomes unlikely and you just keep on skimming in an increasingly detached way.

The popular comedy Portlandia describes this as a 'technology loop' – being caught in a frenzied cycle of overstimulation, unable to drag oneself away from the internet and the torrent of interesting things to do, read and watch which it's impossible for any one person to keep up with. The political theorist Jodi Dean (2013) describes this as getting 'stuck doing the same thing over and over again because this doing produces enjoyment. Post. Post. Post. Click. Click. Click'. It's not necessary to accept the psychoanalytic ideas underpinning Dean's account to recognise the experience she describes. I found myself doing it on Facebook a few minutes ago before a track change on the music I have playing in the background jolted me back into attention and reminded me that I'm supposed to be writing a chapter about sustaining your focus in an age of social media. The more general problem is a distractedness produced by digital technology in an age of informational abundance. The issue here is not only the multiplication of distractions, it's also the sheer scale of what we're missing out on and our growing awareness of all the other things we could and perhaps should be doing (Carrigan 2016).

The most obvious way to prevent this is simply to recognise that you're doing it. Putting a name to the experience makes it easy to identify what you're doing and so help you drag yourself out of an impending technology loop. If you find yourself drifting into such a state repeatedly, even as you pull yourself out each time, perhaps it's worth taking a break or at least shifting to a different activity? The website www.donothingfor2minutes.com offers a helpful antidote to the frenzied hyperactivity which characterises the technology loop. There are also more preventative means which can be taken: using tools like Anti-Social and Freedom or switching off the WiFi if you're having this problem at home (it's presumably not feasible to do this at a coffee shop or in an office but I must admit I've never tried). More indirectly, it can help to minimise distractions by turning off pop-up notifications (pop up e-mail alerts are effectively designed to fracture your focus) and maybe isolating your social media use to another device such as writing on your laptop and only using Twitter on your smart phone. Pang (2013) offers a really thorough discussion of the range of tools available for these purposes, as well as a philosophy of 'contemplative computing' in terms of which we can understand their utility.

All these suggestions are basically preventative though. This problem can be tackled in a different way by thinking about how you approach your work. Do you have a strategy for managing your time and attention? One such strategy can be seen in the Pomodoro Technique, a popular working method which is predicated on the understanding that 'taking short, scheduled breaks while working eliminates the "running on fumes" feeling you get when you've pushed yourself too hard' (Cirillo 2015). It involves working on a larger task through small chunks of intense work punctuated by repeated breaks: you work intensively for a set period of time, take a break and then do another chunk of work. Any extraneous tasks, whether connected to your present focus or something else entirely, should be recorded on a piece of paper before you immediately return to the task at hand. Its developer Francesco Cirillo suggests 25 minute-long sessions of work followed by 5 minute-long breaks.

However these are optional really, as is the tomato-shaped timer which he sells via his website (though I must admit writing this has left me tempted to finally buy one of these). There are many apps which can do the same thing and which have the advantage of recording your results in a way that can be useful for measuring your own productivity as well as filling out timesheets if necessary. The idea of this is to minimise task interruption and to ensure frequent breaks to prevent precisely the depletion of attentional energy which Paul Dolan (2015) described earlier. This sounds deceptively easy but it's remarkable how easy it is to get distracted in the space of 25 minutes.

Committing to working for a specific period of time helps heighten your aware-ness of all the distraction events which intervene and can so chronically drag your attention away from the task at hand: committing to not checking your e-mails for 25 minutes helps you notice those often imperceptible whims arising – 'I'll just check my e-mails quickly and see if I've got a response from earlier'. This point holds for other forms of distraction as well but it would be a mistake to overlook e-mail given the concerns of this chapter. We don't tend to think of e-mail as social media. It's certainly not an example of what used to be called web 2.0 before that term largely gave way to that of social media. But in the broader sense addressed in this book of *media* that are *social* then e-mail surely falls into this category. It's also a pervasive source of stress and concern across the academy, as Ros Gill (2009) points out in her insightful account of the 'hidden injuries' of the contem-porary academy:

> 'Addiction' metaphors suffuse academics' talk of their relationship to e-mail, even as they report such high levels of anxiety that they feel they have to check e-mail first thing in the morning and last thing at night, and in which time away (on sick leave, on holiday) generates fears of what might be lurking in the inbox when they return. Again, inventive 'strategies' abound for keeping such anxiety at bay e.g. put-ting on your 'out of office' reply when you are actually in the office.

However, it is not only the always-on culture of e-mails that has led to the marked intensification of our workloads and the almost constant experience of high levels of stress. In fact it is paradoxical, given how much time we spend on it, that e-mail is mostly experienced as what stops us getting on with our 'real' work (Gill 2009).

I've tried to clear my inbox on a daily basis simply because it largely removes the stress from the process. I recognise this won't be possible for everyone but I'd also maintain it's nowhere near as unfeasible for many people as might first seem to be the case. The time spent avoiding e-mail and being stressed out by e-mail is time that could be spent getting it out of the way in one go. I don't recall it ever taking me more than an hour to entirely clear my inbox, even if this can be quite dispiriting when it immediately leads to a rapid expansion of my to-do list. It works most effectively when I do e-mail first thing in the morning. Replies are the exception rather than the rule before 8am, whereas trying to clear my inbox in the middle of day can produce despair as replies and new e-mails hurtle into my inbox faster than I can clear the backlog. The description of the 'stupid e-mail ritual' offered by the protagonist of Cory Doctorow's novel *Homeland* is quite apt: 'Download download download. Spam spam spam. Delete delete delete' (Doctorow 2013: 17). I find it hard to read about things like e-mail apnoea – breath-holding or shallow breathing associated with checking e-mail – without wondering about the psychosocial costs of our communications system (Stone 2012). The stress caused by e-mail is so widely recognised as to make discussion of it a cliché. But it's something which crops up time and time again, at least if you make a habit of reading academics blogging about academic life.

One final useful suggestion comes from the social media scholar danah boyd (2011) who describes how she takes an occasional e-mail sabbatical in order to cope with its intrinsically Sisyphean nature. While many people can step back from social media (though not everyone! – see the Potential Pitfalls box above), it's far more difficult to do this with e-mail. This is getting worse because, as Pat Thompson (2014) suggests, the e-mail auto-responder is becoming pretty useless in the contemporary academy. Being 'out of office' while retaining internet access means continuing to respond to e-mails or watching them build up in a way which quickly undermines any of the potential benefits of 'disconnection'. There are other strategies it's possible to adopt: I recently bought a pay-as-you-go phone for when I *really* want to get away from the internet, and have sometimes deleted the mail settings on my iPhone when I want to disconnect but nonetheless retain the capacity to consult Google Maps when, as so often happens, I get lost on my way somewhere. However, in these cases it just displaces the moment when you reconnect and confront the masses of mail that have piled up while you were elsewhere enjoying the benefits of 'disconnection':

> We all need time off. Like serious time off. Time when we feel like we're able to truly rejuvenate without the little panicked voice chirping away in the back of our heads fretting about the backlog of things we are going to have to deal with when we come in. Information overload can be a very taxing issue for many people. Luckily, many services allow us to go zen without making us feel guilty. Most of us can scan Twitter without obsessing over all that we missed. And there's simply too many blogs to think about all that we haven't read. Unfortunately, email is the one app that we feel guilty about turning off. Why? Cuz the interface is designed to put you on a hamster wheel, rarely ever succeeding at letting you reach empty. You feel accomplished when you get to inbox zero. And then you sleep and it's all back to haunt you. For this reason, I recommend taking an email sabbatical. (boyd 2011)

How much time do you really spend on social media?

The interruptions encouraged by Twitter can be almost imperceptible. To give a personal example: towards the end of writing this book I have, as a matter of necessity, set myself a daily target of timed writing. This is something that's proved very effective for me in the past and it's largely working as I write this in June 2015 towards the end of what has been a much longer project than I anticipated. It feels good when I meet the goal and 'goal streaks', as tracked in a wonderful iOS app of the same name, inevitably translate into rapid progress towards the finish line. Nonetheless, I suddenly find myself flicking to Twitter without having made any deliberate decision to do so. The habit this represents is a dangerous one. It is nonetheless a habit – an acquired tendency that can be counteracted. The technologist Alex Soojung-Kim Pang (2013) insightfully questions whether such a tendency can be accurately blamed on the technology itself and whether this notion is something which helps abdicate the responsibility of sustaining our own focus. In other words, things like Twitter might give us an excuse to get distracted but this doesn't change the fact that we are letting ourselves get distracted.

Nonetheless, it's necessary to be realistic about how much time you spend on social media. I would be the last person to deny these can be a dangerous distraction. If it appears as if I have been suggesting that at times, it's not my intention. I've only sought to show how the situation is not as unambiguous as some amongst the sceptics might tend to suggest. Fortunately, there are many tools which can be drawn upon if social media are becoming a problem. Freedom and Anti-Social are two I suggested earlier. But it's a category of application which, as Pang (2013) discusses, continues to expand. However one problem I've noticed is that these don't really address the compulsivity, they only block it. I've sometimes found myself seizing upon Twitter at the moment my social media block expires, launching myself into a flurry of tweets and completely losing any focus upon what I'd previously been doing. This isn't necessarily a problem. I usually set the timer for at least two hours and so I've usually got a lot done in the meantime. But it can nonetheless be ironically disruptive at times, as I go from being engrossed in writing to being engrossed in Twitter purely because an arbitrary unit of time has expired.

How to reduce the time you spend on social media

There is nonetheless a straightforward way to reduce the amount of time you spend on social media: *scheduling* and *automation*. This might be a matter of scheduling posts in WordPress – writing them at a time of your convenience rather than one at a time as the mood strikes you. There are also scheduling tools for Twitter, such as Buffer and HootSuite, which allow you to collate tweets and publish them on multiple accounts to a defined schedule. This makes it possible to keep a Twitter feed regularly updated without necessitating a continued presence online. You might for instance spend an hour or two a week scheduling a feed, as opposed to this being a regular and potentially interruptive part of most working days.

An obvious factor which might lead you to want to reduce the time you spend on social media is the demand of managing multiple social media profiles. Having multiple profiles can be effective. Using them for different purposes will lead the time demands to multiply, but if they're connected together it can be an incisive way to access multiple and different audiences. For instance, Stuart Elden's strategy for this is to connect Progressive Geographies to a Facebook page and Twitter feed, using WordPress to post updates to each of these. This is using the functionality built into WordPress itself, with cross-platform compatibility an increasingly likely option to be found across social media. However a new breed of online services, such as If This Then That (IFTTT), allow you to establish functionality of this sort across a dizzying array of online services. The way this works in practice can be slightly difficult to grasp until you try it yourself but the underlying idea is quite simple. For instance IFTTT works by linking up services for which you are registered through commands that operate under particular conditions: if THIS happens then do THAT. So the link between my WordPress blog and Twitter feed could be reproduced using IFTTT in the following form: if new post on markcarrigan.net then tweet this post at @mark_carrigan. This is a very simple example which is unnecessary because WordPress allows the same thing to be done more easily. But there are many other uses towards which a service like IFTTT can be put. For instance, it's possible to link Google Documents, Evernote and Dropbox (amongst many others) to IFTTT and create an automatic spreadsheet archive of your blog posts or fill an Evernote notebook with a record of the tweets you favourite on Twitter. If you use the service Pocket, it's possible to automatically save PDF versions of articles you favourite to Dropbox. These are just a few suggestions. Mostly I just use these to link the different blogs I run with different Twitter feeds. As well as automatically tweeting new blog posts on my personal Twitter feed, IFTTT then uses Buffer to schedule a tweet sharing this new post at a later date on the sociology feed I maintain @soc_imagination. New posts at the associated blog sociologicalimagination.org are automatically tweeted via WordPress, but also, via IFTTT, are scheduled to be released again at a later date on the @soc_imagination feed. There are many other more esoteric uses and browsing the 'recipes' which IFTTT indexes gives a sense of the many varied uses to which the service has been put. The value of the service is obviously dependent upon the potential uses to which it can be put. This will vary a lot but hopefully I've managed to convey how this could be useful, even if you're still slightly unclear as to precisely what use you might make of it. It's certainly worth experimenting with if you find yourself maintaining profiles across a range of sites. While the academically-orientated services like ResearchGate and Academia. edu are not yet represented on IFTTT, it is surely only a matter of time before they are included. This would make it possible to automatically tweet new pre-publications documents you upload or automatically download PDF copies of new articles shared relating to a topic you work on. The long-term relevance of services like IFTTT is particularly interesting if we really do enter the much hyped 'Internet of Things'. They could play a crucial role in allowing us to establish the relationship between the many smart devices which might increasingly feature in our lives, as well as define the functionality that might allow them to act as more than the sum of their parts.

However, that said, there's a real risk that maintaining too many profiles simply leads to a lot of wasted time and little identifiable reward. While an enthusiasm for engaging online can sometimes give rise to an inclination to engage wherever and whenever there's an opportunity to do so, it's worth considering whether maintaining a presence across multiple platforms serves any real purpose. Perhaps ask yourself each time you consider setting up a new account 'what's the point of this?' In some cases it might simply be to try something out so as to clarify whether there is a point to it. This is fine but it should be accompanied by a willingness to recognise that something might not be for you and to delete an account once you've experimented with a particular service. The fear of missing out thrives online and this can sometimes lead people to assume there is a risk entailed in not having a presence on any service where their peers are active. However the real risk is undermining your online presence by spreading it too thinly. It's also easy to over-estimate how many people are actually using a particular service. LinkedIn and ResearchGate in particular seem to thrive on creating the impression that everyone you know is using them, whereas in actual fact these platforms are simply adept at ensuring invitations are sent to people in your address book. As a general rule, it's unlikely that a service will be useful to you unless there is a potential audience there which can be gathered with the time and energy available to you. The more profiles you attempt to cultivate, the less of this time and energy you'll have available to expend on any one online presence.

In other words, it's more useful to engage a lot on the right service than it is to engage a little bit across the full range of services. The clearer you are about your reasons for using it, the more likely it is that you'll get what you want out of your engagement, assuming that your assessment of that service is accurate.

Further reading

- *Pressed for Time: The Acceleration of Life in Digital Capitalism* by Judy Wajcman (2015) is an insightful exploration of how we experience and manage time under conditions of 'constant connectivity'.
- *The Organized Mind: Thinking Straight in the Age of Information Overload* by Daniel Levitin (2014) offers a thorough and practical account of time management informed by the latest scientific findings.
- *The Activity Illusion* by Ian Price (2010) is a provocative critique of familiar habits which lead us to inadvertently intensify our workloads and undermine our capacity to keep work from intruding on life.

The future landscape of academic social media

9

Chapter themes

This chapter will:

- Explore the concept of the 'marketplace of ideas' and its application to higher education
- Examine the politics of openness and what this means for digital scholarship
- Discuss how the popularity principle can shape social media discourse
- Look at the potential for crowdfunding in academic research
- Analyse institutional attitudes to social media and their implications for academic freedom

As I stated at the start of this book, writing about social media inevitably leaves you plagued by an awareness of quite how fast things are moving. At certain points I wanted nothing more than to be able to press a 'pause' button on the development of academic social media, fantasising about how much easier this book would be to write if its subject matter wasn't changing at such a rapid pace. I began it with some data from the Internet Live Stats project to illustrate the speed of change but the numbers don't really capture the extent of it. The entire landscape of social media has continued to alter over the period in which I've been writing. Pinterest, Snapchat, WhatsApp and Instagram were relative newcomers when I began planning this project. With the exception of the latter all were founded since 2010. Yet they're now titans of the technology industry, with WhatsApp and Instagram being purchased for many billions of dollars and all being the subject of vast market capitalisations in spite of their relative insubstantiality as organisations and lack of any obvious capacity to make a profit.

In large part this reflects the sheer size of the user base they've accumulated. Over 105,000,000 photos were uploaded on Instagram on the day I wrote this sentence (Internet Live Stats 2015). WhatsApp and Instagram, both now owned by Facebook, have more than 900 million active users between them (Dolle 2015). Their growth is particularly pronounced within certain demographics: over half of internet-using young American adults use Instagram and half of these use the site on a daily basis; 42% of online American woman use Pinterest, compared to 13% of online American men (Duggan et al. 2014). The 'winner-takes-most' character of competitive fields within the technology sector leads investors to tolerate a lack of profit in the hope that they've backed the company that will ultimately come out on top (Stone 2013). More recently, they've been joined by the companies of the so-called sharing economy, most prominently Airbnb and Uber, who have given rise to spiralling controversy around the world and united otherwise polarised boosters and critics in a shared perception of their sheer significance.

Higher education itself has continued to undergo profound changes during this time, though not to the extent or in the manner that advocates of 'disruption' had claimed or pressed for (Morozov 2013). The newer platforms in social media have begun to be taken up: platforms like Snapchat and Pinterest have been used creatively by universities, even as others have attributed a deadening triviality to them. Measurement and data become ever more integral to higher education, posing questions about the politics of information which as yet go unanswered (Johnson 2015). The convergence of students and academics on the same social media platforms raises issues which are only now beginning to emerge, as well as all manner of practical and theoretical questions posed by a changing relationship between academics and the media.

In this chapter I offer an overview of these trends, beginning with two of the most significant for higher education: the new 'marketplace of ideas' being brought about by social media and the 'politics of openness' which is emerging within it. In each case, my focus is upon the practical implications of these trends for different aspects of the working lives of academics – their public face and scholarly writing respectively. I then discuss what I see as two potential outcomes of these long-term trends, one pessimistic and one optimistic. These are intended as illustrative of potential outcomes rather than definitive predictions. But I'm hoping to give a sense of where this *might* all be leading, as well as how it will be bound up in potential changes within academic life. These are themes that I would wish to explore in much greater length on my blog over the coming years.

Academic life and the marketplace of ideas

The 'marketplace of ideas' is a term I found irritatingly trite when I first heard it. I've since come to think it captures something important, namely the environment in which ideas of whatever sort are communicated and received. It is incidental as to whether your share my initial irritation or begrudging acceptance of this terminology, what's more pressing here is the question of how this environment is changing and how academics could, or should, respond to the new pressures which these changes bring. Academics are far from being the only professionals whose working lives are subject to new pressures. In early 2014 an internal report on digital strategy produced by the *New York Times* was leaked and became the subject of widespread analysis online. It began with the claim that while the venerable newspaper was 'winning at journalism' it was failing at 'the art and science of getting our journalism to our readers' (Benton 2014). What concerned the authors of the report was not the familiar fear about the long-term consequences of digital technology to journalism itself, but rather their capacity to ensure their quality journalism thrives in a marketplace of ideas saturated by digitally native publishers.

This is a much bigger topic than social media alone. But it is nonetheless an important element in it, with implications for how academics utilise social media and the environment they encounter when they do. The key question here is how what van Dijck (2012) calls the *popularity principle* might influence the behaviour and practices of academics as they embrace social media. As she defines it, the popularity principle holds that 'the more contacts you have and make, the more valuable you become, because more people think you are popular and hence want to connect with you' (van Dijck 2012: loc 310). This concept is coded into the architecture of social media platforms in a way that is impossible to avoid, reflecting the broader attention economy in which 'attention means eyeballs or (unconscious) exposure, and this value is an important part of Internet advertising in the form of banners, pop-ups, and paid ad space on websites'. There's money to be made from popularity, or rather turning popularity (often, as van Dijck points out, equated with values of truth, trust and objectivity) into a quantifiable commodity (van Dijck 2012: loc 1281). It might feel like you would be immune to this, but if you encounter a popular Twitter feed, previously unknown to you, how does the high follower count influence your perceptions of it in the absence of any other information? At the very least, it's likely to factor into a sense that there's something authoritative or valuable about the account. After all, surely those followers must have arrived for a reason? The popularity principle is insidious and it is built into social media platforms themselves. Value comes to be quantified in terms of the accumulation of followers, likes, retweets and reblogs. Yet as van Dijck (2012: loc 1360) notes, the 'concept of "liking" pushes popular ideas or things with a high degree of emotional value … "difficult but important" is not a judgement prompted by social media sites'. In using social media, academics are entering into an attention economy heavily structured around the popularity principle.

What are the implications of this attention economy for scholarship? The risk is that, as the political blogger Ezra Klein (2015) puts it, '[t]he incentives of the social web make it a threat to the conversational web'. The increasing reliance upon social media to drive traffic to blogs encourages certain ways of writing posts. The most obvious manifestation of this can be seen in the rise of viral content websites but there are more subtle manifestations as well. Klein's point is that 'the social web' encourages an atomisation of content because individual posts circulate on their own rather than relying on readers' repeated visits to the author's blog. He presents this as a negative thing because it mitigates against the intensely conversational style that used to characterise the political blogosphere in which arguments were developed through mutual engagement across whole sequences of blog posts (Rosenberg 2010). While he may be undervaluing the conversations which emerge on social media in response to blog posts, he nonetheless makes an important point about the implications of content needing to 'travel' in a way that was not formerly the case. Obviously these pressures aren't inexorable but their influence can be surprisingly effective, as the obvious desire of bloggers to gain an audience for their posts gradually chips away at a principled opposition to changing how they write in order to better solicit a readership. The growing reliance upon social media to drive traffic to blogs, something which is compounded by Facebook's desire to be 'a gateway to social content, a toll road to a data infrastructure that facilitates all forms of online commercialized sociality', only adds to the pressures inherent in the popularity principle around which social media platforms are structured (van Dijck 2012: loc 1391).

The centrality of the popularity principle may be most pronounced in the case of Facebook but it's far from being unique to it. One of Amazon's most ground-breaking innovations was the extension of their initial Hot 100 bestseller list to encompass everything on the site, drawing authors into a neurotic fixation with where they ranked on this all-encompassing list (Stone 2013: 75). The choices YouTube users make are heavily guided by selection mechanisms, including search engines and ranking algorithms, which inevitably favour some producers over others. Selection of the 'most popular' videos is the most pronounced manifestation of this but the guiding of user choices is built into the interface of the platform itself (van Dijck 2012: loc 2328). In part this can be fairly attributed to the practical challenge of dealing with the sheer scale of the content uploaded to YouTube. Without filtering it would be difficult to find relevant content in the 3000 hours of video that have been uploaded in the ten minutes or so I've been writing this paragraph, let alone the entire content of the site's archive (YouTube 2015). But contrary to the rhetorical focus on the blurring of boundaries between viewers and producers, evidence suggests that the site's architecture is designed to favour their official partners, allowing some professionalised amateurs to make a living out of the system and entrenching a sense of possibility that one will be 'discovered' through YouTube (van Dijck 2012: loc 2396–2610). The most obvious example however is the ranking facilitated by Google, a service which has sought to identify the most popular content from the outset. As Vaidhyanathan (2012) asks, 'Does anything (or anyone) matter if it (or she) does not show up on the first page of a Google search?'. The simplicity of the interface and the objectivity of its ordering belie the biases ('valuing popularity over accuracy, established sites over new, and rough rankings over more fluid or multidimensional models of presentation') that are built into it (Vaidhyanathan 2012: 7).

However, perhaps the most pertinent examples for academics using social media can be seen with Twitter. As van Dijck (2012: loc 1569) puts it, '[t]he sheer number of followers has become a barometer for measuring popularity and influence, ascribing more power to few users in the twitterverse'. The potential implications of this can be seen by examining what might initially seem to be an extremely obscure feature of the culture emerging around academics using social media. One of the most striking developments in the last year has been the emergence of natively academic viral marketing accounts. I discussed two of these, Nein Quarterly and Shit Academics Say, in terms of their distinctive approach to communicating visually and what can be learnt from it. The former is inarguably aphoristic in a manner that has a clear philosophical pedigree, utilising social media as part of '[a]n aesthetic and intellectual experiment only slightly less pretentious than it sounds'. In contrast, the latter relies upon viral content of a form likely to be familiar from non-academic contexts, though the selection and execution of it is undoubtedly hugely effective. Yet a recent account with a comparable approach, Grad School Elitist, found itself embroiled in controversy at the point I was completing this book. Accused of plagiarising the content on the account, accusations backed up with substantial evidence, the person controlling the account began to block anyone who questioned their authorship of the material they posted (including myself). My point here is not to intervene in this debate, which is likely to be tedious to the overwhelming majority of people who are less immersed in social media than I am, but simply to highlight this trajectory and what it might suggest about the tensions between scholarship and the logic of popularity built into social media platforms.

Each successive academic viral marketing account seems to have less intellectual value than the last, relying mechanically upon content likely to have the most impact through retweets and favourites, thus contributing to the progressive growth of its follower counts. Virality can soon become an end in itself. The problem arises because, as van Dijck (2012: loc 1569) notes, users 'quickly learned how to play the system and accumulate a lot of clout on Twitter'. In some cases, discussed further in the next section, this might involve straightforwardly copying and pasting content that can be seen to be popular – a judgement that's easy to make because each tweet has its metrics incorporated into its own presentation. But the more subtle aspect of this concerns the manner in which popularity accumulates in a winner-takes-all-manner: 'the more people follow someone, the trendier he or she becomes; the more people retweet a quote, the more impact it has in the twitterverse' (van Dijck 2012: loc 3227). It's in the interests of social media platforms to ensure the prominence of those users with a proven capacity to generate engagement on their site. After all, this amounts to more traffic for advertising, more buzz to draw users into the site, and higher statistics with which to appeal to the markets for more capital. These incentives, and the ease with which they can be accommodated within algorithms which serve other more immediately practical purposes, leave some users objectively positioned as more valuable than others within the platform (van Dijck 2012: loc 2353).

This doesn't mean that all roads inevitably lead to BuzzFeed. It also doesn't mean that academics using social media will inevitably entail the deterioration of scholarly standards, as a neurotic preoccupation with the accumulation of influence (as measured in follower counts and retweets) increasingly encourages simple communication likely to prove popular at the expense of complex ideas which may not thrive because of their difficulty and ambiguity. Using social media doesn't mean academics will inevitably come to talk in TED soundbites and forego things of intellectual worth. But the risk of a drift in this direction is there and that's why it's important to be aware of this at the outset, not least of all in order to reflect on your motivations if you find yourself engaging online with some regularity. It also helps us to be critical of the rhetoric of democratisation, such that it is assumed social media will 'disrupt' the hierarchies of academia. It won't. It might however make them more complex, as influence and esteem accumulate through a more diverse set of mechanisms than was formerly the case. But, as I discuss later in this chapter, it's easy to see how academics might get drawn into the logic of self-evaluation through metrics: if your h-index can be understood as tracking success then is it really a stretch to imagine the same being true of your quantity of Twitter followers? More worryingly, it's easy to imagine managers embracing such measures as an attempt to evaluate a capacity for impact and engagement.

Crowdfunding and social media metrics

The fear here is that the figurative marketplace of ideas is becoming too much of an actual market. In the next section I offer a more positive framing of this trend, discussing ideas concerning the 'publish then filter' principle that many have argued could revolutionise scholarly communication, although I also think aspects of this are extremely worrying. Morozov (2013) sees evidence of this trend in the popularity of sites like Google Scholar and Mendeley, worrying that they will further entrench an existing dependence upon 'the ability to get published and quoted by others' as the driver of career success by offering an ever-expanding array of metrics in terms of which academics will be expected to perform. Metrics are used in different ways across higher education systems internationally and this vast topic could easily constitute a book in its own right (Jump 2015). But if academic use of social media continues to expand, it seems inevitable that what Lupton (2014c) calls the 'Academic Quantified Self' will be shaped by this trend, as all manner of new metrics come to supplement those already used within higher education (Burrows 2012). The optimism of people like Clay Shirky (2008) needs to be countered with a reassertion of the distinction between systems of measurement and the value of what they measure, as well as recognition of how biases are woven into the very fabric of the social media platforms that might be drawn upon to provide new metrics. We need to avoid a 'wisdom of crowds' rhetoric in which popularity on social media comes to function as a cypher of value (Surowiecki 2005). I find it easy to see how things like *crowdfunding* and *crowdsourcing* could begin to thrive in higher education if this problematic rhetoric becomes embedded. The notion that significant funds can be raised by ordinary people coming together in large numbers, each making a small pledge which nonetheless adds up to a significant total, coheres powerfully with the broader cultural moment (Couldry 2014). Examples of crowdfunding for academic research are beginning to emerge, often accomplished by a breathless invocation of such mechanisms as holding the potential to radically change research culture (da Silva 2015). Through cutting out self-interested intermediaries, it *appears* to hold the promise of liberating creative activity from the narrow concerns of gatekeepers and opening up entirely new funding streams.

The reality is of course more complex, not least of all because of the inherent difficulty of running a successful crowdfunding campaign, something which is unlikely to succeed without a vast existing network to draw upon. Nonetheless, it's inevitable that crowdfunding would attract academic attention under circumstances where the funding environment is inhospitable while the expectations of fundraising placed upon academics are continually being ratcheted up in a way that Pop (2015) has argued is leading to a tragedy of the commons: 'Rational individuals (or individuals responding to their employers' rational demands) will write more grant applications, since doing so still probably increases one's chances of being funded. And if everyone else is working harder and harder to secure grant funding, maintaining constant effort will likely result in a decreasing payoff'. Can anyone blame academics who have explored crowdfunding under such circumstances? While crowdfunding for academic research might initially seem exciting, particularly for those who feel they spend ever greater proportions of their time negotiating the imperatives of established funding bodies, it's unlikely that the inevitable hype coming to surround it will prove justified.

The logistical challenges of running a successful crowdfunding campaign privilege those who already have well-developed networks and institutional support. Such people are already best placed to capture funding under existing conditions, suggesting that crowdfunding for the social sciences might open up an entirely new stream of funding only for it to be immediately captured by those least in need of more resources to fund their research. This could even prove enticing for institutions as a carefully planned Twitter campaign from an institutional feed coupled with a relatively small amount of time commitment from communications staff could represent a potentially fruitful means to win new funding. The nature of running such a crowdfunding campaign – relying on social media to recurrently share messages about what the planned project is and why it's important – obviously leaves this within the terrain of communications and marketing in a way that isn't the case with an application to a traditional funding body.

This isn't necessarily a bad thing, as crowdfunding campaigns like this could serve a valuable public engagement function, perhaps even regardless of their success or lack thereof. Could this help improve public understanding of the social sciences? If campaigns were well thought-out and carefully executed then it seems likely to me that it could. But the risk is that this subjugates research funding to the logic of a marketplace dominated by distraction and fragmented attention spans (Carr 2011, Carrigan 2016). What appears to be democratic could more accurately be said to be demotic, bringing people into the process but in a way that treats them as individual consumers rather than as participants in a citizen social science (Turner 2010). It might also encourage a further retrenchment of funding that could intensify these negative trends. Why fund social scientific research through government if individual consumers are already doing it on a large scale? You don't have to agree with this argument to see how it might take hold in a wider context of austerity politics and the unravelling of the public university (Holmwood 2011b, McGettigan 2013). There's a risk of being too negative here. Crowdfunding could provide a lifeline for interesting small-scale projects in an era where 'big science' is coming to dominate, even within the social sciences, while research deemed not to be 'useful' is under political attack, most emphatically in the United States (Todd 2014). We need to be open to the possibility that addressing the wider world as consumer-funders isn't something that can be relied upon, particularly when we're talking about projects that are niche and counterintuitive, going against common sense in the way so much good social science inevitably does. As Morozov (2013: 24–29) convincingly argues, '[s]ome content is simply unlikely to get crowdfunded'.

The future of publishing and the politics of openness

Chapter 2 discussed how social media can be used to publicise your existing publications. My concern throughout this book has been to avoid a simplistic opposition between social media and existing forms of scholarly communication. This is a matter of *both/and* rather than *either/or* (Carrigan 2013b, Daniels 2013*)*. Nonetheless, it's undeniable that social media in particular, as well as digital technology more generally, can bring about changes in what it is for scholars to communicate over-and-above their additional use of social media tools. One of the most striking differences concerns the *openness* of scholarly communication using social media. Many of the scholars I've drawn upon in this book are critical of the concept of 'openness', suggesting it's an ideological term which conceals more than it conveys. Nonetheless, what we might call an *ethos* of openness seems to thrive in the social media sphere. My favourite articulation of this is offered by Cory Doctorow:

> When my daughter was born, I became keenly aware of how much stock we mammals put into the copies we make of ourselves (yes, a child isn't a "copy" exactly, but go with it for a moment). Mammalian reproduction is a major event, especially for us primates, and we want to be sure that every "copy" we make grows up healthy, strong and successful.
>
> But there are other life forms for whom copying is a lot more casual. Dandelions produce two thousand seeds every spring, and when a good, stiff breeze comes around, those seeds are blown into the air, going every which way. The dandelion's strategy is to maximise the number of blind chances it has for continuing its genetic line — not to carefully plot every germination. It works: every summer, every crack in every sidewalk has a dandelion growing out of it. (Doctorow 2014: 143)

The analogy breaks down slightly when we consider it in terms of higher education but I think there's still an interesting point here. The difference between social scientists and the creative producers to whom Doctorow was speaking is that the former are not reliant upon payment for their creative products while the latter obviously are. But while the hoped for pay-off might be different (though this difference can be overstated in a world where creative producers struggle to make a living and many academics are precariously employed) the challenge each group encounters is remarkably similar: how to thrive professionally under networked conditions of cultural abundance.

If the potential royalties to be made from scholarly publishing, discounting textbooks and trade books remain insufficient to purchase a single copy of your book, then there certainly is not a financial incentive mitigating against more open forms of publication. So what is it that's holding people back? In part it might be a matter of prestige, but there's nothing intrinsically suspect about a book that is freely available. Even so, it perhaps remains the case that a 'book' consisting of little more than a loosely formatted word document exported as a PDF lacks something crucial which, in spite of its superficiality, allows the item to be widely recognised as a book in the traditional sense. Initiatives by established publishers certainly have a role to play here. Scholarly publishers still serve a prestige function for authorship, even if it's in decline. As Graham (2013) convincingly argues, the institutional character of higher education mitigates against some of the more 'disruptive' possibilities opened up by new technology. New publishing initiatives, with PressBooks being a particularly exciting example, have great promise but it's unlikely these will disrupt traditional forms of publication.

There are also cultural obstacles to embracing the ethos of openness. As we saw in the previous section copyright claims are on the rise on Twitter, as the service tries to respond to the growing problem of people nakedly passing off others' work as their own in order to maximise their popularity on the service (Mohan 2015). One particularly high profile case emerged in the final stages of writing this book: the comedian Conan O'Brien was sued for allegedly stealing jokes from Twitter (Gardner 2015). But this is only the tip of the iceberg, with its visibility ensured by the prominence of the accused. These issues are only going to get more pronounced with time and there's an obvious risk that claims are made on a malicious basis, raising the question of how social media platforms like Twitter will respond. Will they equip this function with sufficient resources to ensure robust governance? Or will they simply err on the side of caution, taking things down upon request to demonstrate that they will react effectively to infringement? Unfortunately all the evidence we have from similar quandaries suggests a tendency towards the latter (Doctorow 2014). This seems even more likely when we consider the scale of the problem we're discussing here, as well as the resources required to ensure a proper investigation in each case. There's an understandable fear that sharing work freely online opens it up to plagiarism and misunderstanding. As I've tried to argue elsewhere in the book, although these fears might be exaggerated at points they are hardly unfounded. The possibility that mass takedowns of online content become common, on often contentious grounds, as social media platforms seek to minimise discord by reacting emphatically in the face of allegations of plagiarism, will only compound the aforementioned unease.

These understandable obstacles seem likely to impede a move from a *filter-then-publish* to a *publish-then-filter* model of scholarly communication. As Gauntlett (2012) observes, the logistical necessity of gatekeeping has largely dissolved because the financial constraints upon publishing have been radically diminished by digital technology. If we publish then filter, we rely upon responses to the article in question rather than gatekeepers to ensure its quality. As he observes, it's both immediate and cuts out the peer review process in which 'anonymous random people force you to make pointless changes to your carefully-crafted text'. I don't think a naive faith in the peer review system is necessary in order to find this slightly uncomfortable – all the more so because of the *wisdom of crowds* logic underpinning it, in which we can rely on the aggregation of judgements (often as mediated through digital technology) in order to establish the quality of work. As he acknowledges, '[t]he academic community – or rather, different academic communities – would need to develop tools that would support the process of reviewing and rating research and research articles'. This wouldn't necessarily entail that we dispense with the *principle* of peer review, only that exactly how peers evaluate the scholarly virtues of a piece of work might change radically.

The need for caution in these activities seems obvious to me, lest we too hastily abandon something that has slowly evolved, admittedly to be much less than perfect, but perhaps can't be reclaimed easily if it seems more valuable in retrospect. It's also worth observing how enthusiastically this impulse has been embraced by people like Amazon CEO Jeff Bezos, who sees the removal of 'expert gatekeepers' as facilitating innovation and believes in the reception of creative work by its audience as the most reliable assessment of value (Stone 2013). There's a very strong argument to be made that the *logistical* necessity of pre-publication filtering is rapidly eroding, but this doesn't necessarily mean that gatekeeping of this sort serves no purpose. In fact, if there are ever reasons to preserve it, they would surely be in such a specialised field of cultural production. This is only a note of caution rather than a defence of the status quo: the repository arXiv facilitates publish-then-filter (subsequently moderated to filter out inappropriate material but not peer reviewed) and has long been a key resource in the natural sciences. A similar model for the social sciences can be seen in the Social Science Research Network. In both cases the uploaded contents are usually pre-publication versions of papers later submitted to journals, thus we might see this as a hybrid model rather than an absolute publish-then-filter system, but this is by no means true of all submissions.

In a broader sense, I found openness a compelling idea at the level of scholarly practice: as Weller (2011: loc 192) articulates it, 'Openness then refers not only to the technology but also to the practice of sharing content as default'. I've invoked this idea at various points in this book in terms of being an 'open-source academic' (a possibility which Daniel Little so concretely embodies) and of 'continuous publishing' as a style of scholarly labour. These have many practical advantages but I think their widespread uptake would contribute to a greater dynamism of academic life, more interactive and exciting when freed from the temporal rhythms which have defined the existing landscape of scholarly communication.

What if social media become just another thing to do?

Earlier in the book, I argued for the aforementioned possibilities of being an 'open-source academic' as a way of ensuring that social media are not simply another demand placed upon you, alongside many others. If they just become *one more thing to do* then doing so is unlikely to be enjoyable. But over the last few years, it seems as if what was once seen as vaguely questionable now finds itself increasingly regarded as a necessary activity for researchers (Lupton 2014a). Whereas people once felt the need to justify their use of social media, it now seems as if we might be approaching a point where people feel the need to justify *not* using it. It certainly seems as if what Daniels and Feagin (2011) wrote about as the *coming* social media revolution in the academy has pretty much arrived. Social media are becoming central to debates about impact and public engagement. Training is offered with growing frequency in universities, implying the desirability of developing these skills. Calls for contributions to scholarly blogs and other digital projects now supplement the more familiar calls for papers that circulate throughout the academy, suggesting that many colleagues have already adapted to this new multi-dimensionality of academic publication. We also sees stories about career success circulating which stress the role played by online presence, contributing to a diffuse sense that this is crucial for career opportunities, though perhaps with a lack of specificity about precisely *how* this is so or about *who* gained from this in the way suggested. If you find yourself at a conference where everyone is live tweeting, while you're unsure about precisely what this means, it's likely you'll probably feel under pressure to find out. I could continue. My point is that the more academics embrace social media, the more likely it is their colleagues will begin to feel subject to the pressure to do so as well, even if this remains diffuse and unspoken.

Even if social media don't become obligatory in this way, other kinds of pressure might arise over time. It's possible that not being on social media is something which will lead to people missing out on valuable opportunities. Perhaps they might even find themselves penalised, either indirectly through marginalisation or maybe even directly as a result of institutional policies which require engagement through media. Given how recently social media have been seen as a distraction at best, and something profoundly questionable at worse, this might seem unlikely. All the more so if you encounter people who still hold these views on a regular basis. But such a state of affairs is less far away than it might seem.

If academics are using social media because of a fear that they'll fall behind others if they don't then they're not going to enjoy what they're doing. More seriously, this will contribute to the intensification of work in a context already characterised by widespread stress (Shaw and Ward 2014). The psychological dynamics underpinning the fear of missing out (FoMo) could come to be terrifyingly pernicious within an institutional environment characterised by what some have described as 'a culture of acceptance around mental health issues in academia' (Anonymous 2014). Social media activity undertaken out of a sense of fear potentially represents a significant time pressure which could intensify an already problematic level of stress in someone's life. I argued in a previous chapter that social media don't have to be a significant drain upon anyone's time and in fact there are many ways in which these can help enhance the professional activities which academics engage in as a matter of course. I stand by this argument but nonetheless think it's unlikely this will hold true of someone doing it out a sense they have to, lest they fall behind their colleagues. Undertaken with such a mentality, I'd worry that social media can foster what social psychologists describe as 'pluralistic ignorance' – a situation in which group members don't realise that their private experiences are being shared by the collective.

The risks of engaging online and institutional over-reaction

There are real risks entailed by social media in higher education. Moreover, it's easy to see how universities would be increasingly sensitive to these in a climate in which demonstrable success at student recruitment and defending a positive and particularistic corporate brand are seen as increasingly central to the institution's mission. As Helena Webb from the Digital Wild Fire project observed to me, social media are a potent source of stories for journalists. For instance, the profanity-laden tweets of an Australian journalism professor were published on the website of a national newspaper by a right-wing journalist, provoking disciplinary action and a public apology (Davey 2014). Grievances published online by students or staff can be seized upon, either as stories in their own right or as illustrative asides accompanying other higher education stories. In some cases, students have surreptitiously recorded staff in a way that has provoked widespread media attention (Reichman 2015). In one particularly worrying case, a student at another university who had founded what was intended to be a BuzzFeed for conservatives provoked a right-wing outcry over the allegedly racist analysis of white privilege offered by the incoming Boston University professor Saida Grundy (Hetter 2015). Social media can be used by students to abuse and harass each other, as well as staff, often with complete anonymity (Mahler 2015). Systems like Rate Your Lecturer represent alternative evaluation frameworks that are feral and public, with the possibility of 'public scolding' this entails (Morgan 2013). Students at many universities have created Overheard At Facebook groups seen by some as harmless fun (see for instance Datoo, 2014), but which can be forums for sexism and harassment. YouTube videos showing often deeply offensive student misbehaviour risk going viral, providing a justification for mainstream media to report on these videos and in turn contributing to a further circulation, as ever more people see the video in question.

The risks are everywhere. It's a wonder therefore that university communications offices don't try and clamp down on social media use entirely. Having not undertaken a comprehensive review of social media policies across universities (though having read enough to this end to be sure that it's a massive undertaking, not least of all because of the extent to which these practices are still in their earliest stages) I'm reluctant to generalise. There are also important questions to be asked of the degree to which policies are enforced: to what extent are powers being reserved for purposes of crisis management, as opposed to representing an intention to manage the day-to-day communications of academics? One of the most controversial and widely debated social media policies was introduced by Kansas University, following anti-NRA tweets by the journalism professor David Guth after a shooting at the Washington Navy Yard. As well as being inundated with threats and abuse, he was suspended to 'avoid disruption'. The incident provoked the introduction of a social media policy that threatened suspension or dismissal for 'improper use of social media', a category defined in terms so broad they could easily be applied to any imaginable act of communication which the university management found troublesome or problematic (Reichman 2015). The policy was later rescinded in the face of the outrage it provoked, but it nonetheless indicates the potential direction in which institutions might over-react to threats and risks being deeply detrimental to academic freedom.

When I discussed this with her, Helena Webb made the astute observation that the logistical challenge of active monitoring, even with the use of tools like Google

Alerts, probably mitigates against the possibility of active scrutiny and enforcement. But will these policies encourage students to avoid being critical of their university online? Will the notion of 'inappropriate' content inflate over time, encompassing ever more of what might once have been seen as legitimate critique? A sequence of events at my own university (a policing incident on campus, an outcry over the university's new brand, and the attempted creation of a new agency to administer casual teaching) certainly provoked widespread criticism of university management by staff and students on social media. To their credit, there was no attempt whatsoever to suppress this online criticism and in fact management was extremely responsive in the face of it, but will this freedom of expression for staff and students be preserved in confrontation with the many risks social media pose in higher education and the obvious interest of communications offices in preventing these from coming to pass? As Reichman (2014) notes, 'Some politicians and university leaders now act as though the principles of academic freedom should not be applied when it comes to social media'.

My broader fear here is that a concern for managing corporate identity sits uneasily with the potentially radical possibilities for communication and collaboration afforded by social media. In saying this, I'm not attacking people who work in communications. Far from it. On many occasions my social media work has brought me into close contact with them: I like many of the people I've met and I've learnt a lot from them. But I nonetheless think it's necessary to recognise that this is a very different orientation to the possibilities opened up by social media from those which we might loosely group under the catch-all concept of digital scholarship (Weller 2011). There's a real need to introduce the concept of academic freedom into this debate, clarifying the status of social media as a public forum in which academic opinion has a social and political value. The impulse to manage controversy and regulate the online sphere risks stifling academic freedom, even discounting for the additional risks tied up in the impulse to protect the university brand. Thomas Docherty, a professor at my university who was himself subject to disciplinary action many saw as a violation of academic freedom, suggests that under these circumstances 'If one speaks in a tone that stands out from the brand … then, by definition, one is in danger of bringing the branded university into disrepute' (Docherty 2015).

Nonetheless, there's a real need for some governance. Reichman (2014, 2015), vice president of the American Association of University Professors, stresses the need for management and faculty to work together to formulate appropriate policy. This is a commendable goal but it's important to recognise the inequality which would likely characterise such a collaborative endeavour. As the University and College Union make clear, the security of employment in a profession is a crucial safeguard of academic freedom (UCU 2015). Its absence, for instance in the case of fixed term staff or those otherwise precariously employed, makes it difficult to see how any seat at a negotiating table would be offered on fair terms. Could contentious opinion imperil future employment? Might academics concerned about their job security in a fiscally challenged climate fail to exercise their academic freedom in order to avoid potential conflict? If the increasing centrality of the university brand is recognised throughout the institution, might academics come to pre-emptively censor themselves to avoid a conflict with management? Daniel Nehring (2015) makes the worrying suggestion that we are already approaching a tipping point. Once lost, it's unlikely that academic freedom will be regained because each new cohort of academics will have internalised the newfound constraints of the job. It's possible he is overstating this case. I certainly hope he is. But avoiding such an outcome is precisely why we need to attend to these issues which are emerging with what seems like ever greater frequency on social media. Each one inevitably generates a petition, debate and backlash. It's possible over time this might give rise to a general fatigue and growing disinterest. But they're important and will become ever more so with time. The future of academic freedom is being negotiated on each occasion. It's an issue that extends far beyond social media but this is nonetheless a crucial terrain on which issues of significance for the whole of the academy are being played out.

Networked publics and a new collegiality?

Earlier in the chapter I discussed the problem of pluralistic ignorance and the harm it does within academic life. But what if social media could contribute to ending it? I'd like to bring the book to a close on a positive note by suggesting that we can see the outlines of a *new collegiality*, facilitated by social media, in which academics are beginning to exhibit the characteristics of a networked public. Many are rightfully sceptical of the idea that new technology inexorably brings about radical change within any social sphere. Doing so usually entails a determinism about technology, in which complex changes are reduced to the unfolding of the inner logic of the new tools. Even if these changes in fact take place, such explanations miss the point about why they're happening. Furthermore, as Graham (2013: 79–80) observes, '[a]cademic funding, research and dissemination have a deep institutional embeddedness that works against any sort of radical change'. The academy doesn't change simply because the tools used within it have changed. But recognising this shouldn't lead us to over-look the potential significance of those tools for the academy as a whole. Though Graham (2013) is certainly correct that the 'core governance mechanisms' of academia haven't changed, it seems to me that the uptake of social media by academics has foregrounded these in an unprecedented way through what is increasingly a backchannel within the academy itself rather than at particular conferences.

This might seem implausible in light of the triviality still seen to characterise much of how social media are used. But such apparent triviality is bound up in the history of the internet. As Cory Doctorow observes,

> the U.S. government created a military and scientific network for information shar-ing, and its users promptly started a Star Trek discussion forum. Tim Berners-Lee created the World Wide Web for sharing high-energy physics papers, and its users promptly started posting pictures of their cats, their failed cake-baking adventures, and the titanic snowfall that had just been dumped outside their lab windows. (Doctorow 2014: 51).

None of this undermined the serious work to which this technology was expected to give rise. In fact we could make a plausible case that this was cru-cial to the development of the internet, helping to draw ever more people into its orbit. Examples of what I've been pointing to can be seen in many of the cases described in the previous section, in which academics have organised peti-tions and lobbied in support of those who are subject to disciplinary action on contentious grounds. Such action obviously isn't new. But the networked and mediated form it takes is, often instigated by, but extending far beyond, existing peer networks and the formal support structures of trade unions and profes-sional associations. The same trend can be seen in a very different sort of case, the inane sexism of 'computer engineer Barbie' (who created the design ideas, but needed Steven and Brian's help to turn these into a game) which attracted widespread condemnation online, leading to an apologetic withdrawal of the offending book and a re-mixed title by Casey Fiesler, a computer science grad-uate student (Fiesler 2014, Flood 2014). We can see it again in the reaction to a cringeworthy initiative by the European Union to 'overturn clichés and show women and girls, and boys too, that science is not about old men in white coats' which provoked uniform ridicule and widespread offence on social media, with its almost beyond satire message 'Science, it's a girl thing' communicated through the iconography of lipstick and bunsen burners (Gill 2012). Another more prominent example can be seen in the #distractinglysexy hashtag which emerged on Twitter after Nobel laureate Tim Hunt remarked at a conference that women could not be trusted in the lab because 'You fall in love with them, they fall in love with you and when you criticise them, they cry'. These remarks were widely circulated through social media and picked up by print and broadcast media, often framed in terms of the gender gap within Science, Engineering and Technology in which 84% of full-time professors at UK universities are men (Ratcliffe 2015).

The ensuing hashtag featured a wide range of humorous responses from female scientists outraged by Hunt's remarks, including 'distractingly sexy' pictures in full lab gear and hazard signs warning of crying women, ready to fall in love, printed and affixed to labs across the UK (Shaw 2015). The platform very readily lent itself to this sort of networked humour, as scientists across the UK and beyond shared their condemnation of Hunt's attitudes in a way orientated towards viral media. These were even the subject of a post on the viral content site BuzzFeed, viewed 1,470,332 times at the time of writing, in turn contributing to the visibility of the backlash and inciting others to share their own jokes, pictures and condemnations (Karlan 2015). But it only takes a cursory glance back through the tweets using the search term 'Tim Hunt' to see that the same dynamics seem to have been in operation for those who saw Hunt's remarks as an acceptable statement that was the subject of an unjustified and punitive backlash. At the time of writing, over a month since the story broke, it continues to run and does so in a way which doesn't seem to be leading to an amicable conclusion.

Beyond these forms of networked solidarity, as well as the backlash they can provoke, we can see a helpfulness (unevenly) facilitated by social media. The limited time commitment entailed by a tweet helps encourage conversations across disciplinary boundaries that might not otherwise happen, not due to a lack of interest but because busy and stressed people will put off things like this in order to focus on more immediate demands (Carrigan 2015a). Perhaps I'm being naive. But throughout the time I've spent engaging with academic social media, I've seen example after example in which people go out of their way to help others, driven either by sheer helpfulness or curiosity about what the other is doing. If we consider this in terms of time management, it doesn't seem implausible. All manner of factors mitigate against the expression of this co-operative impulse in everyday working life. There's always something else to do, an impending deadline or an unmet commitment looming on the horizon, leaving those small acts of helpfulness, possibly important but certainly not urgent, feeling like an unjustifiable use of time that always seems to be running out (Wajcman 2015). The lack of time commitment involved in particular acts on social media *can* short-circuit the temporal accounting which inevitably dominates our working life when we're busy and stressed. Social media as a whole may occupy significant amounts of time, though as I've argued earlier in this book it isn't a straightforward matter of subtracting from the time available for scholarship, but any one individual use of it does not. At the most extreme end of the spectrum, using 140 characters to answer a question within your area of expertise, asked by a colleague or student outside of it, can literally take a matter of seconds. Likewise can asking someone from another discipline about the work they're undertaking, something which you feel a certain curiosity about but are unlikely to ever read any of the scholarly literature on the topic in question. So too their response to you, pointing towards a blog post they wrote in the past, offering an introduction to the subject for those who are unfamiliar with it, itself something which might have taken an hour or two, but represents a useful resource for others which becomes increasingly rewarding to have produced as each person finds value in it.

I could go on with these imagined examples. They're only imagined in the sense that I'm offering them now, stripped of specifics, in order to illustrate my point. But social media are filled with academics engaging with each other like this, often in ways that get squeezed out by the temporal pressures of working life in a changing academy within which people are expected to do more with less (Carrigan 2016). There are, of course, many counter-examples here: instances of academics behaving badly online, acting in thoughtless or disreputable ways, sometimes with real consequences and many times without. But I do think there's an important aspect to academic social media which can be seen in these everyday acts of helpfulness and co-operation, even if they take place against a background of occasionally very questionable behaviour by some and rather mundane behaviour most of the time for most using these platforms within the academy.

Conclusion

Things are changing. They're changing with a rapidity which makes it difficult to keep up. The inherent difficulty of writing a book comes from the fixity entailed by the format, the anticipation and evasion of the point where you have to declare it finished and send it off. I'm on the verge of reaching that point as I write this conclusion. But already today, I've experimented with Microsoft's new story-telling tool Sway, found an interesting comparison of the Twitter following of an academic viral media account with that of the most established academic institutions, and encountered reports of the controversy being caused by the anonymous social networking tool Yik Yak on American campuses. This is all from a few hours intermittent browsing as I spent the morning drinking coffee and tidying up the rest of the manuscript. It's hard to declare a book finished because there's always more that could be said about any topic large enough to warrant a book about it. It's much harder still when the phenomenon in question is changing and expanding on a daily basis. Not only is there always something *new* to find, the nature of social media platforms also means that you'll inevitably stumble across it as an unintended consequence of your own engagement. This can be fascinating. But it can also be distracting. I've shared some ideas in the book about how to mitigate against this distraction, some from my own experience and others from relevant literature. Nonetheless, the fact I'm submitting it over six months later than planned speaks to the fact that these strategies are not exactly foolproof.

Not only are there new topics I've inevitably missed or recent topics I was only able to add during the later stages of writing, there are also important topics I've only been able to cover in a limited way due to constraints of space (for instance the implications of social media for academic journals and how they are being influenced by open access publishing). There are undoubtedly other topics that simply haven't occurred to me. Plus there's teaching (such a big topic that I felt it was best to defer to the books that have been devoted to this). Social media for academics is such a vast and fast-moving topic that it would be impossible to avoid these gaps in any attempt to capture the field in a single book. Thankfully though, social media provide a partial solution. Much as my own thinking on these topics was initially developed in large part through my blogging, and so too will I continue to blog regularly about these topics over the coming years. Feel free to get in touch if you'd like to discuss anything in the book. Likewise if there's anything you'd like to discuss which *isn't* in the book. I really mean that. You can find me on Twitter @mark_carrigan, on the web at www.markcarrigan.net, or e-mail me at mark@markcarrigan.net.

To bring the book to a close, I thought it would be nice to hear some voices other than my own. So I asked the academics who have featured throughout this book:

What advice would you offer to other academics about social media?

1. 'Treat ideas with seriousness. Don't just think that a blog is a first draft. Take the time to think about it carefully. If blogs are going to be taken seriously, the author needs to take it seriously'. (Daniel Little)

2. 'Engaging with people is crucial. You've just got to get stuck in and plunge into conversations. Nobody's going to think you're rude because you've tweeted them when you've just followed them'. (Charlotte Mathieson)

3. 'If you're using social media in a social way then be yourself. The clue to social media is in the name: it's social'. (Dave O'Brien)

4. 'Just write when you're in the place for it. You need to create a little bit of space around your other work, such that when something occurs to you, you can write it then and there. Write it when it's fresh'. (MJ Barker)

5. 'You need to spend a bit of time on it. Just run with it, rather than just see it as a chore. To get the most out of Twitter, you need to be genuine and engaged, present and willing to communicate'. (Ele Belfiore)

References

Adkins, L. & Dever, M. (2015) 'Academic labour on-the-move', *Australian Feminist Studies*, 30(84): 105–108.

Agger, B. (2000) *Public Sociology: From Social Facts to Literary Acts*. Lanham, MD: Rowman & Littlefield.

Agger, B. (2004) *Speeding Up Fast Capitalism: Internet Culture, Work, Families, Food, Bodies*. Boulder, CO: Paradigm.

Altmann, E.M. & Trafton, J.G. (2007) 'Timecourse of recovery from task interruption: Data and a model', *Psychonomic Bulletin & Review*, 14(6): 1079–1084.

Anonymous (2014) There is a culture of acceptance around mental health issues in academia. *Guardian Higher Education Network Blog*, 1 March. Available at www.theguardian.com/higher-education-network/blog/2014/mar/01/mental-health-issue-phd-research-university (last accessed 22 June 2015).

App Annie (2015) Insights Into App Engagement Q1 2015. *App Annie*. Available at http://go.appannie.com/app-usage-report-q1–2015/ (last accessed 24 May 2015).

Archer, M.S. (2007) *Making Our Way Through The World*. Cambridge: Cambridge University Press.

Back, L. (2007) *The Art of Listening*. Oxford: Berg.

Back, L. (2008) 'Sociologists talking', *Sociological Research Online*, 13(6): 3.

Bady, A. (2013) 'The MOOC moment and the end of reform', *The New Inquiry*.

Bartlett, J. (2014) *The Dark Net*. London: Heinemann.

Bastow, S., Dunleavy, P. & Tinkler, J. (2014) *The Impact of the Social Sciences: How Academics and Their Research Make a Difference*. London: SAGE.

Bauman, Z. (2015) Keynote at Re:Publica 2015.

Baym, N.K. (2010) *Personal Connections in the Digital Age*. Cambridge: Polity.

Becker, H. (2008) *Writing for Social Scientists: How to Start and Finish Your Thesis, Book, or Article.* Chicago: University of Chicago Press.

Beer, D. (2012) 'Open access and academic publishing: Some lessons from music culture', *Political Geography*, 31(8): 479–480.

Beer, D. (2013) 'Public geography and the politics of circulation', *Dialogues in Human Geography*, 3(1): 92–95.

Beer, D. & Burrows, R. (2007) 'Sociology of and in Web 2.0: Some initial considerations', Sociological Research Online, 12(5): 17.

Benton, J. (2014) The leaked New York Times innovation report is one of the key documents of this media age. *Nieman Lab*, 15 May. Available at www.niemanlab.org/2014/05/the-leaked-new-york-times-innovation-report-is-one-of-the-key-documents-of-this-media-age/ (last accessed 22 May 2015).

Benton, J. (2015) A eulogy for Politiwoops, killed by Twitter's confusion over privacy, politics, and journalism. *Nieman Lab*, 4 June. Available at www.niemanlab.org/2015/06/a-eulogy-for-politwoops-killed-by-twitters-confusion-over-privacy-politics-and-journalism/ (last accessed 4 June 2015).

Bergen, A., Watson, G. & Hotton, C. (2013) Three views on using Evernote to improve personal productivity and transform academic knowledge mobilization. *LSE Impact of Social Sciences Blog*, 5 July Available at http://blogs.lse.ac.uk/impactofsocialsciences/2013/07/05/using-evernote-to-improve-academic-productivity (last accessed 10 August 2015).

Berry, D.M. (2012) *Understanding Digital Humanities*. Basingstoke: Palgrave Macmillan.

Berry, J. (2005) *Reclaiming the Ivory Tower: Organizing Adjuncts to Change Higher Education*. New York: Monthly Review Press.

Biswas, A. & Kirchherr, J. (2015) Citations are not enough: Academic promotion panels must take into account a scholar's presence in popular media. *LSE Impact of Social Sciences Blog*, 9 April. Available at http://blogs.lse.ac.uk/impactofsocialsciences/2015/04/09/academic-promotion-scholars-popular-media/ (last accessed 10 August 2015).

Blum, A. (2012) *Tubes: Behind the Scenes at the Internet*. London: Penguin.

Boden, R. & Epstein, D. (2011) 'A flat earth society? Imagining academic freedom', *The Sociological Review*, 59(3): 476–495.

Bohannon, J. (2013) 'Who's afraid of peer review?', *Science*, 342(6154): 60–65.

boyd, d. (2011) How to take an email sabbatical. *Zephoria*. Available at www.danah.org/EmailSabbatical.html (last accessed 18 May 2015).

boyd, d. (2014) *It's Complicated: The Social Lives of Networked Teens*. New Haven, CT: Yale University Press.

Bozarth, J. (2014) *Show Your Work*. San Francisco, CA: Wiley.

Brooker, C. (2013) Too much talk for one planet: why I'm reducing my word emissions. *The Guardian Comment Is Free*, 28 July. Available at www.theguardian.com/commentisfree/2013/jul/28/too-much-talk-charlie-brooker (last accessed 20 May 2015).

Brown, L., Griffiths, R., Rascoff, M. & Guthrie, K. (2007) 'University publishing in a digital age', *Journal of Electronic Publishing*, 10(3).

Brown, M. (2015) Hashtag named UK children's word of the year #important. *The Guardian,* 28 May. Available at www.theguardian.com/technology/2015/may/28/ hashtag-named-uk-childrens-word-of-the-year-important (last accessed 21 June 2015).

Burawoy, M. (2005) 'For public sociology', *American Sociological Review,* 70(1): 4–28.

Burawoy, M. (2008) 'Open letter to C. Wright Mills', *Antipode,* 40(3): 365–375.

Burrows, R. (2012) 'Living with the h-index? Metric assemblages in the contemporary academy', *The Sociological Review,* 60(2): 355–372.

Butler, A. (2015) The things people say. Available at http://nosecretsonthenet.tumblr.com (last accessed 10 August 2015).

Carr, N. (2011) *The Shallows: What the Internet is Doing to Our Brains.* New York: Norton.

Carrigan, M. (2013a) Continuous publishing and being an open-source academic. *LSE Impact Blog,* 23 December. Available at http://blogs.lse.ac.uk/impactofsocialsciences/2013/12/23/ continuous-publishing-and-being-an-open-source-academic (last accessed 7 August 2015).

Carrigan, M. (2013b) Academic blogging – both/and rather than either/or. *Mark Carrigan,* 10 January. Available at http://markcarrigan.net/2013/01/10/academic-blogging-bothand-rather-than-eitheror/ (last accessed 10 August 2015).

Carrigan, M. (2014a) 'Becoming Who We Are: Theorizing Personal Morphogenesis'. Unpublished PhD dissertation, University of Warwick.

Carrigan, M. (2014b) 'Asexuality and its implications for sexuality studies', *Psychology of Sexualities Review,* 1(4): 6–13

Carrigan, M. (2015a) Life in the Accelerated Academy. *LSE Impact Blog,* 7 April. Available at http://blogs.lse.ac.uk/impactofsocialsciences/2015/04/07/life-in-the-accelerated-academy-carrigan/ (last accessed 11 August 2015).

Carrigan, M. (2015b) President of Imperial College London: 'Professors are really like small business owners'. *Mark Carrigan,* 17 April. Available at http://markcarrigan. net/2015/04/17/president-of-imperial-college-london-professors-are-really-like-small-business-owners/ (last accessed 10 August 2015).

Carrigan, M. (2016) 'The Fragile Movements of Late Modernity', in M.S. Archer (ed.), *Morphogenesis and Normativity.* Heidelberg: Springer.

Carrigan, M. & Brumley, C. (2013) Combining journalism with academia: how to read a riot. *LSE Impact Blog,* 5 January. Available at http://blogs.lse.ac.uk/politicsandpolicy/combining-journalism-with-academia-how-to-read-a-riot/ (last accessed 10 August 2015).

Carrigan, M. & Kremakova, M. (2013) Your 'daily dose of Sociological Imagination' reflections on social media and public sociology. *The Sociological Imagination.* Available at http://sociologicalimagination.org/archives/14861/ (last accessed 10 August 2015).

Carrigan, M. & Lockley, P. (2011) Continual publishing across journals, blogs and social media maximizes impact by increasing the size of the 'academic footprint'. *LSE Impact of Social Sciences Blog,* 26 October. Available at http://blogs.lse.ac.uk/impactof socialsciences/2011/10/26/academic-footprint/ (last accessed 7 August 2015).

Carrigan, M. & Mahoney, N. (2013) A critical social science will help inform and shape the wider debate around public engagement. *LSE Impact of Social Sciences*

Blog, 3 December. Available at http://blogs.lse.ac.uk/impactofsocialsciences/ 2013/12/03/social-science-and-the-politics-of-public-engagement/ (last accessed 22 May 2015).

Chen, K. (2015) How much publicity work should book authors do? *OrgTheory*, 17 March. Available at https://orgtheory.wordpress.com/2015/03/17/how-much-publicity-work-should-book-authors-do/ (last accessed 9 August 2015).

Cirillo, F. (2015) Pomodoro in action: Try it out now! *The Pomodoro Technique*. Available at http://pomodorotechnique.com/get-started/ (last accessed 21 May 2015).

Cohen, S. (1979) 'The last seminar', *The Sociological Review*, 27(1): 5–20.

Coleman, G. (2014) *Hacker, Hoaxer, Whistleblower, Spy: The Many Faces of Anonymous*. London: Verso.

Corbyn, Z. (2010) All about me, dot com. *Times Higher Education,*19 August. Available at www.timeshighereducation.co.uk/features/all-about-me-dot-com/413005.article (last accessed 30 July 2015).

Cottom, T.M. (2015a) '"Who The Fuck Do You Think You Are?": Academic engagement, microcelebrity and digital sociology from the Far Left of the matrix of domination', *Ada: A Journal of Gender, New Media, and Technology*.

Cottom, T. (2015b) Everything but the burden: Publics, public scholarship, and institutions. *TressieMc*, 21 May. Available at http://tressiemc.com/2015/05/12/everything-but-the-burden-publics-public-scholarship-and-institutions/ (last accessed 22 May 2015).

Couldry, N. (2014) 'A necessary disenchantment: Myth, agency and injustice in a digital world', *The Sociological Review*, 62(4): 1–18.

Crawford, M. (2015) *The World Beyond Your Head: How to Flourish in an Age of Distraction*. London: Penguin.

Da Silva, M. (2015) I crowdfunded my PhD research. This model could change the world. *TED Fellows,* 12 June. Available at https://medium.com/ted-fellows/i-crowdfunded-my-phd-research-this-model-could-change-the-world-28a079b7a0af (last accessed 10 August 2015).

Daniels, J. (2013) From tweet to blog post to peer-reviewed article: How to be a scholar now. *LSE Impact Blog,* 25 September http://blogs.lse.ac.uk/impactofsocial sciences/2013/09/25/how-to-be-a-scholar-daniels/ (last accessed 10 August 2015).

Daniels, J. & Feagin, J. (2011) 'The (coming) social media revolution in the academy', *Fast Capitalism*, 8(2).

Datoo, S. (2014) The 42 funniest things overhead at British universities. *BuzzFeed,* 23 May. Available at www.buzzfeed.com/sirajdatoo/funniest-things-overheard-at-british-universities (last accessed 10 August 2015).

Davey, M. (2014) Journalism professor's job safe despite troll tweet raising Andrew Bolt's ire. *The Guardian*, 30 July. Available at www.theguardian.com/world/2014/jul/30/journalism-professors-job-safe-despite-troll-tweet-raising-andrew-bolts-ire (last accessed 10 August 2015).

Dean, J. (2013) *Blog Theory: Feedback and Capture in the Circuits of Drive*. Cambridge: Polity.

Dijck, J. Van (2012) *The Culture of Connectivity: A Critical History of Social Media.* Oxford: Oxford University Press.

Docherty, T. (2015) Fear of terror and offence pushing critical voices out of UK universities. *Index on Censorship,* 22 June. Available at www.indexoncensorship.org/2015/06/magazine-fear-terror-offence-pushing-criticial-voices-out-uk-universities (last accessed 8 August 2015).

Doctorow, C. (2002) My blog, my outboard brain. *O'Reilly Web Devcenter,* 31 May. Available at http://archive.oreilly.com/pub/a/javascript/2002/01/01/cory.html (last accessed 7 August 2015).

Doctorow, C. (2013) *Homeland.* London: Titan.

Doctorow, C. (2014) *Information Doesn't Want to Be Free: Laws for the Internet Age.* San Francisco, CA: McSweeney's.

Dolan, P. (2015) *Happiness By Design.* London: Penguin.

Dolle, M. (2015) The social (media) class system. *The Economist Group,* 24 July. Available at www.economistgroup.com/leanback/channels/social-media-consolidation-class-system-kantar-marie-dolle (last accessed 10 August 2015).

Driver, S. (2008) *Queer Youth Cultures.* New York: SUNY.

Duggan, M., Ellison, N.B., Lampe, C., Lenhart, A. & Madden, M. (2014) *Demographics of Key Social Networking Platforms.* Pew Research Centre, available at http://www.pewinternet.org/2015/01/09/demographics-of-key-social-networking-platforms-2/ (last accessed 12 December 2015).

Dunleavy, D. (2014a) Why do academics choose useless titles for articles and chapters? Four steps to getting a better title. *LSE Impact of Social Sciences Blog,* 5 February. Available at http://blogs.lse.ac.uk/impactofsocialsciences/2014/02/05/academics-choose-useless-titles/ (last accessed 19 May 2015).

Dunleavy, P. (2014b) Are you an academic hermit? Here's how to easily change, if you want to. *Writing For Research,* 1 March. Available at https://medium.com/advice-and-help-in-authoring-a-phd-or-non-fiction/are-you-an-academic-hermit-6d7ae5a0f16a (accessed 22 May 2015).

Elden, S. (2015) Foucault's last decade and Foucault: The Birth of Power. *Progressive Geographies.* Available at http://progressivegeographies.com/future-projects/foucaults-last-decade/ (last accessed 10 August 2015).

Engle, R.K. (2001) 'The neo sophists: Intellectual integrity in the Information Age', *First Monday,* 6(8).

Fiesler, C. (2014) Barbie, Remixed: I (really!) can be a computer engineer. *Casey Fiesler,* 18 November. Available at http://caseyfiesler.com/2014/11/18/barbie-remixed-i-really-can-be-a-computer-engineer (last accessed 20 July 2015).

Fitzpatrick, K. (2012) Advice on academic blogging, tweeting, whatever. *Kathleen Fitzpatrick,* 1 October. Available at www.plannedobsolescence.net/advice-on-academic-blogging-tweeting-whatever/ (last accessed 10 August 2015).

Flood, A. (2014) Barbie computer engineer story withdrawn after sexism row. *The Guardian,* 21 November. Available at www.theguardian.com/books/2014/nov/21/barbie-computer-engineer-story-withdrawn-sexist-mattel (last accessed 10 August 2015).

Franzen, J. (2007) *How to be Alone: Essays.* New York: Picador.

French, R.D. (2012) 'The professors on public life', *The Political Quarterly,* 83(3): 532–540.

Fuchs, C. (2014) *Social Media: A Critical Introduction.* London: SAGE.

Fuller, S. (2003) 'Can universities solve the problem of knowledge in society without succumbing to the knowledge society?', *Policy Futures in Education,* 1(1): 106–124.

Fuller, S. (2005) *The Intellectual.* Cambridge: Icon.

Fullick, M. (2012) Tweeting out loud: Ethics, knowledge and social media in academe. *LSE Impact Blog,* 16 October. Available at http://blogs.lse.ac.uk/impactof socialsciences/2012/10/16/fullick-tweeting-out-loud/ (last accessed 1 August 2015).

Garden, A. (2015) Students, don't rate me on my appearance but on my teaching. *Guardian Higher Education Network,* 21 April. Available at www.theguardian.com/ higher-education-network/2015/apr/21/students-dont-rate-me-on-my-appearance-but-on-my-teaching (last accessed 10 August 2015).

Gardner, E. (2015) Conan O'Brien is being sued for allegedly stealing jokes from Twitter. *Business Insider,* 28 July. Available at www.businessinsider.com/conan-obrien-is-being-sued-for-allegedly-stealing-jokes-from-twitter-2015–7 (last accessed 29 July 2015).

Gauntlett, D. (2011) *Making is Connecting: The Social Meaning of Creativity, from DIY and Knitting to YouTube and Web 2.0.* Cambridge: Polity.

Gauntlett, D. (2012) How to move towards a system that looks to 'publish, then filter' academic research. *LSE Impact Blog,* 10 July. Available at http://blogs.lse.ac.uk/impact ofsocialsciences/2012/07/10/publish-then-filter-research/ (last accessed 13 July 2015).

Geary, D. (2009) *Radical Ambition: C. Wright Mills, the Left, and American Social Thought.* Oakland, CA: University of California Press.

Gilbert, D. (2009) *Stumbling on Happiness.* Toronto: Vintage Canada.

Gill, M. (2012) 'Science, it's a girl thing!' says EU Commission, holding lipstick and bunsen burner. *New Statesman,* 22 June. Available at www.newstatesman.com/blogs/martha-gill/ 2012/06science-its-girl-thing-says-eu-commission-holding-lipstick-and-bunsen-burn (last accessed 10 August 2015).

Gill, R. (2009) 'Breaking the Silence: The Hidden Injuries of Neo-liberal Academia', in R. Ryan-Flood, and R. Gill (eds), *Secrecy and Silence in the Research Process: Feminist Reflections.* Abingdon: Routledge.

Ginsberg, B. (2011) *The Fall of the Faculty.* Oxford: Oxford University Press.

Gitlin, T. (2007) *Media Unlimited: How the Torrent of Images and Sounds Overwhelms Our Lives* (revised edn). New York: Holt.

Graham, M. (2013) 'Social media and the academy: New publics or public geographies?', *Dialogues in Human Geography,* 3(1): 77–80.

Gratton, L. (2011) *The Shift: The Future of Work is Already Here.* London: Harper Collins.

Greenhow, C. & Gleason, B. (2014) 'Social scholarship: Reconsidering scholarly practices in the age of social media', *British Journal of Educational Technology,* 45(3): 392–402.

Gregg, M. (2006) 'Feeling ordinary: Blogging as conversational scholarship', *Continuum: Journal of Media & Cultural Studies,* 20(2): 147–160.

Grollman, E. (2014) On dealing with online criticism and trolls for academics. *Conditionally Accepted,* 10 July. Available at http://conditionallyaccepted. com/2014/10/07/trolls (last accessed 10 August 2015).

Grollman, E. (2015a) 'Academic freedom won't protect us', 19 May. Available at http:// conditionallyaccepted.com/2015/05/19/academic-freedom/ (last accessed 10 August 2015).

Grollman, E. (2015b) 'For marginalized scholars, self-promotion is community promotion', 23 July. Available at http://blogs.lse.ac.uk/impactofsocialsciences/2015/07/23/self-promotion-imposter-syndrome-marginalized-scholars/ (last accessed 10 August 2015).

Hayles, N.K. (2012) *How We Think: Digital Media and Contemporary Technogenesis.* Chicago: University of Chicago Press.

Helft, M. (2011) Facebook, foe of anonymity, is forced to explain a secret. *New York Times,* 13 May. Available at www.nytimes.com/2011/05/14/technology/14facebook. html (last accessed 10 August 2015).

Hetter, K. (2015) Online fury over Boston University professor's tweets on race. *CNN,* 13 May. Avilable at http://edition.cnn.com/2015/05/13/living/feat-boston-university-saida-grundy-race-tweets/ (last accessed 10 August 2015).

Hoffman, R. & Casnocha, B. (2012) *The Start-up of You: Adapt to the Future, Invest in Yourself, and Transform Your Career.* New York: Crown Business.

Holmwood, J. (2010) 'Sociology's misfortune: disciplines, interdisciplinarity and the impact of audit culture', *British Journal of Sociology,* 61(4): 639–658.

Holmwood, J. (2011a) 'Viewpoint – the impact of 'impact' on UK social science', *Methodological Innovations Online,* 6(1): 13–17.

Holmwood, J. (2011b) *A Manifesto for the Public University.* London: A&C Black.

Holmwood, J. (2013a) The 'avalanche of change' in higher education must be contextualized in terms of the government's broader neoliberal policies. Available at http:// blogs.lse.ac.uk/impactofsocialsciences/2013/03/18/the-avalanche-of-change-must-be-contextualised/ *LSE Impact of Social Sciences Blog,* 18 March (last accessed 10 August 2015).

Holmwood, J. (2013b) Markets versus dialogue: The debate over open access ignores competing philosophies of openness. *LSE Impact of Social Sciences Blog,* 21 October. Available at http://blogs.lse.ac.uk/impactofsocialsciences/2013/10/21/markets-versus-dialogue/ (last accessed 10 August 2015).

Instagram Press Pages (2015) Available at https://www.instagram.com/press/ (last accessed 12 December 2015).

Internet Live Stats (2015) Available at www.internetlivestats.com

Jeffries, S. (2014) Jean-Paul Sartre: more relevant now than ever. *The Guardian,* 22 October. Available at www.theguardian.com/books/2014/oct/22/jean-paul-sartre-refuses-nobel-prize-literature-50–years-book (accessed 10 August 2015).

Jenkins, H., Ford, S. & Green, J. (2013) *Spreadable Media: Creating Value and Meaning in a Networked Culture.* New York: NYU Press.

JISC (2012) Available at www.webarchive.org.uk/wayback/archive/20140614040703/ http://www.jisc.ac.uk/publications/reports/2012/researchers-of-tomorrow.aspx

Johnson, A. (2013) Best practice for tagging academic notes. *LSE Impact of Social Sciences Blog,* 5 July. Available at http://blogs.lse.ac.uk/impactofsocialsciences/2013/07/05/best-practice-for-tagging-academic-notes/ (last accessed 22 May 2015).

Johnson, C.A. (2012) *The Information Diet: A Case for Conscious Consumption.* Sebastopol, CA: O'Reilly Media.

Johnson, J. (2015) On the frontline: What is the data in Big Data? *Discover Society,* 3 August. Available at http://discoversociety.org/2015/08/03/on-the-frontline-what-is-the-data-in-big-data/ (accessed 3 August 2015).

Jones, R.H. & Hafner, C.A. (2012) *Understanding Digital Literacies: A Practical Introduction.* Abingdon: Routledge.

Jump, P. (2015) Metrics: how to handle them responsibly. *Times Higher Education,* 9 July. Available at www.timeshighereducation.co.uk/features/metrics-how-to-handle-them-responsibly (accessed 10 August 2015).

Jurgenson, N. (2011) Jeff Jarvis and Multiple Identities: A Critique. *Cyborgology,* 25 March. Available at http://thesocietypages.org/cyborgology/2011/03/25/jeff-jarvis-and-multiple-identities-a-critique (accessed 10 August 2015).

Karlan, S. (2015) Women scientists are tweeting 'sexy' photos of themselves at work to shut down sexism. *BuzzFeed,* 11 June. Available at www.buzzfeed.com/skarlan/biohazard-suits-are-nsfw (last accessed 20 July 2015).

Keen, A. (2012) *Digital Vertigo: How Today's Online Social Revolution is Dividing, Diminishing, and Disorienting Us.* New York: Macmillan.

Keen, A. (2015) *The Internet is Not the Answer.* New York: Atlantic Books.

Klein, E. (2015) What Andrew Sullivan's exit says about the future of blogging. *Vox,* 30 January. Available at www.vox.com/2015/1/30/7948091/andrew-sullivan-leaving-blogging (last accessed 22 May 2015).

Kitchin, R. (2014) 'Big Data, new epistemologies and paradigm shifts', *Big Data & Society,* 1(1).

Koh, A. (2012) *Twittergate: What are the Ethics of Live-tweeting at Conferences?* Available at https://storify.com/adelinekoh/what-are-the-ethics-of-live-tweeting-at-conference.html (last accessed 10 August 2015).

Kolowich, S. (2012) *The Academic Twitterazzi.* Available at https://www.insidehighered.com/news/2012/10/02/scholars-debate-etiquette-live-tweeting-academic-conferences (last accessed 12 December 2015).

Lanier, J. (2014) *Who Owns The Future?* London: Allen Lane.

Lee, H. (1960/1997) *To Kill a Mockingbird.* London: Arrow.

Lee, K. (2015) The eternally clickable headlines of Buffer (and how to write and find your own). *buffer social,* 9 April. Available at https://blog.bufferapp.com/clickable-headlines (last accessed 21 May 2015).

Levitin, D.J. (2014) *The Organized Mind: Thinking Straight in the Age of Information Overload.* London: Viking.

Lewis, M. (2014) *Flash Boys: A Wall Street Revolt.* New York: Norton.

Lingard, M. (2010) Twitter at LSE Teaching Day. *Reluctant Technologist,* 25 June. Available at https://mattlingard.wordpress.com/2010/06/25/twitter-at-lse-teaching-day/ (last accessed 25 July 2015).

Little, D. (2014) Five years of understanding society. *Understanding Society*, 6 November. Available at http://understandingsociety.blogspot.co.uk/2012/11/five-years-of-under-standingsociety.html (last accessed 22 May 2015).

Losse, K. (2014) Wierd Corporate Twitter. *The New Inquiry*, available at http://thenew inquiry.com/essays/weird-corporate-twitter/ (last accessed 12 December 2015).

Lupton, D. (2013a) *Digital Sociology: Beyond the Digital to the Sociological*, 15 November. Available at www.slideshare.net/dlupton/digital-sociology-beyond-the-digital-to-the-sociological (last accessed 6 August 2015).

Lupton, D. (2013b) Opening up your research: a guide to self-archiving. *LSE Impact of Social Sciences Blog*, 20 September. Available at http://blogs.lse.ac.uk/impactof socialsciences/2013/09/20/opening-up-your-research-self-archiving-for-sociologists/ (last accessed 10 August 2015).

Lupton, D. (2014a) 'Feeling better connected: Academics' use of social media', 10 June. Available at www.canberra.edu.au/about-uc/faculties/arts-design/attachments2/pdf/n-and-mrc/Feeling-Better-Connected-report-final.pdf (last accessed 10 August 2015).

Lupton, D. (2014b) *Digital Sociology*. Abingdon: Routledge.

Lupton, D. (2014c) The academic quantified self: the role of data in building an academic professional sense of self. *LSE Impact Blog*, 13 January. Available at http://blogs.lse.ac.uk/impactofsocialsciences/2015/04/09/academic-promotion-scholars-popular-media/ (last accessed 10 August 2015).

Mahler, J. (2015) Who spewed that abuse? *New York Times*, 8 March.

Maile, S. & Griffiths, D. (eds) (2014) Public Engagement and Social Science. Bristol: Policy.

Malesky Jr, L.A. & Peters, C. (2012) Defining appropriate professional behavior for faculty and university students on social networking websites, *Higher Education*, 63(1): 135–151.

Marsh, A. (2013) Blogging and 'writing'. *Alex's Archives*, 29 September. Available at www.alexsarchives.org/2013/09/blogging-and-writing/ (last accessed 23 May 2015).

Marwick, A.E. (2014) *Status Update: Celebrity, Publicity, and Branding in the Social Media Age*. New Haven, CT: Yale University Press.

Mayer-Schönberger, V. (2011) *Delete: The Virtue of Forgetting in the Digital Age*. Princeton, NJ: Princeton University Press.

Maynard, A. (2015) Is public engagement really career limiting? *Times Higher Education*, 14 July. Available at www.timeshighereducation.co.uk/blog/public-engagement-really-career-limiting (last accessed 10 August 2015).

McDonald, P. & Thompson, P. (2015) 'Social media(tion) and the reshaping of public/private boundaries in employment relations', *International Journal of Management Reviews*.

McGeeney, E. (2015) 'Live tweeting and building the digital archive: NFQLR – who and what is it for?', *International Journal of Social Research Methodology*.

McGettigan, A. (2013) *The Great University Gamble*. London: Pluto.

Medvetz, T. (2012) *Think Tanks in America*. Chicago: University of Chicago Press.

Mewburn, I. & Thomson, P. (2013) 'Why do academics blog? An analysis of audiences, purposes and challenges', *Studies in Higher Education*, 38(8): 1105–1119.

Miller, D. (2011) *Tales From Facebook*. Cambridge: Polity.

Miller, D. & Sinanan, J. (2014) *Webcam*. Cambridge: Polity.

Mills, C.W. (2000) *The Sociological Imagination*. Oxford: Oxford University Press.

Mirowski, P. (2013) *Never Let A Serious Crisis Go To Waste: How Neoliberalism Survived The Financial Meltdown*. London: Verso.

Mohan, P. (2015) Copied someone's joke on Twitter? Your tweet may be deleted. *Fast Company,* 27 July. Available www.fastcompany.com/3049084/fast-feed/copied-some-ones-joke-on-twitter-your-tweet-may-be-deleted (last accessed 27 July 2015).

Morgan, J. (2013) *Times Higher Education*, available at https://www.timeshighereducation.com/news/rate-your-lecturer-urges-new-uk-website/2004274.article (last accessed 12 December 2015).

Morozov, E. (2012) *The Net Delusion: The Dark Side of Internet Freedom*. London: Penguin.

Morozov, E. (2013) *To Save Everything, Click Here: Technology, Solutionism, and the Urge to Fix Problems that Don't Exist*. London: Penguin.

Murthy, D. (2012) *Twitter: Social Communication in the Twitter Age*. Cambridge: Polity.

NCCPE (2010) Available at www.publicengagement.ac.uk/sites/default/files/reputational%20risk_0.pdf

Nehring, D. (2015) What's wrong with academic freedom in the UK? *Social Science Space*, 28 May. Available at www.socialsciencespace.com/2015/05/whats-wrong-with-academic-freedom-in-the-uk/ (last accessed 1 August 2015).

Nickel, P. (2011) 'The man from somewhere: Author, affiliation, and letterhead', *Fast Capitalism*, 8(2).

O'Shea, K. (2009) Creepy Treehouse Effect – How do we social network in Higher Ed? *Instructional Development Center Blog*, 24 August. Available at www.purdue.edu/learning/blog/?p=210 (last accessed 2 August 2015).

Pang, A.S.K. (2013) *The Distraction Addiction: Getting the Information You Need and the Communication You Want, Without Enraging Your Family, Annoying Your Colleagues, and Destroying Your Soul*. London: Hachette.

Pariser, E. (2011) *The Filter Bubble: What the Internet is Hiding From You*. London: Viking.

Pearce, N., Weller, M., Scanlon, E. & Kinsley, S. (2012) 'Digital scholarship considered: How new technologies could transform academic work', *Education*, 16(1).

Pedersen, S., Burnett, S., Smith, R. & Grinnall, A. (2014) 'The impact of the cessation of blogs within the UK police blogosphere', *New Technology, Work and Employment*, 29(2): 160–176.

Pink, D.H. (2001) *Free Agent Nation: How America's New Independent Workers Are Transforming the Way We Live*. New York: Business Plus.

Plunkett, J. (2010) Andrew Marr says bloggers are 'inadequate, pimpled and single'. *The Guardian,* 11 October. Available at www.theguardian.com/media/2010/oct/11/andrew-marr-bloggers (last accessed 22 May 2015).

Poe, M. (2012) What can university presses do? *Inside Higher Ed*, 9 July. Available at www.insidehighered.com/views/2012/07/09/essay-what-university-presses-should-do (last accessed 10 August 2015).

Poore, M. (2016) *Using Social Media in the Classroom: A Best Practice Guide,* 2nd edn. London: SAGE.

Pop, E. (2015) The grant economy as tragedy of the commons. *OrgTheory*, 16 March. Available at https://orgtheory.wordpress.com/2015/03/16/the-grant-economy-as-tragedy-of-the-commons/ (last accessed 10 August 2015).

Porpora, D. (2016) 'The Great Normative Changes of the Twentieth Century', in M.S. Archer (ed.), *Morphogenesis and Normativity*. Heidelberg: Springer.

Price, I. (2010) *The Activity Illusion*. Leicester: Troubadour.

Rainie, L. & Wellman, B. (2012) *Networked: The New Social Operating System*. Cambridge, MA: MIT Press.

Ratcliffe, R. (2015) Nobel scientist Tim Hunt: female scientists cause trouble for men in labs. *The Guardian*, 10 June. Available at www.theguardian.com/uk-news/2015/jun/10/nobel-scientist-tim-hunt-female-scientists-cause-trouble-for-men-in-labs (last accessed 20 July 2015).

Ratwani, R.M., Trafton, J.G. & Boehm-Davis, D.A. (2008) 'Thinking graphically: Connecting vision and cognition during graph comprehension', *Journal of Experimental Psychology: Applied*, 14(1): 36.

Reed, J. (2014) How social media is changing language. *OxfordWords Blog,* 18 June. Available at http://blog.oxforddictionaries.com/2014/06/social-media-changing-language/ (last accessed 21 June 2015).

Reichman, H. (2014) When academic freedoms and modern media collide. *EdTech Magazine,* 7 May. Available at www.edtechmagazine.com/higher/article/2014/05/when-academic-freedoms-and-modern-media-collide (last accessed 10 August 2015).

Reichman, H. (2015) Can I tweet that? Academic freedom and the new social media. *The Academe Blog*. Available at http://academeblog.org/2015/04/01/can-i-tweet-that-academic-freedom-and-the-new-social-media/ (last accessed 10 August 2015).

Remler, D. (2014) Are 90% of academic papers really never cited? Reviewing the literature on academic citations. *LSE Impact of Social Sciences Blog,* 23 April. Available at http://blogs.lse.ac.uk/impactofsocialsciences/2014/04/23/academic-papers-citation-rates-remler/ (last accessed 20 July 2015).

Rettberg, J.W. (2008) *Blogging*. Cambridge: Polity.

Rettberg, J.W. (2014) *Seeing Ourselves through Technology: How We Use Selfies, Blogs and Wearable Devices to See and Shape Ourselves*. Basingstoke: Palgrave Macmillan.

Rey, P.J. (2010) 'Social media: Have we built a society without closets?', 29 July. Available at http://thesocietypages.org/sociologylens/2010/07/29/social-media-have-we-built-a-society-without-closets/ (last accessed 10 August 2015).

RIN (2011) 'If you build it, will they come? How researchers perceive and use web 2.0'. Available at www.rin.ac.uk/system/files/attachments/web_2.0_screen.pdf (last accessed 10 August 2015).

Rojas, F. (2015) Blogging will not ruin your career. *Org Theory*, 6 August. Available at https://orgtheory.wordpress.com/2015/08/06/blogging-will-not-ruin-your-career/ (last accessed 10 August 2015).

Ronson, J. (2015) *So You've Been Publically Shamed*. London: Pan Macmillan.

Rosa, H. (2013) *Social Acceleration: A New Theory of Modernity*. New York: Columbia University Press.

Rose, N. (2007) *The Politics of Life Itself: Biomedicine, Power, and Subjectivity in the Twenty-first Century*. Princeton, NJ: Princeton University Press.

Rosenbaum, S. (2011) *Curation Nation: How to Win in a World Where Consumers are Creators*. London: Continuum.

Rosenberg, S. (2010) *Say Everything: How Blogging Began, What it's becoming, and Why it matters*. New York: Three Rivers Press.

Sapiro, G. (2010) *Sociology is a Martial Art: Political Writings by Pierre Bourdieu*. New York: The New Press.

Savage, M. & Burrows, R. (2007) 'The coming crisis of empirical sociology', *Sociology*, 41(5): 885–899.

Scoble, R. & Israel, S. (2014) *Age of Context: Mobile, Sensors, Data and the Future of Privacy*. Charleston, SC: CreateSpace.

Sennett, R. (2008) *The Craftsman*. New Haven, CT: Yale University Press.

Shaw, C. (2015) #Distractinglysexy Twitter campaign mocks Tim Hunt's sexist comments. *The Guardian*, 11 June. Available www.theguardian.com/higher-education-network/2015/jun/11/distractinglysexy-twitter-campaign-mocks-tim-hunts-sexist-comments (last accessed 20 July 2015).

Shaw, C. and Ratcliffe, R. (2015) Academics under pressure to bump up student grades, Guardian survey shows. *Guardian Higher Education Network*, 18 May. Available at www.theguardian.com/higher-education-network/2015/may/18/academics-under-pressure-to-bump-up-student-grades-guardian-survey-shows (last accessed 23 May 2015).

Shaw, C. & Ward, L. (2014) Dark thoughts: why mental illness is on the rise in academia. *Guardian Higher Education Network Blog*, 6 March. Available at www.theguardian.com/higher-education-network/2014/mar/06/mental-health-academics-growing-problem-pressure-university (last accessed 22 June 2015).

Shirky, C. (2008) *Here Comes Everybody: The Power of Organizing Without Organisations*. New York: Penguin Press.

Shirky, C. (2011) *Cognitive Surplus: Creativity and Generosity in a Connected Age*. London: Allen Lane.

Slade, G. (2012) *Big Disconnect: The Story of Technology and Loneliness*. Amherst, NY: Prometheus.

Stewart, B.E. (2015) 'In abundance: Networked participatory practices as scholarship', *International Review of Research in Open and Distributed Learning*, 16(3).

Stone, B. (2013) *The Everything Store: Jeff Bezos and the Age of Amazon*. New York: Random House.

Stone, L. (2012) 'The connected life: From email apnea to conscious computing', 5 July. *Huffington Post*, 5 July. Available at www.huffingtonpost.com/linda-stone/email-apnea-screen-apnea-_b_1476554.html (last accessed 30 May 2015).

Sugimoto, C., Hank, C., Bowman, T. & Pomerantz, J. (2015) 'Friend or faculty? Social networking sites, dual relationships, and context collapse in higher education', *First Monday*, 20(3).

Surowiecki, J. (2005) *The Wisdom of Crowds*. New York: Anchor.

Terras, M. (2012) The verdict: Is blogging or tweeting about research papers worth it? *LSE Impact Blog*, 19 April. Available at http://blogs.lse.ac.uk/impactofsocialsciences/2012/04/19/blog-tweeting-papers-worth-it/ (last accessed 10 August 2015).

Thompson, P. (2014) What's the use of 'out of office' notices? *Patter*, 29 September. Available at http://patthomson.net/2014/09/29/whats-the-use-of-out-of-office-notices/ (last accessed 23 May 2015).

Thompson, P. (2015) 'Constructing a Sociological Career'. Talk given at the University of Manchester, 20 February.

Todd, M. (2014) Whither, or wither, social sciences at the NSF? *Social Science Space*, 2 June. Available at www.socialsciencespace.com/2014/06/whither-or-wither-social-science-at-the-nsf/ (last accessed 10 August 2015).

Turner, G. (2010) *Ordinary People and the Media: The Demotic Turn*. London: SAGE.

UCU (2009) Academic Freedom. *UCU*. Available at www.ucu.org.uk/index.cfm?articleid=2283 (last accessed 25 July 2015).

UCU (2015) Academic Freedom: A guide for early career researchers. Available at https://www.ucu.org.uk/media/pdf/6/b/Academic-freedom-leaflet.pdf (last accessed 12 December 2015).

Vaidhyanathan, S. (2012) *The Googlization of Everything (and Why We Should Worry)*. Oakland, CA: University of California Press.

Veletsianos, G. (2012) 'Higher education scholars' participation and practices on Twitter', *Journal of Computer Assisted Learning*, 28(4): 336–349.

Veletsianos, G. & Kimmons, R. (2012) 'Networked participatory scholarship: Emergent techno-cultural pressures toward open and digital scholarship in online networks', *Computers & Education*, 58(2): 766–774.

Verhaeghe, P. (2014) *What About Me? The Struggle for Identity in a Market-Based Society*. London: Scribe.

Vostal, F. (2014) 'Thematizing speed between critical theory and cultural analysis', *European Journal of Social Theory*, 17(1): 95–114.

Vostal, F. (2015) 'Academic life in the fast lane: The experience of time and speed in British academia', *Time & Society*, 24(1): 71–95.

W3C (2012a) Available at www.w3.org/WAI/intro/people-use-web/diversity

W3C (2012b) Available at www.w3.org/WAI/intro/people-use-web/principles

Wajcman, J. (2015) *Pressed for Time: The Acceleration of Life in Digital Capitalism*. Chicago: University of Chicago Press.

Wang, X. (2014) From attention to citation: What are altmetrics and how do they work? *LSE Impact Blog*, 28 October. Available at http://blogs.lse.ac.uk/impactofsocialsciences/2014/10/28/from-attention-to-citation-what-and-how-do-altmetrics-work/ (last accessed 10 August 2015).

Watermeyer, R. & Lewis, J. (2015) Public engagement: hidden costs for research careers? *Times Higher Education*, 22 January. Available at www.timeshighereducation.co.uk/comment/opinion/public-engagement-hidden-costs-for-research-careers/2018045.article (accessed 10 August 2015).

Watermeyer, R. (2015) 'Public intellectuals vs. new public management: The defeat of public engagement in higher education', *Studies in Higher Education* (ahead-of-print), 1–15.

WebAxe (2011) Available at www.webaxe.org/25–ways-to-make-your-website-accessible/

WebAxe (2012a) Available at http://webaim.org/intro

WebAxe (2012b) Available at http://webaim.org/articles/userperspective

Weller, M. (2011) *The Digital Scholar: How Technology is Transforming Scholarly Practice.* London: Bloomsbury.

Williams, L. (2013) Academic blogging: A risk worth taking? *Higher Education Network*, 4 December. Available at www.theguardian.com/higher-education-network/blog/2013/dec/04/academic-blogging-newspaper-research-plagiarism (last accessed 10 August 2015).

Wolmers, J. (2015) How economists came to dominate the conversation. *The Upshot*. Available at www.nytimes.com/2015/01/24/upshot/how-economists-came-to-dominate-the-conversation.html?_r=0&abt=0002&abg=0 (accessed 20 July 2015).

Wordnik (2015) 'Hobby', *Wordnik*. Available at www.wordnik.com/words/hobby (last accessed 23 May 2015).

Wren-Lewis, S. (2013) Advice for potential academic bloggers. *LSE Impact of Social Sciences Blog*, 14 January. Available at http://blogs.lse.ac.uk/impactof socialsciences/2013/01/14/advice-for-potential-academic-bloggers/ (last accessed 19 May 2015).

YouTube (2015) Statistics. *YouTube*. Available at www.youtube.com/yt/press/en-GB/statistics.html (last accessed 10 August 2015).

Index